# 2201 Fascinating FACTS

# 2201 Fascinating FACTS

## Two Volumes in One

By David Louis

Greenwich House
Distributed by Crown Publishers, Inc.
New York

Previously published in separate volumes under the titles:
*Fascinating Facts* copyright © 1977 by The Ridge Press, Inc. and
Crown Publishers, Inc.
*More Fascinating Facts* copyright © 1979 by The Ridge Press, Inc.
and Crown Publishers, Inc.

The 1983 edition is published by Greenwich House,
a division of Arlington House, Inc.,
distributed by Crown Publishers, Inc.,
225 Park Avenue South, New York, New York 10003
by arrangement with Crown Publishers, Inc.

Prepared and Produced by The Ridge Press, Inc.

Manufactured in the United States of America

Library of Congress Cataloging in Publication Data

Carroll, David, 1942-
2201 fascinating facts.

Reprint (1st work). Originally published: Fascinating facts. New York : Ridge Press : [Distributed by] Crown Publishers, c1977.
Reprint (2nd work). Originally published: More fascinating facts. New York : Ridge Press : [Distributed by] Crown Publishers, c 1979.
1. Curiosities and wonders. I. Carroll, David, 1942- . More fascinating facts. II. Title. III. Title: Two thousand two hundred one fascinating facts. IV. Title: Two thousand two hundred and one fascinating facts.
[AG243.C37 1982] 031',02 82-12113

ISBN: 0-517-395746

s r q p o

# Contents

# Volume One

# Animals

The largest living species of kangaroo has a head the size of a sheep's and may stand 7 feet tall. An extinct species of kangaroo had a head the size of a Shetland pony's and reached a height of more than 10 feet. There are miniature kangaroos, such as the musk kangaroo, that are no bigger than a jackrabbit.

Greyhounds have the best eyesight of any breed of dog.

Every 9.6 years there is a peak in Canada's wildlife population, especially among muskrats, red fox, skunks, mink, lynx, and rabbits. The population of grasshoppers in the world tends to rise and fall rhythmically in 9.2-year cycles.

A rodent's teeth never stop growing. They are worn down by the animal's constant gnawing on bark, leaves, and other vegetable matter.

Beaver, one of the largest rodents in the world, gnawing on a tree branch

One million stray dogs and about 500,000 stray cats live in the New York City metropolitan area. There are about 100 million dogs and cats in the United States. Americans spend $5.4 billion on their pets each year. Every hour, 12,500 puppies are born in the United States.

Elephant herds post their own sentries. When danger threatens, the sentry raises its trunk and though it may be as far as a half-mile away, the rest of the herd is instantly alerted. How this communication takes place is not understood.

The whale has the slowest metabolism of all animals. Despite its great size, it lives on one of the smallest of all creatures, the microscopic plankton found throughout the sea.

A horse focuses its eye by changing the angle of its head, not by changing the shape of the lens of the eye, as humans do.

Deer have no gall bladders.

A mole can dig a tunnel 300 feet long in one night.

The average porcupine has more than 30,000 quills. Porcupines are excellent swimmers because their quills are hollow and serve as pontoons to keep them afloat.

Wildlife biologists estimate that as many as five out of six fawns starve to death during a hard winter in Vermont.

The now-extinct ancestor of the horse, eohippus, had a short neck, a pug muzzle, and stood no higher than a medium-sized dog.

The kinkajou's tail is twice as long as its body. Every night it wraps itself in its tail and uses it as a pillow.

The ring-tailed lemur, a primate found only on the island of Madagascar, meows like a cat.

Genuine ivory does not come only from elephants. It can come from the tusks of a boar or a walrus.

A horse can sleep standing up.

A rat can go without water longer than a camel can.

An elephant may consume 500 pounds of hay and 60 gallons of water in a single day.

Cats have no ability to taste sweet things.

There is no single cat called a panther. The name is commonly applied to the leopard, but it is also used to refer to the puma and the jaguar. A black panther is really a black leopard.

Guinea pigs were first domesticated by the Incas, who used them for food, in sacrifices, and as household pets.

A male baboon can kill a leopard.

The hippopotamus is born underwater.

Cows have four stomachs. Often when a calf is born the farmer will make it swallow a magnet. This is to attract the various nails, staples, tacks, bits of wire, and so on that the cow may ingest while grazing. (This odd hunger is known to farmers as "hardware disease.") When the animal is slaughtered, the butcher will remove the magnet along with the metallic debris and sell the mass of iron and steel for scrap.

The hippopotamus (*Hippopotamus amphibius*):

is, next to the elephant, the heaviest of all land mammals, larger even than the rhinoceros. It may weigh as much as 8,000 pounds.

is a close relative of the pig.

can open its mouth wide enough to accommodate a 4-foot-tall child.

has skin an inch and a half thick, so solid that most bullets cannot penetrate it.

has a stomach 10 feet long, capable of holding 6 bushels of grass.

---

The crocodile *(Crocodylus sp.):*

is a cannibal; it will occasionally eat other crocodiles.

does not chew its food, but swallows it whole. It carries several pounds of small stones in its stomach to aid in grinding up and digesting its nourishment.

does cry tears, but they are crocodile tears—not real tears at all, but glandular excretions that serve to expel excess salt from the eyes.

continually grows new sets of teeth to replace old teeth.

cannot move its tongue (a crocodile's tongue is rooted to the base of its mouth).

is surprisingly fast on land. If pursued by a crocodile, a person should run in a zigzag motion, for the crocodile has little or no ability to make sudden changes of direction.

---

The frigate bird can fly at a speed of 260 miles per hour. The snail moves at a rate of 0.000362005 miles per hour. The fastest animal on four legs is the cheetah, which races 70 miles per hour over short distances and can accelerate to 45 miles per hour in two seconds. An elephant, despite its ponderous appearance, can do 25 miles per hour on an open stretch, and a charging rhino has been clocked at 30. The fastest of all fish in the sea is the swordfish, streaming forward at 68 miles per hour. Man's best speed in the water is 4.1 miles per hour; the maximum speed at which a human being can run on land is 24 miles per hour.

A squirrel has no color vision; it sees only in black and white. Every part of its field of vision, however, is in perfect focus, not just straight ahead, as with man.

Weimaraner dogs were first bred in Germany for hunting deer in a special manner: the dogs were trained to pursue stags low and from behind, and to leap at their victims' genitals and rip off these most vulnerable organs in a single bite. Today, if given a chance, many members of this breed will instinctively perform the same feat.

A baby turkey is called a "poult." A group of lions is known as a "pride," and a group of hogs is a "herd." Geese in collection are a "gaggle," and when in the air they are a "skein." A gathering of foxes is referred to as a "skunkel," a gathering of quail as a "covey." A baby kangaroo is a "joey." A baby fish is a "fry."

An ox is a castrated bull. A mule is a sterile cross between a male ass and a female horse. A donkey is an ass, but an ass is not always a donkey. The word "ass" refers to any of several hoofed mammals of the genus *Equus,* including the onager.

A kangaroo cannot jump if its tail is lifted off the ground. It needs its tail for pushing off.

Snakes picking up sound vibrations by flicking their tongues

A snake has no ears. However, its tongue is extremely sensitive to sound vibrations, and by constantly flicking its tongue the snake picks up these sound waves. In this sense a snake "hears" with its tongue.

Contrary to popular belief, dogs do not sweat by salivating. They sweat through the pads of their feet.

When a hippopotamus exerts itself, gets angry, or stays out of the water for too long, it exudes red sweatlike mucus through its skin.

Every day of the year 100 whales are killed by whale fishermen.

Early U.S. whaling ship off California coast

A newborn Chinese water deer is so small it can almost be held in the palm of the hand.

Every year more people are killed in Africa by crocodiles than by lions.

Antlers and horns are not the same. Horns grow throughout an animal's life and are found on both the male and female of a species (such as a cow). Antlers, composed of a different chemical substance, are shed every year. Usually, though not invariably, they are found on males.

A hippopotamus can run faster than a man.

The Mojave ground squirrel, found mainly in the American West, hibernates for two-thirds of every year.

The sea lion *(Eumetopias jubata):*

can swim 6,000 miles, stopping only to sleep.

is susceptible to sunburn, and if put on board a ship will get as seasick as man.

Male sea lions may have more than 100 wives and sometimes go three months without eating.

There once were more sea lions on earth than people.

The venom of the king cobra is so deadly that one gram of it can kill 150 people. Just to handle the substance can put one in a coma.

King cobra

A whale's heart beats only nine times a minute.

A cat uses its whiskers to determine if a space is too small to squeeze through. The whiskers act as feelers or antennae, helping the animal to judge the precise width of any narrow passage.

Of all known forms of animal life ever to inhabit the earth, only about 10 percent still exist today.

The lesser mole rat not only digs an entire subterranean house for itself, complete with storerooms, halls, bedrooms, and a "wedding chamber" where all mating takes place, but actually constructs a separate bathroom which, when filled, is sealed off from the rest of the house.

Elephants are covered with hair. Although it is not apparent from a distance, at close range one can discern a thin coat of light hairs covering practically every part of an elephant's body.

Male monkeys lose the hair on their heads in the same way men do.

The flying snake of Java and Malaysia *(Chrysopelea ornata)* is able to flatten itself out like a ribbon and sail like a glider from tree to tree.

A good milking cow will give nearly 6,000 quarts of milk every year.

There are buffalo in Poland. They live mainly in the area of the Bialowieza Forest and are known as *zubra*. The well-known Polish vodka Zubrowka, which means "buffalo brand," takes its name from these animals.

Sheep will not drink from running water. Hence the line in the Twenty-third Psalm: "He leadeth me beside the still waters."

A completely blind chameleon will still take on the colors of its environment.

Camels were used as pack animals in Nevada and Arizona as late as 1870.

Male moose have antlers 7 feet across. The antlers often weigh 60 pounds.

The fur of the vicuña, a small member of the camel family which lives only in the Andes Mountains of Peru, is so fine that each hair is less than two-thousandths of an inch thick. The animal was considered sacred by the Incas, and only royalty could wear its fleece.

A female mouse may spawn as many as ten litters of eight to ten young during her lifetime—which generally is less than a year. The gestation period is three weeks, and the young mice reach maturity in only ten weeks.

The chameleon, a small lizard generally measuring 6 or 7 inches, has a tongue several inches longer than its body. With a thrust of this remarkable appendage it can catch insects some 10 inches away.

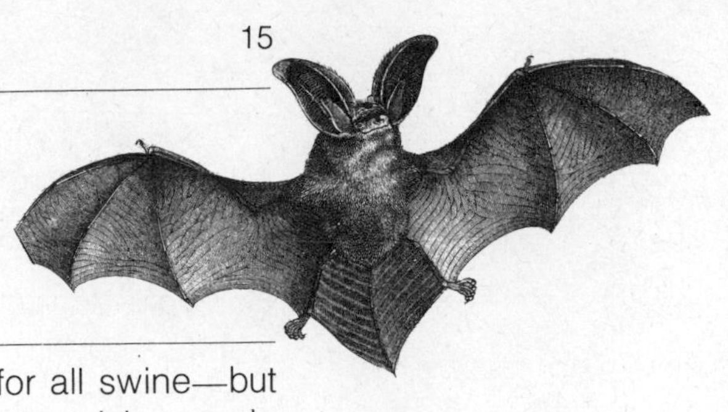

The bat is the only mammal that can fly.

A pig is a hog—hog is a generic name for all swine—but a hog is not a pig. In the terminology of hog raising, a pig is a baby hog less than ten weeks old.

The bottle-nosed whale can dive to a depth of 3,000 feet in two minutes.

## Architecture & Construction

The Egyptian pyramids were once faced completely with marble. The Parthenon was once painted.

Nobody knows who built the Taj Mahal. The names of the architects, masons, and designers that have come down to us have all proved to be latter-day inventions, and there is no evidence to indicate who the real creators were.

Boulder Dam is as thick at its base (660 feet) as a city block is long.

The Washington Monument sinks 6 inches every year.

The Statue of Liberty's mouth is 3 feet wide.

The largest pyramid in the world is not in Egypt but in Cholulu de Rivadahia, Mexico. It is 177 feet tall and covers 25 acres. It was built sometime between 6 and 12 A.D.

Bricks are the oldest manufactured building material still in use. Egyptians used them 7,000 years ago.

The world's two largest dams are both in Russia. They are the Inguri (988 feet high) and the Nurek (984 feet high).

Face of Statue of Liberty before assemblage

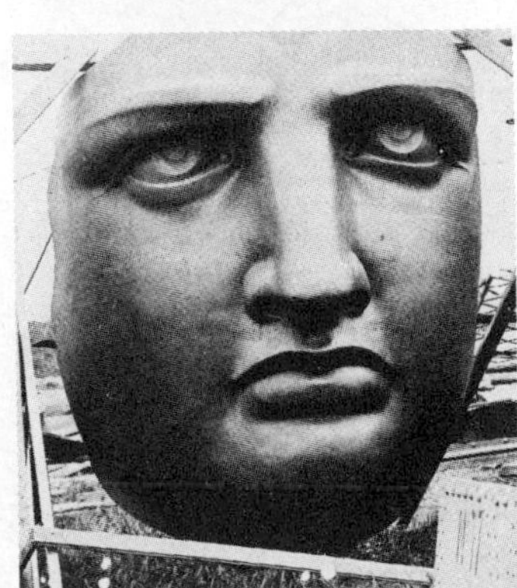

There is a house in Rockport, Massachusetts, built entirely of newspaper. The Paper House at Pigeon Cove, as it is called, is made of 215 thicknesses of newspaper. "All the furniture is made of newspaper," its builder reports, "including a desk of newspapers relating Lindbergh's historic flight."

The pyramids in Egypt contain enough stone and mortar to construct a wall 10 feet high and 5 feet wide running from New York City to Los Angeles.

Empire State Building

Many of the first houses in the American colonies (including the home of William Penn) were built from bricks used as ballast in the holds of ships. These ships arrived in the New World filled with bricks, the bricks were unloaded and sold, and the cargo hatches were refilled with export goods in their place. The bricks were then used by the colonists to construct their homes.

In 1830 the Taj Mahal was sold to a British merchant who planned to dismantle it stone by stone and ship the marble back to England, where it would be used to embellish English estates. Though wrecking machinery was brought into the gardens of the Taj, the plan was discouraged: the project turned out to be too expensive.

In 1931 an industrialist named Robert Ilg built a half-size replica of the Leaning Tower of Pisa outside Chicago and lived in it for several years. The tower is still there.

In the city of Washington, D.C., no building may be built taller than the Capitol.

The Empire State Building (1,250 feet) exceeds the height of the Eiffel Tower (984.5 feet) by only 265.5 feet.

The Empire State Building was built with 60,000 tons of steel, 3 million square feet of wire mesh, 70,000 cubic yards of concrete, 10 million bricks, and can accommodate 15,000 people.

In 1711, when work on St. Paul's Cathedral in London was completed and was shown to George I, the King is reported to have exclaimed to its architect, Christopher Wren, that the work was "aweful" and "artificial." In the eighteenth century, "aweful" meant awe-inspiring, and "artificial" meant full of great art.

## Art & Artists

During the Napoleonic Wars, Napoleon's soldiers bivouacked in the chapel of Santa Maria delle Grazie in Milan, where Leonardo's *Last Supper* is located. The soldiers used the painting in target practice, shooting at the central figure of Christ's head. This is why the face of Christ is almost obliterated in the painting.

The largest stained-glass window in the world is at Kennedy International Airport in New York City. It can be seen on the American Airlines terminal building and measures 300 feet long by 23 feet high.

Indian-miniature painters of the Kangra school used brushes so fine that they were sometimes made of a single hair. A painter of Indian miniatures would often apprentice for ten years before he was allowed to pick up a brush. The colors used by this school of artists were made of such strange substances as crushed beetles, ground lapis lazuli, and blood.

The statue by Auguste Rodin that has come to be called *The Thinker* was not meant to be a portrait of man in thought. It is a portrait of the poet Dante.

There is only one picture by an American hanging in the Louvre—*Whistler's Mother. Whistler's Mother*, however, is only the painting's popular name; its official title is *Arrangement in Black and Gray: The Artist's Mother.*

In his last days, the painter Pierre Renoir was so crippled

with arthritis that he had to have the brushes tied to his arms in order to execute his paintings.

---

Equestrian statues: traditionally when all four of the horse's hooves are on the ground, it signifies that the rider died a natural death. One hoof in the air indicates that he died of wounds sustained in action. If two are raised, it means that the rider was killed on the field of battle.

---

Peter Paul Rubens

The seventeenth-century Flemish artist Peter Paul Rubens often did not paint his own pictures. His procedure was to set up the canvas, draw in preliminary outlines, sketch in the various figures, and design the color scheme. He turned the actual painting over to members of his atelier, a veritable factory of skilled painters, some of whom specialized in painting flowers, some in fruit, some in birds, candles, or even beards. Van Dyck, one of the greatest of all Flemish painters, was a member of this great studio.

---

The horns protruding from the head of the famous statue of Moses by Michelangelo were a mistake! It is true that the Bible describes Moses as having horns coming from his head. This, however, was an error on the part of the translators. In Hebrew the words for "horn" and "ray of light" are spelled identically. The translators misinterpreted "ray" for "horn" and thus Moses is often portrayed in western art as looking like a devil.

Detail of Michelangelo's *Moses*

The Spanish painter Velázquez was official court painter to King Philip IV when he was twenty-six.

Currier and Ives published more than 7,000 prints. They ran a large factory with hundreds of employees, including many full-staff artists. Though their prints are rare and expensive today, they originally sold for 10 cents apiece.

Detail of 12th-century Chinese painting of women preparing silk. Note that girl's and woman's feet are not shown.

Things you may not know about the *Mona Lisa:*

She has no eyebrows (it was the fashion in Renaissance Florence to shave them off).

The real name of the painting is not *Mona Lisa.* It is *La Giaconda.* It is a portrait of a middle-class Florentine woman, the wife of a merchant named Francesco del Giacondo.

The painting measures less than 2 feet by 2 feet.

An entire opera was written about the painting by Max von Schillings.

X-rays of the *Mona Lisa* show that there are three completely different versions of the same subject, all painted by Leonardo, under the final portrait.

Ancient Chinese artists freely painted scenes of nakedness and coition. Never, absolutely never, would they depict a simple bare female foot.

## Aviation

Houdini was the first man to fly an airplane solo in Australia.

The top of the tower on the Empire State Building was originally intended (though never used) as a mooring place for dirigibles.

According to the Federal Aviation Authority, United States airlines are four times safer than the airlines of any other country.

The name of the first airplane flown at Kitty Hawk by the Wright Brothers was *Bird of Prey.* The maiden flight of the

*Bird of Prey,* however, was less than a flight—the plane stayed in the air only long enough to sail 59 feet.

---

Charles Lindbergh was not the first man to fly the Atlantic. He was the sixty-seventh. The first sixty-six made the crossing in dirigibles and twin-engine mail planes. Lindbergh was the first to make the dangerous flight *alone.*

---

Castor oil is used as a lubricant in jet planes.

---

An airplane uses more fuel flying at 25,000 feet than at 30,000 feet. The higher it flies, the thinner the atmosphere and the less atmospheric resistance it must buck.

---

## Babies & Birth

---

Newborn babies are not blind. Studies have shown that newborns have approximately 20/50 vision and can easily discriminate between degrees of brightness.

---

A fetus in the womb can hear. Tests have shown that fetuses respond to various sounds just as vigorously as they respond to pressures and internal sensations.

---

A survey conducted at Iowa State College in 1969 suggests that a parent's stress at the time of conception plays a major role in determining a baby's sex. The child tends to be of the same sex as the parent who is under less stress.

---

Statistics based on more than a half-million births occurring in New York City hospitals between 1948 and 1957 show a significantly greater number of births taking place during the waning moon than during the waxing moon.

---

Until the 1920's, babies in Finland were delivered in saunas. The heat was thought to help combat infection, and the warm atmosphere was considered pleasing to the infant.

---

Children born in the month of May are on the average 200 grams heavier at birth than children born in any other month.

Up to the age of six or seven months a child can breathe and swallow at the same time. An adult cannot do this. (Try it.)

Midgets and dwarfs almost always have normal-sized children, even if both parents are midgets or dwarfs.

Twins are born less frequently in the eastern part of the world than in the western.

## The Bible

Studies of the Dead Sea Scrolls indicate that the passage in the Bible known as the Sermon on the Mount is actually an ancient Essene prayer dating to hundreds of years before the birth of Christ.

The American Bible Association has published almost a billion Bibles since it was founded in 1816.

The Lord's Prayer appears twice in the Bible, in Matthew VI and Luke XI.

Two chapters in the Bible, 2 Kings 19 and Isaiah 37, are alike almost word for word.

The shortest verse in the Bible consists of two words: "Jesus wept" (John 11:35).

The King James version of the Bible has 50 authors, 66 books, 1,189 chapters, and 31,173 verses.

In the history of printing, several early English Bibles are famous not so much for their workmanship or their beauty as for their textual idiosyncrasies. A few famous examples, much sought after by rare-Bible collectors, are:

*The Breeches Bible (1560)*—so named because it states that Adam and Eve "sewed fig tree leaves together and made themselves breeches."

*The Bug Bible (1551)*—so named because of an incorrect translation of a line in the Ninety-first Psalm. The line "Thou shalt not be afraid for the terror by night" reads "Thou shalt not be afraid of any buggies by night."

*The Treacle Bible (1568)*—so named because it uses the word "treacle" for "balm" in the line "Is there no balm in Gilead?"

## Birds

Eagle with young deer in its talons

An eagle can attack, kill, and carry away an animal as large as a young deer. The harpy eagle of South America feeds on monkeys.

The penculine titmouse of Africa builds its home in such a sturdy manner that Masai tribesmen use their nests for purses and carrying cases.

The female knot-tying weaverbird will refuse to mate with a male who has built a shoddy nest. If spurned, the male must take the nest apart and completely rebuild it in order to win the affections of the female.

The average hummingbird weighs less than a penny. It has a body temperature of 111 degrees and beats its wings more than 75 times a second. Its newborn are the size of bumblebees and its nest is the size of a walnut. The hummingbird is the only bird that can fly backward.

When attacked, the petrel, a giant bird of the Antarctic, repels its enemies either by regurgitating food in their faces or by squirting a jet of viscous oil from its nostrils with a force great enough to knock down a person.

Bald eagles are not bald. The top of their head is covered with slicked-down white feathers; from a distance they appear hairless.

The tailorbird of Africa makes its nest by sewing together two broad leaves. It uses fiber as the thread and its bill as the needle.

In one year, hens in America lay enough eggs to encircle the globe a hundred times.

Male bowerbirds build and decorate nests to be used exclusively for mating. They ornament the nests with flowers, bits of string, berries, feathers, even pieces of glass or brightly colored paper. After these decorations are in place, the male bowerbird paints the entire nest with blueberry juice that he has extracted by pressing the berries in his beak. After courtship and mating have taken place, the nest is deserted and a separate one is constructed for rearing the young.

Above: Flamingos
Left: Passenger pigeon

Flamingos are not naturally pink. They get their color from their food, tiny blue-green algae that turn pink during digestion.

In 1880 there were approximately 2 billion passenger pigeons in the United States. By 1914 the species was extinct.

The penguin has an apparatus above its eyes that enables it to transform salt water into fresh. The penguin takes only one mate during its life and is such a conscientious parent that it will, if necessary, starve to death in order to provide its children with food.

The albatross drinks sea water. It has a special desalinization apparatus that strains out and excretes all excess salt.

The optimum depth of birdbath water, says the Audubon Society of America, is 2½ inches. Less water makes it difficult for birds to take a bath; more makes them afraid.

Ducks will lay eggs only in the early morning.

An ostrich egg can make eleven and a half omelets.

## The Body

A sneeze can travel as fast as 100 miles per hour.

As men and women get older their ability to hear high-pitched sounds diminishes. The ability to taste sweet foods also decreases with age.

The human nose can detect the odor of artificial musk in such low concentrations as one part musk to 32 billion parts of air.

The easiest sounds for the human ear to hear, and those which carry best when pronounced, are, in order, "ah," "aw," "eh," "ee," and "oo."

The sound heard by a listener when holding a seashell to his ear does *not* come from the shell itself. It is the echo of the blood pulsing in the listener's own ear.

A person's nose and ears continue to grow throughout his or her life.

The nose cleans, warms, and humidifies over 500 cubic feet of air every day.

Human eyes are so sensitive that on a clear night when there is no moon, a person sitting on a mountain peak can see a match struck 50 miles away.

It is impossible to sneeze and keep one's eyes open at the same time.

While reading a page of print the eyes do not move continually across the page. They move in a series of jumps, called "fixations," from one clump of words to the next.

Two out of three adults in the United States wear glasses at some time.

It takes the human eyes an hour to adapt completely to seeing in the dark. Once adapted, however, the eyes are about 100,000 times more sensitive to light than they are in bright sunlight.

The human eyes can perceive more than 1 million simultaneous visual impressions and are able to discriminate among nearly 8 million gradations of color.

The average person's field of vision is 180 degrees.

Sight accounts for 90 to 95 percent of all sensory perceptions.

The pupil of the eye expands as much as 45 percent when a person looks at something pleasing.

Blue eyes are the most sensitive to light, dark brown the least sensitive.

It takes 17 muscles to smile, 43 muscles to frown.

The average person's hand flexes its finger joints 25 million times during a lifetime.

One-fourth of the 206 bones in the human body are located in the feet.

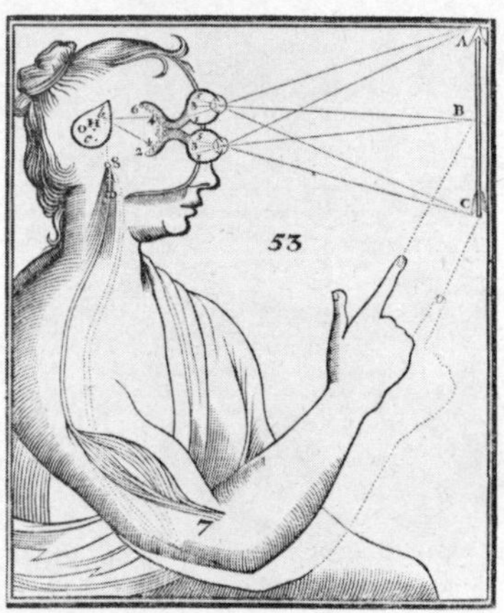

17th-century woodcut showing how image of arrow is transmitted from eyes to brain

Drinking *lowers* rather than raises the body temperature. There is an illusion of heat because alcohol causes the capillaries to dilate and fill with blood. In very cold weather drinking alcoholic beverages can lead to frostbite.

---

The strongest bone in the body, the thigh bone, is hollow. Ounce for ounce it has a greater pressure tolerance and bearing strength than a rod of equivalent size cast in solid steel.

---

Type O is the most common blood type in the world. Type AB is the rarest. There is also a subtype called A-H, but to date only three people in the world are known to have it.

---

The substance that human blood resembles most closely in terms of chemical composition is sea water.

---

There are almost 6 million red blood cells in a cubic millimeter of human blood. The entire body contains about 30 trillion red blood cells. When a person inhales several breaths of carbon monoxide, more than half of the blood's hemoglobin combines with the gas, leaving only half the red blood cells to carry oxygen. This has the same effect on the body as a sudden loss of 50 percent of one's red blood cells. Fifteen million red blood cells are produced and an equal number are destroyed every second.

---

The average brain comprises 2 percent of a person's total body weight. Yet it requires 25 percent of all oxygen used by the body, as opposed to 12 percent used by the kidneys and 7 percent by the heart.

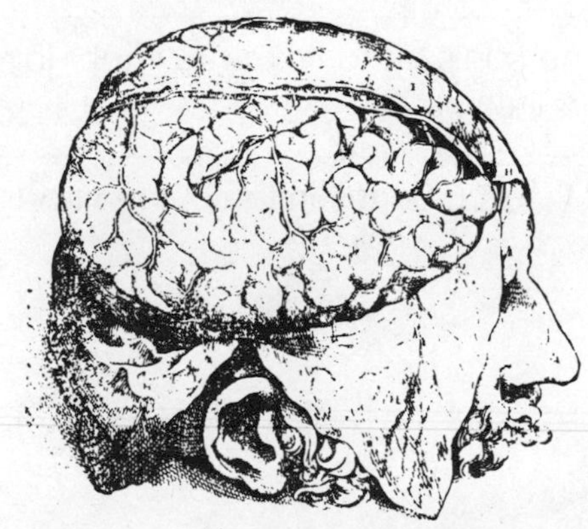

The body has 70,000 miles of blood vessels. The heart pumps blood through this labyrinth and back again once every minute.

A person breathes 7 quarts of air every minute.

The average person takes from twelve to eighteen breaths per minute.

The right lung takes in more air than the left.

The human brain is 80 percent water, more watery than our blood.

The human brain is insensitive to pain. The suffering of a headache comes not from the organ itself but from the nerves and muscles lining it.

Neanderthal man, the first human being in the true sense, had a brain capacity 100 cc larger than modern man's.

The average human heart beats about 100,000 times every 24 hours. In a seventy-two-year lifetime the heart beats more than 2.5 billion times.

A woman's heart beats faster than a man's.

During pregnancy, the uterus expands to 500 times its normal size.

During menstruation, the sensitivity of a woman's middle finger is reduced.

The human tongue tastes bitter things with the taste buds toward the back. Salty and pungent flavors are tasted in the middle of the tongue, sweet flavors at the tip.

The average person's total skin covering would weigh about 6 pounds if collected into one mass.

The average woman's thighs are 1½ inches larger in circumference than the average man's.

An average man on an average day excretes 2½ quarts of sweat.

The palms of the hands and soles of the feet contain more sweat glands than any other part of the body.

A skin graft can be taken only from the skin of one's own body or from the body of an identical twin.

False teeth are often radioactive. Approximately 1 million Americans wear some form of denture; half of these dentures are made of a porcelain compound laced with minute amounts of uranium to stimulate fluorescence. Without the uranium additive the dentures would be a dull green color when seen under artificial light.

16th-century drawing by Andreas Vesalius showing network of nerves in human body

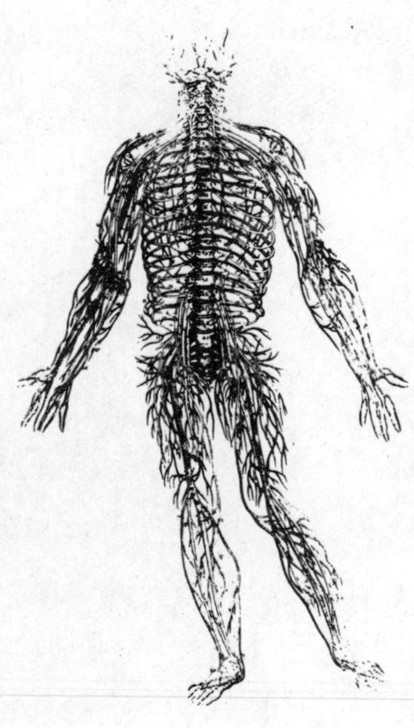

For many years after the Battle of Waterloo, dentures known as "Waterloo teeth" were sold throughout Europe. These were actual human teeth extracted from the corpses of soldiers on the Waterloo battlefield. They were especially esteemed among denture wearers because most of them came from young, healthy boys.

The older a person gets the less sleep he requires. A child should get from 8 to 9 hours a night. An elderly adult can do well with 4 to 6 hours.

The liver is a gland, not an organ.

There are 10 trillion living cells in the human body.

Tongue prints are as unique as fingerprints.

The human body has 45 miles of nerves.

The fingernails and the hair are dead. Both are made of a tissue called keratin, which is similar to the dried skin cells that continually flake off the body. Hair and nails, however, originate from living cells. Growth occurs at the base, and new cells push the dead hair and nails upward. Then these cells themselves die, to be pushed up and replaced by more from below.

While 7 men in 100 have some form of color blindness, only 1 woman in 1,000 suffers from it. The most common form of color blindness is a red-green deficiency.

The mouth produces a quart of saliva a day.

Human nails and hair do *not* grow after death. They are simply the last part of the body to disintegrate.

The fingernails grow faster on the hand you favor. If you are right-handed your right fingernails will grow faster; if left-handed, your left. The middle fingernail grows faster than all other nails.

## China

In *Tales from Early Histories,* the Chinese historian Ssu-ma relates that the Yin dynasty king, Chou-hsin (1154–1122 B.C.) used the following mixtures as aphrodisiacs:

*The Hunting Lion*—the paws of bears simmered over a slow fire, and flavored with the horn of a rhinoceros and distilled human urine.

*Celestial Thunder*—the tongues of a hundred peacocks spiced with chili powder from the western provinces and flavored with the sperm of pubescent boys.

*Three-Day Glory*—soy beans mixed with fresh ginseng, the penis of an ox, and dried human placenta.

In ancient China, towns were often arranged in specific patterns so that if seen from the air the whole community resembled an animal or a symbolic design. The city of Tsuenchen-fu was built in the shape of a carp. Wung-chun was laid out in the shape of a fish net. Other towns were arranged to resemble snakes, stars, sunbursts, and dragons.

---

In sixteenth- and seventeenth-century Peking, one took revenge against one's enemies by placing finely chopped tiger's whiskers in their food. The numerous infinitesimal whisker barbs would get caught in the vicitim's digestive tract and cause hundreds of painful sores and infections.

---

The famous Boxer Rebellion in China received its name from its association with an ancient Chinese martial art, Kung-fu. During this bloody uprising in northern China in 1900, traditionalist members of a secret society called *I-ho-ch'uan* ("Harmonious and Righteous Fists") set out to destroy all foreign influences in China, including schools, churches, and places of commerce and trade. The members of this society were well trained in the ancient fighting art of Kung-fu, which, because there was no equivalent word in English to describe it, became known to westerners simply as "boxing." Hence the uprising was termed the "Boxers' Rebellion."

---

In third-century China, kites were used as games, ritual objects, musical instruments, transmitters of messages, distance-measuring devices, weapons, and parachutes.

---

The willow-leaf pattern commonly found on Chinese plates and cookware is descended from a series of signs and emblems used by ancient Chinese secret societies. The original pattern, designed in the fifteenth century and used as a means of communication among members of these societies, was discovered by the Manchu government, which ordered all the plates destroyed. The pattern turned up again in Europe in the eighteenth century. It had been copied by a western merchant who had managed to smuggle a few of the original plates out of China.

---

In the early fifteenth century, scholars in China compiled an encyclopedia consisting of 11,095 volumes.

---

---

The men who served as guards along the Great Wall of China in the Middle Ages were often born on the wall, grew up there, married there, died there, and were buried within it. Many of these guards never left the wall in their entire lives.

---

Chang Hsien-chung, a Chinese bandit, is credited with having killed 40 million people between 1643 and 1648. He completely wiped out the population of Szechwan province.

---

At funerals in ancient China, when the lid of a coffin was closed, mourners took a few steps backward lest their shadows get caught in the box.

---

In ancient China people committed suicide by eating a pound of salt.

---

There are more than 40,000 characters in Chinese script.

---

Some Chinese typewriters have 5,700 characters. The keyboard is almost 3 feet wide on some models, and the fastest one can type on these machines is 11 words per minute.

---

Until the modernization of China, and to some extent still today, the Chinese did the following things:

When they met a friend they shook their own hand, not his.

When serving tea they placed the saucer over the cup (to keep it warm), not under it.

They drank hot beverages to cool themselves.

After bathing they dried themselves with a wet towel.

When building a house they constructed the roof first.

Their compasses pointed south, not north.

They said "westsouth," not "southwest."

Their surnames came first, not last.

They addressed letters in the following manner: New York City, Street Blank, 50, Jones, John Mr.

They read books from back to front and put footnotes at the top of the page.

Noon was any time between 12:00 and 2:00 P.M., midnight any hour before dawn.

They used paper in their windows instead of glass.

---

Confucius, from a design of the Tang dynasty (7th–10th century)

Centuries before Christ, the Chinese were using natural gas for lighting. Gas was brought to the surface from beds of rock salt 1,600 feet beneath the ground, conveyed through bamboo pipes, and used for illuminating home interiors in Szechwan province.

---

Confucius is not a Chinese name. In China the sage's name is K'ung Fu-tzu. Further, the words "mandarin," "junk," "coolie," and "pagoda" are all English. None of them is Chinese in origin.

---

In the Chinese written language, the ideograph that stands for "trouble" represents two women under one roof.

---

The abacus was not invented in China. It originated in Egypt in 2000 B.C., almost a millennium before it reached the Orient.

---

The Chinese invented eyeglasses. Marco Polo reported seeing many pairs worn by the Chinese as early as 1275, 500 years before lens grinding became an art in the West.

## Churches

The first gold brought back by Christopher Columbus from the Americas was used to gild the ceiling of the church of Santa Maria Maggiore in Rome. The ceiling and the gold are still there.

---

In the original architectural design, the French cathedral of Chartres had six spires. (It was built with two spires.)

---

Many Gothic churches of the Middle Ages were built in the following way: a quarry site was established, often as much as 50 miles from the place where the church was to be erected. When the rocks were mined, volunteers from all over the countryside would form a living chain from the quarry to the building site. The rocks would then be passed from hand to hand all the way to the construction grounds.

---

The world's largest Gothic cathedral is in New York City. It is the Cathedral of St. John the Divine on Amsterdam Avenue and 112th Street. The cathedral measures 601 feet long, 146 feet wide, and has a transept measuring 320 feet from end to end.

---

## The Classical World

Nero did not fiddle while Rome burned. The fiddle had not yet been invented. Nor was Nero there. He was at his villa in Antium, 50 miles away.

---

The Colosseum of ancient Rome was occasionally filled with water and an entire naval battle was staged there, complete with armed vessels and fights to the death.

Remains of the Roman Colosseum

The ancient Greeks were the first to use bed springs. They fashioned them out of braided leather thongs and hung them between opposite sides of the bed.

At the time of Titus in fourth-century Rome, the Circus Maximus held 380,000 spectators.

Florentine engraving depicting the death of Aeschylus

According to several Greek historians, the great playwright Aeschylus was killed by a tortoise dropped on his head from a great height by an eagle.

The Roman pantheon included a god whose only function was to rule over mildew. His name was Robigus. Each year on April 25th a procession wound through the streets of Rome to Robigus' sacred grove, where a red puppy was sacrificed in his name. The Romans hoped the sacrifice would appease the mildew god's hunger for their crops.

Until the time of the Caesars, all Romans were vegetarians.

Suetonius Tranquillis reported in his *Life of Augustus* that the great Roman poet Vergil once held a funeral for a dead fly, complete with pallbearers and lengthy eulogies. In ancient Rome, cemetery land was not taxable. By interring a fly on the land surrounding his private villa, the wily poet turned his home into a burial ground and thus made it tax-exempt.

Ancient Romans always entered the home of a friend on their right foot—the left side of the body was thought to portend evil. The Latin word for "left" is *sinister*—thus our English word "sinister" for anything threatening or malevolent.

Christmas-tree ornaments date back to the time of the Romans. During the Saturnalia, which coincided roughly with our Christmas holiday, the Romans hung little masks of Bacchus on pine trees. Vergil refers to these dangling ornaments as *oscilla,* and describes how during the December season evergreens were laden with them.

Roman coins minted during the reign of Diocletian have been excavated in remote parts of Iceland. No one is quite certain what this signifies historically, as the very existence of Iceland was unknown to the ancient Romans.

The ancient Greek leader Pericles was so self-conscious about his pointed head that he would only pose for portraits wearing a helmet.

Roman statues were made with detachable heads, so that one head could be removed and replaced by another.

The month of July is named after Julius Caesar. The month of August is named after Augustus Caesar.

The Roman emperor Caligula bestowed the rank of Consul First Class on his favorite horse, Incitatus. The horse was provided with a gold goblet for drinking wine and with an ivory manger.

Above: Pericles
Below: Roman statuette of theatrical figure with hooked nose

Atomic theory was known to the ancient Greeks. It formed the basis of the Greek philosopher Democritus' theory of "atomism" and his "materialistic" explanation of the universe.

In ancient Greece, no one was born or died on the island of Delos. Whenever someone became pregnant or ill, she or he was quickly removed from the sacred island and was kept away until nature took its course.

In ancient Rome it was considered a sign of leadership to be born with a hooked nose.

A stone phallus was set above the city gates of many ancient Roman towns as a protection against bad luck. Under the phallus appeared the inscription *Hic Habit Felicitas*—"Happiness Dwells Here." The Romans often hung small phalli around children's necks as a protection against the evil eye.

The level and the claw hammer, found in every modern carpenter's tool chest, were invented by the ancient Romans.

## Colleges

The University of Calcutta has 175,000 students.

According to a survey taken by the Standard & Poor Corporation in 1976, 30 percent of the leading executives of United States corporations attended the following twelve colleges: Harvard leads the list and is followed, in order, by New York University, Yale, University of Pennsylvania, University of Michigan, Columbia, Northwestern, City College of New York, Princeton, University of Wisconsin, MIT, and University of Illinois.

John Harvard did not found Harvard University. Harvard, a Puritan minister, simply left his library of 400 books to the college when he died in 1638. The college itself had been founded two years earlier and was first known as Cambridge.

Yale was founded by Harvard men. In 1700 ten educators, nine of them Harvard graduates, met in Killingworth (now Clinton), Connecticut, for the purpose of establishing a college. When it was begun, Yale was not known as Yale but as the Collegiate School of Connecticut. Only in 1718, thanks to donations from Elihu Yale, was it given its present name.

Yale College and State House, New Haven, early 19th century

The famous goldfish-swallowing fad was started at Harvard University in 1938 by a student who downed a fish on a lark, then was challenged to perform the same feat in public. Hundreds of students witnessed the performance, and the fad caught on. The first goldfish-swallowing record was set the following year by a student from Middlesex College who downed 67 live goldfish. In 1967 the fad was revived just long enough for a St. Joseph's College undergrad to consume 199 hapless fish.

There are fewer than a million college graduates each year in the United States.

North Texas State University gives a degree in "dance-band arts."

Dartmouth was the only college in New England to remain open during the entire Revolutionary War.

When Harvard College was founded in 1636 it was surrounded by a tall stockade to keep out prowling wolves and hostile Indians.

## Comic Strips & Cartoons

Mickey Mouse has only four fingers. Early Mickey Mouses can be distinguished from later ones by the fact that the originals have a pie-shaped section of white in their eyes while the later ones do not.

The oldest continuous comic strip still in existence is "The Katzenjammer Kids." It first appeared in newspapers in 1897.

There is a 6-foot-high stone monument dedicated to the comic-strip character Popeye in Crystal City, Texas.

# Communications

The *Boston Nation,* a newspaper published in Ohio during the mid-nineteenth century, had pages 7½ feet long and 5½ feet wide. It required two people to hold the paper in proper reading position.

Almost half the newspapers in the world are published in the United States and Canada.

Of all professionals in the United States, journalists are credited with having the largest vocabulary—approximately 20,000 words. Clergymen, lawyers, and doctors each have about 15,000 words at their disposal. Skilled workers who have not had a college education know between 5,000 and 7,000 words, farm laborers about 1,600.

As of 1976, there were 110,200,000 TV sets in America, 372,000,000 radios, and 125,142,000 telephones.

The average American's vocabulary contains 10,000 words.

There is no known way for a submarine to communicate with land via radio when it is underwater.

According to a Nielsen rating survey taken in 1974, the average three-year-old child in America spends 30 hours a week in front of the television set.

There are more television sets in the United States than there are people in Japan.

As of 1976 in Greece, it cost $250 to get a telephone installed in a private residence and there was a four-year waiting list. The cost per call, however, is cheaper in Greece than in any other country in the world.

When using the first pay telephones (installed in an office building in New Haven, Connecticut, in June, 1880), a caller did not deposit his coins in the machine. He gave them to an attendant who stood next to the telephone. Coin telephones did not appear until 1899.

---

The first operators employed by the Bell Telephone Company were young boys who worked standing up. Only after several years did it occur to anybody to provide them with chairs.

---

The Pentagon building in Arlington, Virginia, has 68,000 miles of telephone lines.

---

There are 5,919,682 telephones in New York City, more phones than in the entire country of Spain. The cables serving the New York City area have 33,072,975 miles of wire.

---

On November 9, 1965, the day of the great blackout in the northeastern United States, 62 million phone calls were placed in New York City during a twenty-four-hour period. That is the greatest number of telephone calls ever made in one day.

---

There is only one country in the world without telephone service: Bhutan.

---

The average American sees or hears 560 advertisements a day.

---

# Crime

The nation with the highest murder rate in the world is Nicaragua—there are 30 homicides per 100,000 people every year. As of 1975, the western nation with the lowest murder rate was Spain, with one killing per million people per year. In Hunza, a small state above Kashmir, only one murder has been recorded in the last seventy-five years.

Marie-Augustin Marquis de Pélier of Brittany was arrested in 1786 and spent the next fifty years of his life in prison. His crime: whistling at Queen Marie Antoinette as she was being ushered into a theater.

A 1975 Gallup poll shows that Latin America has the highest crime rate in the world. Next come Africa and then the United States. According to this poll, people from richer countries report themselves happier, find their lives more interesting, worry less, and would like fewer changes in their existence than those from more impoverished nations. Only 8 percent of Latin Americans and 6 percent of Africans are satisfied with their lives.

According to the National Safety Council, an average of sixty-nine people a day are shot to death with handguns in the United States. Three-quarters of these shootings take place within the inner family circle or among close friends.

According to the International Association of Art Security, art theft is the second most common international crime in the world (the first is narcotics smuggling). In 1975 33,840 thefts were reported world-wide. The United States had the greatest number of art robberies—9,460.

Approximately half the money paid out by fire-insurance companies in the United States is paid for fire loss due to arson.

Murder is the only crime that does not increase during the full moon. Theft, disorderly conduct, larceny, armed robbery, assault and battery, illegal breaking and entering, and rape all statistically increase dramatically during the full moon.

The Center for Studies in Criminology and Criminal Law at the University of Pennsylvania reports that as of 1975 women were responsible for 31 percent of all embezzlement in the United States.

Approximately 80 percent of the men serving terms in American prisons for rape were convicted not of forcible rape but of statutory rape, that is, of fornicating with a girl who is underage.

## Death

After his death, Alexander the Great's remains were preserved in a huge crock of honey. Among the ancient Egyptians, it was common practice to bury the dead in this manner.

Undertakers report that human bodies do not deteriorate as quickly as they used to. The reason for this, they believe, is that the modern diet contains so many preservatives that these chemicals tend to prevent the body from decomposing too rapidly after death.

Obsidian balls, or occasionally brass balls, were placed in

Mummy from the tomb of Tutankhamen, 18th century B.C.

the eye sockets of Egyptian mummies. The bandaging of a mummy often took from six to eight months and required a collection of special tools, including a long metal hook that was used to draw the dead person's brains out through his nose.

---

When a man died in ancient Egypt, the females in his family would smear their heads and faces with mud and wander through the city beating themselves and tearing off their clothes.

---

When a crusader died, his corpse was chopped up and the flesh boiled away. This was done so that the skeleton could be conveniently returned to Europe for a Christian burial.

---

When a person dies, hearing is generally the last sense to go. The first sense lost is usually sight. Then follow taste, smell, and touch.

---

In ancient Egypt, when merchants left the country on business trips they carried small stone models of themselves. If they died while abroad, these figures were sent back to Egypt for proxy burial.

---

In Turkey the color of mourning is violet. In most Moslem countries and in China the color is white.

---

Among the Danakil tribesmen of Ethiopia, when a male dies his grave is marked with a stone for every man he killed.

---

Until the 1950's, Tibetans disposed of their dead by taking the body up to a hill, hacking it into little pieces, and feeding the remains to the birds.

---

It is possible to drown and not die. Technically the term "drowning" refers to the process of taking water into the lungs, not to death caused by that process.

---

More men than women commit suicide in the United States.

---

A recent Gallup poll shows that 69 percent of Americans

believe they will go somewhere after death.

## Demography

In the tenth century A.D. there was not one city in Europe with a population over 400,000.

The black population of Houston, Texas (316,551), is greater than the total population of the entire state of Alaska (302,173).

No one knows how many people live in the country of Bhutan. As of 1975, no census had ever been taken.

In 1790 only 5 percent of the American population lived in cities.

The population of Colombia doubles every twenty-two years.

The population of the American colonies in 1610 was 350.

As of 1976, Chile, Egypt, and Guatemala had the highest birth rates in the world.

Ninety million people are added to the world's population each year. It is estimated that by the year 2000 there will be 1,800,000,000 people in China alone.

Hawaii is the only state in the United States where male life expectancy exceeds 70 years. Hawaii also leads all states in life expectancy in general, with an average of 73.6 years for both males and females.

Every year one out of five American families changes its place of residence.

Roughly a quarter of the world's people live in China.

There are more people in New York City (7,895,563) than

there are in the states of Alaska (302,173), Vermont (444,732), Wyoming (332,416), South Dakota (666,257), New Hampshire (737,681), Nevada (488,738), Idaho (713,008), Utah (1,059,273), Hawaii (769,913), North Dakota (617,761), Delaware (548,104), and New Mexico (1,016,000) combined.

---

If the population of the world continues to expand at its present rate, in the year 2100 there will be 60,000,000,000,000,000 people on the face of the earth.

---

Roughly 40 percent of the population of the underdeveloped world is under fifteen years old.

---

The population of the entire world in 5000 B.C., according to the National Population Council, was 5 million.

---

If the population continues to expand at its present rate, Calcutta, India, will have a population of 66 million in the year 2000.

---

There are more Irish in New York City than in Dublin, more Italians in New York City than in Rome, and more Jews in New York City than in Tel Aviv.

---

It is estimated by the National Population Council that 74 billion human beings have been born and died in the last 500,000 years.

---

New York City has the largest black population of any city in the United States. It is followed by Chicago and Philadelphia.

# Diet

Celery has negative calories—it takes more calories to eat a piece of celery than the celery has in it to begin with.

---

The candies most likely to cause tooth decay are dark

chocolate and fudge. Those least likely to damage the teeth are nut- or coconut-covered candies. The most harmful baked goods are chocolate-chip cookies, frosted cakes, and Graham crackers. The least harmful to the teeth are pies, plain cakes, and doughnuts.

---

One has to eat 11 pounds of potatoes to put on 1 pound of weight—a potato has no more calories than an apple. The potato was not known in Europe until the seventeenth century, when it was introduced by returning Spanish conquistadors. At first potatoes were thought disgusting and were blamed for starting outbreaks of leprosy and syphilis. As late as 1720 in America eating potatoes was believed to shorten a person's life.

---

The United States Postal Service assures its customers that they will not get fat licking stamps. There is no more than one-tenth of a calorie's worth of glue on every stamp.

---

## Drugs

In 1865 opium was grown in the state of Virginia and a product was distilled from it that yielded 4 percent morphine. In 1867 it was grown in Tennessee; six years later it was cultivated in Kentucky. During these years opium, marijuana, and cocaine could be purchased legally over the counter from any druggist.

Cultivating opium poppies

---

In sixteenth-century Europe many druggists sold medicine made from the powder of Egyptian mummies. Such "medicine" was considered good for gout and catarrh and was often incorporated into products known as "mummy balm" or "Egyptian salve." In 1564 someone named Guy de la Fontaine attempted to corner the mummy market in Alexandria, a center for the export of such commodities. He discovered that Alexandrian merchants had for some time been selling the mummified remains of derelicts who had died not so long before from a variety of rather loathsome diseases.

---

In the Andes Mountains of Peru, where porters can work with superhuman endurance for days with little or no food by chewing the leaves of the coca plant (from which cocaine is extracted), distances are measured in *cocadas* rather than miles. A *cocada* is the span of road that can be traveled after chewing one portion of coca leaves.

The drug thiopentone can kill a human being in one second if injected directly into the blood.

Both George Washington and Thomas Jefferson grew *Cannabis sativa* (marijuana) on their plantations.

## The Earth

The earth is estimated to be 4.5 billion years old. It travels through space at 660,000 miles per hour.

The oldest rocks in the world, the so-called St. Peter and St. Paul stones in the Atlantic Ocean, are 4 billion years old.

The earth weighs 6,588,000,000,000,000,000,000,000 tons.

The earth rotates on its axis more slowly in March than in September.

If the earth were compressed to a sphere with a 2-inch diameter, its surface would be as smooth as a billiard ball's.

The temperature of the earth's interior increases by 1 degree every 60 feet down.

If the world were to become totally flat and the oceans distributed themselves evenly over the earth's surface, the water would be approximately 2 miles deep at every point.

Glaciers occupy 5.8 million square miles, or 10 percent of the world's land surface, an area as large as South America.

The world is not round. It is an oblate spheroid, flattened at the poles and bulging at the equator.

## Energy

The average American uses eight times as much fuel energy as an average person anywhere else in the world.

In one night, the World Trade Center in New York City uses more electricity than the entire city of Troy, New York.

A person uses more household energy shaving with a hand razor at a sink (because of the water power, the water pump, and so on) than he would by using an electric razor.

The world consumes 1 billion gallons of petroleum a day.

Petroleum accounts for half the world's energy supply.

One 75-watt bulb gives more light than three 25-watt bulbs.

Ten cords of wood stacked 4 feet wide by 4 feet high by 80 feet long have the same heating potential as 1,400 gallons of oil.

A car operates at maximum economy, gas-wise, at speeds between 25 and 35 miles per hour. A car that shifts manually gets 2 miles more per gallon of gas than a car with automatic shift. A car uses 1.6 ounces of gas idling for one minute. Half an ounce is used to start the average automobile.

# Executions

In the Middle Ages animals were tried and publicly executed. Birds, wolves, insects, all were tried by ecclesiastical courts as witches and heretics, and suffered excommunication, torture, and death. The last such trial took place in 1740, when a French judge found a cow guilty of sorcery and ordered it hanged by the neck until dead. In 1386 at Falaise a judge ordered a pig to have its legs mutilated and then be hanged for killing a little girl. The pig was dressed up in the child's jacket and dragged to the town square with all the ceremony due a first-rate criminal. The execution, it is recorded, cost 6 sous plus a pair of gloves for the executioner so that he might carry out the killing with clean hands.

During the French revolution, a magistrate named Jean Baptiste Carrier, commissioner of the National Convention at Nantes, dispatched a number of boatloads of political prisoners into the Loire River. When the boat was in midstream he ordered a trap door in the bottom of the boat opened, sending an entire group of prisoners to their death. From his merciless methods of extermination the word *noyade,* meaning "mass drownings," was coined.

Beheading of Mary, Queen of Scots

People condemned to the guillotine in France during the French revolution had the top of their head shaved. Two long locks of hair were left hanging at the temples.

Those condemned to die by the axe in medieval and Renaissance England were obliged to tip their executioner to ensure that he would complete the job in one blow. In some executions, notably that of Mary, Queen of Scots, it took fifteen whacks of the blade before the head was severed.

The Nazis used the guillotine to execute prisoners during World War II. Their version of the punishment had the condemned person lying on his back with his eyes forced open so that he had to watch the blade as it descended.

Until recent times, prisoners condemned to death in Mongolia were nailed into wooden boxes and left on the plains to die of exposure and starvation.

## Fashion

Before King George IV of England ordered a set of boots made to fit each of his feet, shoes were designed to be worn on either foot.

In eighteenth-century England eyeglasses were often worn purely as fashionable accessories, not as aids to vision. Such glasses were frequently set in gold frames decorated with precious jewels. Sometimes the lenses were removed completely, leaving only the decorative frame to ornament the face.

Fashionable women in medieval Japan gilded or blackened their teeth. Today many Hindu women in India stain their teeth bright red to enhance their appearance.

The Maya Indians filed their front teeth to points and drilled holes in them so that they could be embellished with precious gems. They filled cavities in their teeth with pieces of jade.

The buttons on the back of a dress coat once served a purpose other than decoration. In seventeenth- and eighteenth-century Europe, the skirts of such coats were very long and the tails flapped about, interfering with movement. An ingenious gentleman had buttons sewn on the back so that when the wearer was in a hurry he could simply button up his skirts.

The pigtail worn for so many years by Chinese men was originally a symbol of abject humiliation. The Manchus, a tribe of Tartars, conquered China in 1644. To emphasize their suzerainty, they ordered each Chinese male to shave the forepart of his head and to permit the hair on the back

Chinese men at a fortuneteller's. All have shaved heads and pigtails.

of his head to grow long. This extended length of hair was then to be braided and tasseled, and in the presence of superiors always hung over the back. The pigtail, however, gradually became so popular among its wearers that in 1912 when the Manchus were defeated and dethroned, most Chinese men were loath to give it up.

---

The natives of Kandahar, Afghanistan, wear turbans which when unwrapped are 20 feet long.

A group of turbaned Afghan chiefs

---

Americans spend more than $125 billion a year on sneakers. One hundred million pairs were sold in 1975.

---

Kilts are not native to Scotland. They originated in France.

The shoestring was invented in England in 1790. Prior to this time all shoes were fastened with buckles.

In the late nineteenth century, it was the fashion among many English women to wear gold rings through their nipples. In an 1899 edition of the British journal *Society,* fascinating details are given about this peculiar fad. The woman who wished to wear such ornaments, the magazine said, had holes bored through her nipples and thin golden rings threaded through the holes. It was believed that wearing such rings made the breasts fuller and rounder, and that the rings were a stimulating sight for men when exposed. The operation was performed not by doctors, but by jewelers, much the way ear piercing is done today.

## Firsts

Benjamin Franklin was the first head of the United States Post Office.

The first macaroni factory in the United States was established in 1848. It was started by Antoine Zegera in Brooklyn, New York.

The first United States Marine Corps officer of Chinese descent was commissioned in 1943. His name was Wilbur Sze. The first black to be commissioned in the Marines, John Rudder, received his commission in 1948.

The first telephone book ever issued contained only fifty names. It was published in New Haven, Connecticut, by the New Haven District Telephone Company in February, 1878.

King George VI of England became the first British monarch to set foot on American soil when he visited the World's Fair in New York City in 1939.

The first Secretary of Health, Education and Welfare was a

woman. Her name was Oveta Culp Hobby and she took office in 1953.

---

The Grand Canyon was not seen by a white man until after the Civil War. It was first entered on May 29, 1869, by the geologist John Wesley Powell.

---

Of the first five men to reach the North Pole, one was black, four were oriental, and one was white. The orientals were Eskimos serving as porters for their white leader, Robert Peary. The black was Matthew Henson, Peary's personal aide.

---

Wyoming was the first state to allow women to vote.

---

*The Adventures of Tom Sawyer* was the first novel ever to be written on a typewriter. It was typed on a Remington in 1875 by Mark Twain himself. Twain, however, wished to withhold the fact. He did not want to write testimonials, he said, or answer questions concerning the operation of the "newfangled thing."

---

Catherine de Medici was the first woman in Europe to use tobacco. She took it in a mixture of snuff.

---

The A & P was the first chain-store business to be established. It began in 1842.

---

Benjamin Franklin was America's first political cartoonist. His drawing of a snake divided into eight parts was published in Philadelphia in 1754.

---

Andrew Jackson was the first president to ride in a railroad train. The first to use a telephone was James Garfield. Theodore Roosevelt was the first president to ride in an automobile.

---

Theodore Roosevelt was the first United States president to visit a foreign country while in office. In November, 1906, he sailed on the U.S.S. *Louisiana* for Panama and Puerto Rico.

---

# Fish

The teeth of the tiger shark rest on a spring. When the shark's mouth is closed, the teeth are pressed back firmly against the gums. When the mouth is opened, the teeth spring out, ready for action.

Head of tiger shark

*The white shark (Carcharodon sp.):*

has teeth that rank on a scale of hardness with steel.

is the only creature in the sea with no natural enemies; even killer whales normally avoid it.

can survive brain damage better than any animal in the world.

never gets sick. It has mysterious antibodies that give it immunity to practically every known bacterial invader. It is also one of the few animals known to be completely immune to cancer.

can hear sounds a mile away.

is always hungry; no matter how much it eats, its appetite is never satisfied—it lives in a state of continual hunger.

Despite their ferocity and reputation, however, sharks rarely attack man. Three times as many people are killed each year by lightning as are killed by sharks. A hundred more people die from bee stings each year than from shark bites.

The lanternfish has a glowing spot on the front of its head that acts like a miner's lamp when the fish is swimming in dark waters. This "lamp" is so powerful that it can shed light for a distance as great as 2 feet. Experiments have shown that when confined to an aquarium, the lanternfish can project enough light to allow a person to read a book in an otherwise totally darkened room.

Atlantic salmon are able to leap 15 feet high.

Most tropical marine fish could survive in a tank filled with human blood.

Minnows have teeth in their throat.

The lungfish can live out of water in a state of suspended animation for three years.

Lungfish

An electric eel can produce a shock of more than 600 volts, five times more powerful than a household outlet. It not only uses this power to kill its prey but to locate it as well—though it is born with eyes, it is blind as an adult and employs its electricity to find food in much the same way as man uses radar.

A marine catfish can taste with any part of its body. The female marine catfish hatches her eggs in her mouth.

The garfish has green bones.

The freshwater eel *(Anguilla rostrata* and *Anguilla anguilla):*

All freshwater eels, both the European and American species, are born in the same place, a seaweed- and vine-clogged section of the ocean south of Bermuda known as the Sargasso Sea. From this location, the eels migrate to

various parts of the world, the American eels to North America, the European eels to Europe. The trips may take as long as three years. Once they arrive at their destination, the males remain at the river mouths while the females move farther upstream, finally settling in small island lakes and ponds. They remain there for ten to fifteen years, until they receive a strange instinctive call back to the sea. Swimming against great river currents, leaping upward like salmon, sometimes leaving the water altogether to crawl along great stretches of land, the female eel finally makes her way back to the sea, where she joins the male. Then they swim together directly to the Sargasso Sea. Here they mate, spawn, and die.

## Flowers, Plants, & Trees

The nasturtium derives its name from the Latin *nasus* ("nose") *tortum* ("to twist"). The flower's smell is so powerful that to inhale it was considered tantamount to having one's nose tweaked.

Nasturtiums

The Japanese have a special method for growing superb melons. They plant a seed, allow it to sprout and form buds, then pick all the buds but one. This one bud is allowed to mature into a full fruit. In this way a single fruit receives all the nutrients originally meant for the whole plant. The result is a remarkably succulent melon.

The cucumber is not a vegetable; botanically, it is a fruit. So are the eggplant, the pumpkin, the squash, the tomato, the gherkin, and the okra. Rhubarb, however, is botanically a vegetable, not a fruit.

Fruits and flowers of the cucumber plant

An orange tree may bear oranges for more than 100 years. The famous "Constable Tree," an orange tree brought to France in 1421, lived and bore fruit for 473 years.

Orange pickers

The General Sherman Tree in Sequoia National Park, California, is the largest tree in the world. It weighs more than 6,000 tons.

---

Poison oak is not oak; poison ivy is not ivy. Both are members of the cashew family (Anacardiaceae).

---

A peanut is not a nut. It is a legume.

---

The bark of the redwood tree is fireproof. Fires in redwood forests take place *inside* the trees.

---

Oak trees are struck by lightning more often than any other tree. This, it has been theorized, is one reason that the ancient Greeks considered oak trees sacred to Zeus, god of thunder and lightning.

---

The angle between the main branches of a tree and its trunk remains constant in each species—and this same angle is found between the principal vein of the tree's leaves and all its subsidiary branching veins.

---

Seedless oranges were not grown in the United States until 1871. The first ones came from Brazil and were planted in California.

---

The banana cannot reproduce itself. It can be propagated only by the hand of man. Further, the banana is not a tree,

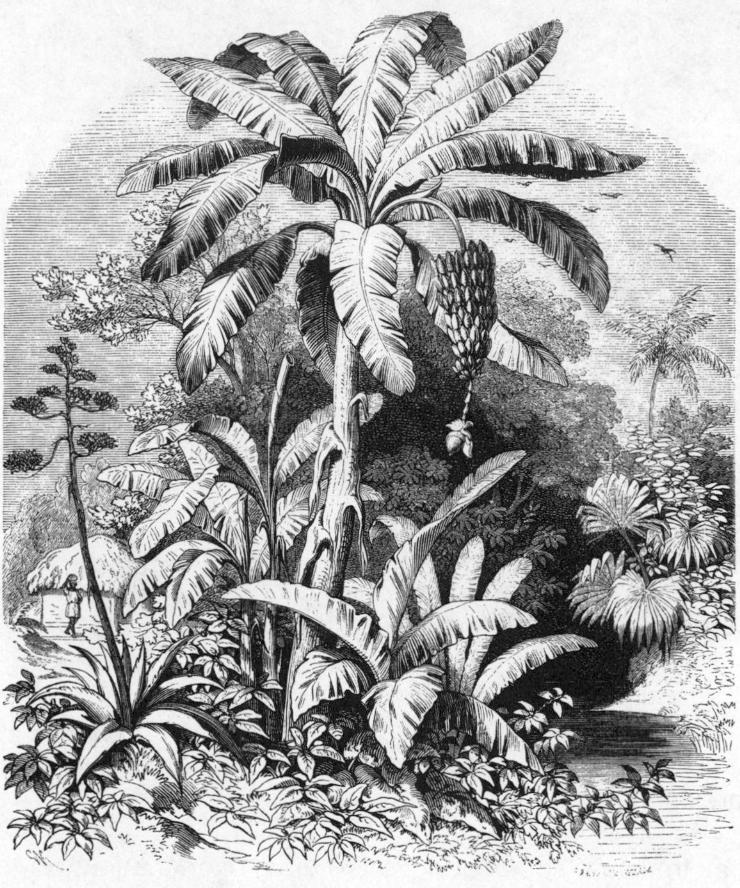

it is an herb, the largest known of all plants without a woody stem or solid trunk.

Right: Banana plant
Below: Leaves and fruit of the baobab tree

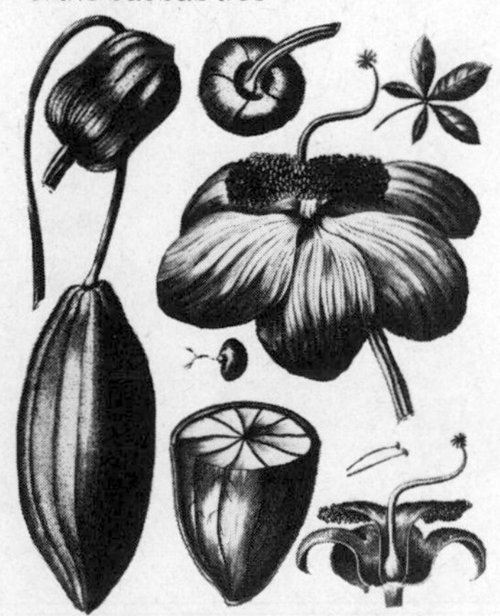

The sequoias and redwoods of the American West Coast are *not* the oldest living trees in the world. The honor belongs to the macrozamia trees of Australia, which live 5,000 to 7,000 years and, some claim, may even reach 15,000 years.

The trunk of the African baobab tree is sometimes as wide as the tree is high. The tree is pollinated by bats, and its blossoms open only in moonlight.

The rings of a tree are always farther apart on the tree's southern side. Woodsmen often read tree rings to find the compass points.

Bamboo is not a tree. It is a wood grass.

The onion is a lily, botanically.

Cork comes from the bark of trees. Specifically, it is harvested from the cork tree, which takes more than ten years to produce one layer of cork.

Life preservers and the linings of aviators' jackets used during World War II were made from fiber found in milkweed pods.

In one day a full-grown oak tree expels 7 tons of water through its leaves.

During midsummer the radical leaves of the compass plant invariably point precisely north and south.

The orchid is named after the male genitalia. Its botanical family name, Orchidaceae, means "testicles" in Greek and may derive from an early notion that the orchid possessed aphrodisiac qualities.

The poinsettia flower is named after a nineteenth-century ambassador to Mexico, Joel R. Poinsett, who first brought the poinsettia plant to America.

The flower of the calla lily *(Amorphophallus titanum)* is 8 feet high and 12 feet wide. It is grown in Sumatra.

Eighty percent of the world's rose species come from Asia.

It takes 4,000 crocuses to produce a single ounce of saffron.

*Bamboo and Rocks,* detail of a 13th-century Chinese hanging scroll

## Food & Drink

Diamond Jim Brady's average breakfast as recorded by a New York restauranteur: a gallon of orange juice, three eggs, a quarter of a loaf of corn bread, sirloin steak with fried potatoes, hominy grits and bacon, two muffins, and several pancakes. For dinner Diamond Jim might eat three dozen oysters, two bowls of turtle soup, and six crabs as an appetizer. Restaurant owners referred to him as the best twenty-five customers they ever had.

A raisin dropped in a glass of fresh champagne will bounce up and down continually from the bottom of the glass to the top.

In medieval England beer was often served with breakfast.

The United States Department of Agriculture reports that the average American eats 8½ pounds of pickles a year. Dill pickles are twice as popular as sweet.

The pickle, an American favorite

Cabbage is 91 percent water.

Lettuce is the world's most popular green.

The term "cocktail" was invented in Elmsford, New York. A barmaid named Betsy Flanagan decorated her establishment with the tail feathers of cocks. One day a patron asked for "one of those cock tails." She served him a drink with a feather in it.

As many as 50 gallons of maple sap are needed to make a single gallon of maple sugar.

Dairy products account for 29 percent of all food consumed in the United States.

The Swedes drink more coffee than any other people in the world.

Potato chips were invented by a black chef in Louisiana in 1865.

Goat's milk is used more widely throughout the world than cow's milk.

Milking goats in India

Wine tasters never drink the wine they taste. They sip it, swish it about, gargle it, and then spit it out. Swallowing wine is believed to dull the palate, not to mention the brain.

Wadakin and Matsuzuka beef, raised in Japan, are considered the two most tender kinds of beef in the world. The steers from which this meat is taken are isolated in totally dark stalls, fed on beer and beer mash, and hand-massaged by specially trained beef masseurs three times a day.

Wine will spoil if exposed to light; hence tinted bottles.

Chop suey was invented in the United States. Its creator was a Chinese dignitary visiting America in the nineteenth century. Requested by American friends to prepare an authentic Chinese meal and not having the proper ingredients, the Chinese gentleman ordered his cook to collect all available foods, pour them into a large pot, and flavor the whole thing with soya sauce, which was still relatively new and exotic to the western palate. Asked the name of this delicious concoction, the dignitary, spotting a pair of chopsticks lying near the bottle of soya sauce, replied, "Chop-soya." Through his heavy Chinese accent this became "chop suey," and so it has remained ever since.

---

Milk is heavier than cream.

---

According to the Nutritional Sciences Department of Cornell University, the best temperature at which to preserve frozen foods is 0° F (−18° C).

---

The purpose of the indentation at the bottom of a wine bottle is to strengthen the structure of the bottle and to trap the sediments in the wine.

---

Vintage port takes forty years to reach maturity.

---

The average person ingests about a ton of food and drink each year.

---

The age recorded on a whiskey bottle refers to the number of years it is aged *prior* to being bottled. Once in the bottle, whiskey does not improve.

---

Honey is the only food that does not spoil. Honey found in the tombs of Egyptian pharaohs has been tasted by archaeologists and found edible.

---

According to *Institutions/Volume Feeding* magazine, a trade journal for fast-food-chain operators, the single most popular entree in American restaurants is the hamburger. Right behind the hamburger are, in order, fried chicken, roast beef, spaghetti, turkey, baked ham, fried shrimp, and beef stew.

---

Haggis, a traditional Scottish dish, is made from the lungs, heart, and liver of a sheep, chopped with onions, seasonings, suet, and oatmeal, and then boiled in a bag made from the sheep's stomach.

More than one-third of the world's commercial supply of pineapples comes from Hawaii.

The strongest any liquor can be is 190 proof. This means the beverage is a little more than 97 percent alcohol.

Argentinians eat more meat than any other nation in the world—an average of 10 ounces per person per day.

The herring is the most widely eaten fish in the world. Nutritionally its fuel value is equal to that of a beefsteak.

The custom of serving a slice of lemon with fish dates back to the Middle Ages; the lemon was originally intended for remedial purposes rather than to flavor the fish. It was believed that if a person accidentally swallowed a fish bone, the lemon juice would dissolve it.

Americans spend $600 million a year on hot dogs. They consume enough of them each year to form a chain stretching from the earth to the moon and back again. The average American eats forty hot dogs a year. But the hot dog is not an American invention; it was first produced in Germany in 1852 by a group of butchers in Frankfurt.

There are professional tea tasters as well as wine tasters.

Tea tasters at work in New York, 1883

In Wilton, Maine, there is a cannery that imports and cans only dandelion greens.

A hard-boiled egg will spin. An uncooked or soft-boiled egg will not.

# Gambling

From a fifty-two-card deck it is possible to deal 2,598,960 different five-card poker hands. Of these 1,088,240 will contain a pair. Other possibilities are 4 royal flushes, 36 straight flushes, 624 four-of-a-kind hands, 3,744 full houses, 5,108 flushes, 10,200 straights, 54,912 three-of-a-kind hands, and 123,552 two-pair hands.

Gamblers in ancient Greece made dice from the ankle-bones and shoulder blades of sheep.

Eskimos don't gamble.

At race tracks, the favorite wins fewer than 30 percent of all horse races.

The opposite sides of a dice cube always add up to seven.

Horse-racing regulations state that no race horse's name may contain more than eighteen letters. (Names that are too long would be cumbersome on racing sheets.) Apostrophes, hyphens, and spaces between words count as letters.

THE FINISH

According to *Gambler's Digest,* more cheating takes place in private, friendly gambling games than in all other gambling games combined.

*The Card Players,* by Lucas van Leyden

There is one slot machine in Las Vegas for every eight inhabitants.

Sir Miles Partridge once played at dice with Henry VIII for the bells of St. Paul's church, won, and collected the bells.

On a bingo card of ninety numbers there are approximately 44 million possible ways to make bingo.

Madame de Montespan, second wife of Louis XIV, once lost 4 million francs in a half-hour at the gambling table.

In 1950 at the Las Vegas Desert Inn, an anonymous sailor made twenty-seven straight passes (wins) with the dice at craps. The odds against such a feat are 12,467,890 to 1. Had he bet the house limit on each roll he would have earned $268 million. As it was, he was so timid with his wagers that he walked away from the table with only $750. The dice today are enshrined in the hotel on a velvet pillow under glass.

---

Residents of Nevada bet an average of $846 a year in gambling casinos.

---

When prevented from gambling, compulsive gamblers often experience physical withdrawal symptoms resembling those undergone by heroin addicts. The reactions range from restlessness to shakiness, severe headaches, and diarrhea.

---

In eighteenth-century English gambling dens, there was an employee whose only job was to swallow the dice if there was a police raid.

---

At Brook's, an eighteenth-century English gambling club, the faro table had a large semicircular section cut out of one of its sides in order to accommodate the enormous stomach of the famous statesman Charles James Fox.

---

There are no clocks in Las Vegas gambling casinos.

---

In poker a pair of aces and a pair of eights is known as a "dead man's hand." The odd name originated in 1876,

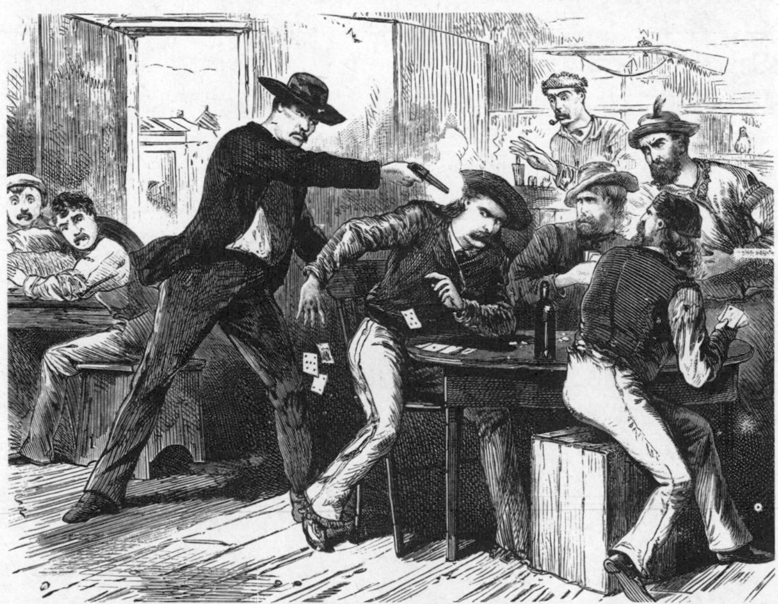

Jack McCall shooting
Wild Bill Hickok, 1876

when Wild Bill Hickok was shot down by Jack McCall during a card game in a saloon in Deadwood, South Dakota. As Wild Bill slumped over the table he exposed his hand for all to see—it showed a pair of eights and a pair of aces.

---

The receipts from illegal gambling each year in the United States surpass the total revenues of America's seventy-five largest industrial organizations combined.

---

According to *Gambler's Digest,* an estimated $1 million is lost at race tracks each year by people who lose or carelessly throw away winning tickets.

---

No patent can ever be taken out on a gambling machine in the United States.

---

Parimutuel betting was invented in 1865 by a Parisian perfume maker named Pierre Oller.

---

## Games & Hobbies

The game of billiards was popularized in France by Louis XIV. The King started playing the game at the recommendation of his physicians. The constant stretching exercise

Louis XIV at a game of billiards

Louis received in playing billiards, his physicians believed, would relieve him of his digestive problems.

---

Modern playing cards were derived from the tarot fortune-telling deck. The original tarot was divided into two sections, the major arcane (dropped from the modern deck) and the minor arcane. The minor arcane was composed of four suits: cups, wands, coins, and swords. In the modern deck these became the hearts, clubs, diamonds, and spades. Similarly, the early tarot had kings, queens, and knights (jacks), plus a page who has been eliminated from contemporary decks.

---

There are 170,000,000,000,000,000,000,000,000 ways to play the ten opening moves in a game of chess.

---

The children's game "Ring Around the Rosy" and the words that accompany it ("Ring around the rosy, pocket full of posy, ashes, ashes, all fall down") derive from the medieval practice of scattering rose petals in a circle around one's bed ("ring around the rosy") and carrying small bouquets ("pocket full of posy") as protection against the Black Plague ("all fall down").

---

Benjamin Franklin was one of the first people to manufacture playing cards in America.

---

The game of dominoes was invented by French monks. It is named for a phrase in the Vesper services: *Dixit Dominus Domineo Meo.*

---

Stamp collecting is the most popular hobby in the world.

---

During the French revolution, because they smacked of royalist influence, kings, queens, and jacks were removed from the standard deck of cards and were replaced by "liberty" (queens), "nature" (kings), and "virtue" (jacks). The hearts, clubs, spades, and diamonds were changed to peace, war, art, and commerce.

---

There are playing cards manufactured especially for left-handed people. Normally the pips on a card are in the upper left-hand corner and lower right for the convenience of right-handed fanners. Left-handed playing cards have pips on all four corners.

---

The practice of using ten pins in the game of bowling originated in colonial America as a means of circumventing a gaming law. An eighteenth-century ordinance in Connecticut ruled that "bowling at nine pins" was illegal, and offenders were often jailed or placed in stocks. To get around this law, bowlers added an extra pin to the game, so that they would be playing "ten pins" rather than "nine pins." The name stuck, and so did the number of pins.

A game of bowls

## Geography

The principality of Monaco consists of only 370 acres.

---

More than 25 percent of the world's forests are in Siberia.

---

The United States would fit into the continent of Africa three and a half times.

---

---

The Sahara Desert comprises an area as large as Europe. Its total land mass is some 3,565,565 square miles.

---

All continents, with the exception of Antarctica, are wider in the north than in the south.

---

Florida is *not* the southernmost state in the United States. Hawaii is farther south.

---

The town of Hamilton, Ontario, Canada, is closer to the equator than it is to the North Pole.

---

More than two-thirds of the earth's land surface lies north of the equator.

---

Of the 3,000 islands in the Bahama chain in the Caribbean, only 20 are inhabited.

---

Israel is one-quarter the size of the state of Maine.

---

The precise geographical center of the North American continent is in a town called Rugby, North Dakota.

---

There are sand dunes in Arcachon, France, that are 350 feet high.

---

Panama (because of a bend in the isthmus) is the only place in the world where one can see the sun rise on the Pacific Ocean and set on the Atlantic.

---

For 186 days a year the sun is not seen at the North Pole.

---

The Hawaiian Islands are the projecting tops of the biggest mountain range in the world. Mauna Kea, on the island of Hawaii and part of this range, is the largest mountain on earth—though partially submerged, its full height from base to crown is 33,476 feet, some 4,000 feet taller than Mount Everest.

---

The distance from Honolulu to New York is greater than the distance from Honolulu to Japan.

Saudi Arabia, which contains one of the largest expanses of desert in the world and through which great camel caravans have traveled for centuries, must import both sand and camels. River sand is sent to Arabia by the ton from Scotland for use in construction; desert sands are not suitable for building purposes. And since camel herds are dwindling in Arabia, camels must be imported from North Africa.

Jacksonville, Florida, has the largest total area of any city in the United States. It takes in 460 square miles, almost twice the area of Los Angeles.

*Question:* If one were to drive from Los Angeles, California, to Reno, Nevada, in which direction would he be going, east or west? *Answer:* West. (Check the map.)

In the Northern Hemisphere water goes down drains counterclockwise. In the Southern Hemisphere it goes down clockwise.

The King Ranch in Texas is bigger than the state of Rhode Island. It comprises 1.25 million acres and was the first ranch in the world to be completely fenced in. At one time its borders were guarded by armed patrol.

# Insects & Spiders

The female praying mantis devours the male while they are mating. The male sometimes continues copulating even after the female has bitten off his head and part of his upper torso!

A male spider's penis is located at the end of one of its legs.

Ants keep slaves. Certain species, the so-called sanguinary ants in particular, raid the nests of other ant tribes, kill the queen, and kidnap many of the workers. The workers are brought back to the captors' hive, where they are coerced into performing menial tasks.

Digger wasp, with cocoon and larva

A house fly lives only two weeks.

Every night, wasps bite into the stem of a plant, lock their mandibles into position, stretch out at right angles to the stem, and, with legs dangling, fall asleep.

In rainy climates, some breeds of termites attach special overhanging eaves to their nests. These eaves deflect downpours and keep the nests dry. The compass termite, an Australian breed, builds its nest in the shape of an axe head, the sides of which always point north and south. African termites in search of water will bore holes as deep as 130 feet into the earth until they find the water table.

After mating, the female black widow spider turns on her partner and devours him. The female may dispatch as many as twenty-five suitors a day in this manner.

Termites are not related to ants. They are part of the cockroach family.

In a beehive, only 1½ ounces of wax are used to build a comb that will hold 4 pounds of honey.

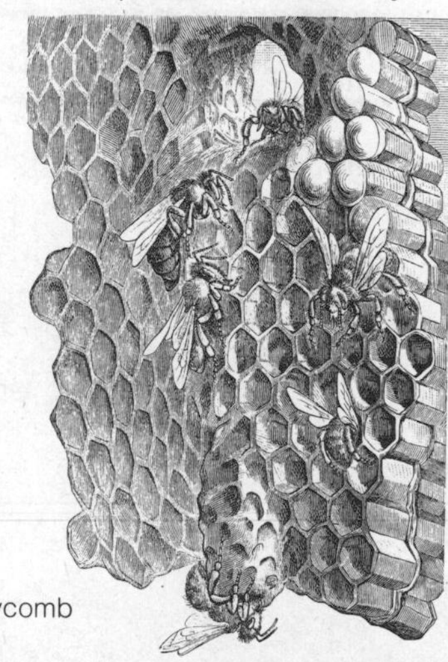

Constructing a honeycomb

Queen termites may live for fifty years.

The Mexican fishing spider attaches itself to a small leaf, floats across a pond as if on a raft, and from this vantage point hunts its prey, large tadpoles and small fish.

According to the United States Department of Agriculture, the best time to spray household insects is 4:00 P.M. Insects are most active and vulnerable at this time.

Only female bees work. Males remain in the hive and literally do nothing, their only mission in life being to fertilize the queen bee on her maiden flight. For this purpose literally

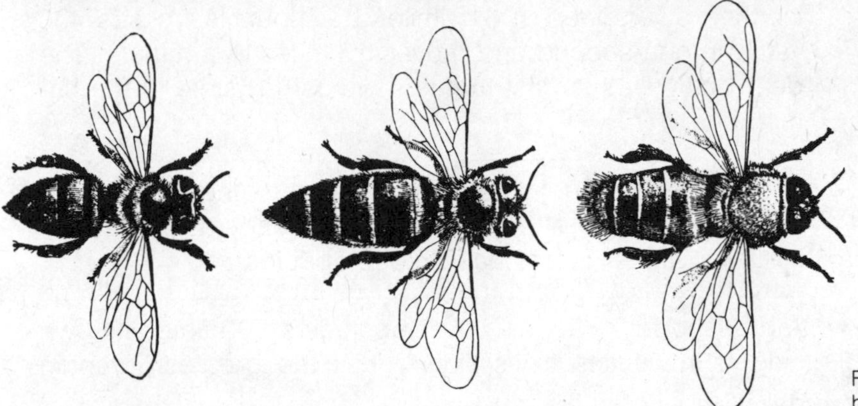

From left: Worker, queen bee, and male (drone)

thousands of males are hatched, out of which only one or two mate with the queen. After they have served their function, the males are not allowed back into the hive but are left outside, where they starve to death.

Flies prefer to breed in the center of a room. This is why experts advise placing flypaper away from corners.

Cockroaches have lived on the earth for 250 million years without changing in any way whatsoever.

The caterpillar has more than 2,000 muscles.

Spiders never spin webs in structures made of chestnut wood. That is why so many European châteaux were built with chestnut beams—spider webs on a 50-foot beamed ceiling can be difficult to clean!

---

The reason a fly swatter is an efficient tool for killing flies while the human hand is not is as follows: a fly's tactile sense is controlled by numerous sensory hairs covering its entire body. These hairs are especially sensitive to air pressure. The movement of a hand or any other solid object creates fluctuations of air and warns the fly well in advance of the blow. The fly swatter, however, has many holes arranged along its surface, so that it displaces little air as it bears down on its victim. Thus the fly is caught unawares.

---

The deer botfly can fly faster than a jet plane. It has been clocked at a speed of 818 miles per hour. It crosses 400 yards in one second and moves 13 miles in a minute. The deer botfly flies so fast that it is almost invisible to the human eye.

---

There are more beetles on earth than any other living creature. The number of *species alone* is nearly a quarter-million (the United States has 28,000 species).

---

A grasshopper can leap over obstacles 500 times its own height. In relation to its size, it has the greatest jumping ability of all animals.

---

An ant can lift 50 times its own weight. A bee can handle 300 times its own weight, which is equivalent to a human being pulling a 10-ton trailer.

---

There are 5 million different species of insects in the world. The insect population of the world is at least 1,000,000,000,000,000,000. The weight of the world's insect population exceeds that of man by a factor of twelve.

---

The animal with the largest brain in proportion to its body size is the ant.

---

The honeybee kills more people each year world-wide than poisonous snakes.

---

Bees can see ultraviolet light.

Butterflies taste with their hind feet.

There are more than 100,000 different species of butterflies.

The leaf-cutter ant sometimes makes anthills 16 feet deep and an acre wide.

If one places a minute amount of liquor on a scorpion, it will instantly go mad and sting itself to death.

Only female mosquitoes bite.

A flea can jump 200 times the length of its own body. This is equivalent to a person jumping almost a quarter of a mile.

Mosquitoes are attracted to the color blue twice as much as to any other color.

A male emperor moth can detect and find a female of his species a mile away.

It would take 27,000 spiders, each spinning a single web, to produce a pound of web.

Bees have five eyes. There are three small eyes on the top of a bee's head and two larger ones in front.

A queen bee may lay as many as 3,000 eggs in a single day.

Ants stretch when they wake up. They also appear to yawn in a very human manner before taking up the tasks of the day.

In September, 1951, seventeen-month-old Mark Bennet of Vancouver, B.C., was stung 447 times by wasps and lived. He was released from the hospital after twenty days of treatment.

A cockroach can live several weeks with its head cut off.

The common house fly, *Musca domestica,* cannot survive in Alaska. It is too cold. Those that do appear there are brought in by boat or plane and perish without reproducing. Mosquitoes, on the other hand, love cold weather. Specimens have been found near the North Pole.

The bumblebee does not die when it stings—it can sting again and again. In bumblebee hives, the entire colony, except for the queen, dies at the end of each summer. Each year an entirely new colony of bees must be produced.

Cicadas have their hearing organs in their stomachs, at the base of the abdomen. Crickets have their hearing organs in their knees, or, more precisely, in the oval slits of their forelegs.

The bombardier beetle, when disturbed, defends itself by emitting a series of explosions, sometimes setting off four or five reports in succession. The noises sound like miniature popgun blasts and are accompanied by a cloud of reddish-colored, vile-smelling fluid.

# Inventions

Orson S. Fowler, who in the mid-nineteenth century popularized the science of phrenology, was also the inventor of the octagon house, an eight-sided dwelling that enjoyed great popularity in America from the 1840's through the 1860's.

The first plastic ever invented was celluloid, which is still used to make billiard balls. It came into use in 1868, when cellulose nitrate was first combined with natural camphor in a laboratory. At the time it was regarded as a mere curiosity.

As of 1940, a total of ninety-four patents had been taken out on shaving mugs.

The Chinese invented the speedometer. In 1027 Lu Tao-lung presented the Emperor Jen Chung with a cart that could measure the distances it spanned by means of a mechanism with eight wheels and two moving arms. One arm struck a drum each time a *li* (about a third of a mile) was covered. Another rang a bell every 10 *li*.

The rickshaw was invented by an American. The Reverend Jonathan Scobie, a Baptist minister living in Yokohama, Ja-

pan, built the first model in 1869 in order to transport his invalid wife through the city streets. Copies were made by the minister's parishioners and soon the rickshaw became a standard mode of transportation in the Orient.

---

In 1875 the director of the United States Patent Office sent in his resignation and advised that his department be closed. There was nothing left to invent, he claimed.

---

Thomas Jefferson invented the dumbwaiter.

---

The telephone was not invented by Alexander Graham Bell. Its first creator was a German, Philip Reis, who in 1861 made a primitive sending-receiving transmitter which he called the "telephone." Twelve years later Elisha Gray of Chicago completed a short-distance telephone communication. Bell's invention, patented in March, 1876, was distinguished by the fact that it was the first sending-receiving mechanism over which the human voice could be transmitted.

---

The postage stamp was invented by an Englishman named James Chambers in 1834. Before that time envelopes had stamps engraved upon them. They were bulky, however, and Chambers' invention caught on immediately. Postage stamps were introduced to America in 1847.

---

James Ramsey invented a steam-driven motorboat in 1784. He ran it on the Potomac River, and the event was witnessed by George Washington.

---

Benjamin Franklin invented crop insurance.

---

Henry Ford did not invent the automobile. It was the invention of several nineteenth-century engineers, paramount among them being two Germans, Gottlieb Daimler and Karl Benz. What Ford did was to mass-produce automobiles and provide cheap service for them.

---

The parachute was invented more than a hundred years before the airplane. It was the creation of a Frenchman,

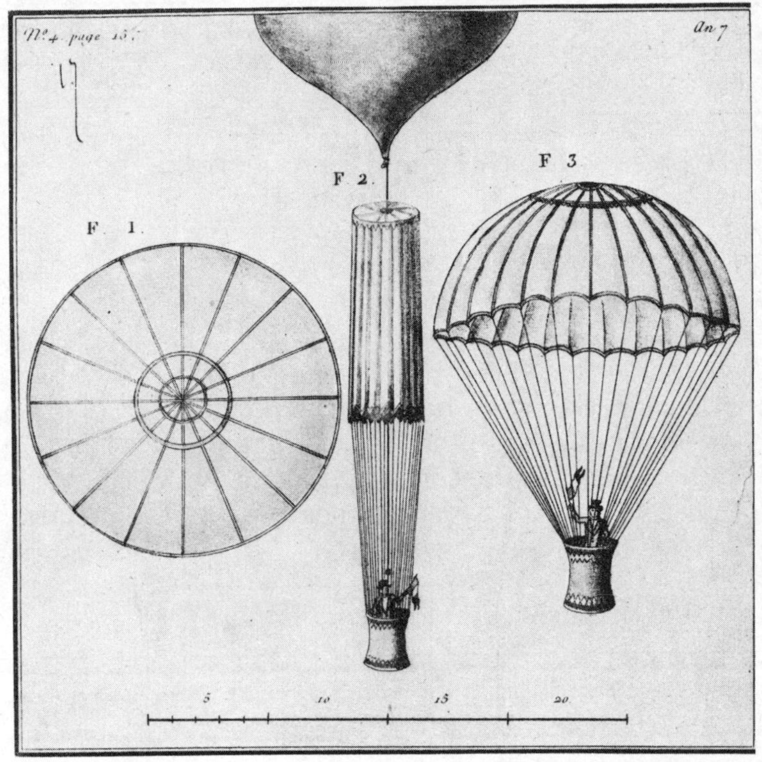


Early French parachute

Louis Lenormand, who designed it in 1783 to save people who had to jump from burning buildings. In 1797 Jacques Garnerin gave a public exhibition of parachuting, descending 3,000 feet from a balloon.

---

Roulette was invented by the great French mathematician and philosopher Blaise Pascal. It was a by-product of his experiments with perpetual motion.

---

The parking meter was invented in Oklahoma City. It was the brainstorm of one Carl Magee, whose first model appeared in 1935. Early models look almost exactly like modern ones: few items have changed as little through the years as the parking meter.

---

James J. Ritty, owner of a tavern in Dayton, Ohio, invented the cash register in 1879 to stop his patrons from pilfering house profits.

---

Joseph Priestley, the English chemist, invented carbonated water. It was a by-product of his investigations into the chemistry of air.

The monkey wrench is named after its inventor, a London blacksmith named Charles Moncke.

Camel's-hair brushes are not made of camel's hair. They were invented by a man named Mr. Camel.

Wallpaper was invented in Philadelphia. The inventor was one Plunket Fleeson, who in 1739 stamped designs on paper with woodblocks and painted them in by hand. In August of that year Fleeson advertised in the Pennsylvania *Gazette* the sale of "bedticks, choice live geese feathers, as well as paper hangings."

Leonardo da Vinci invented the scissors.

## Language

To "decimate" does not mean to obliterate or wipe out. It means to destroy one-tenth of something. Originally the word referred to a Roman military tradition in which an entire troop would be punished for disobedience by decimation, that is, by the killing of every tenth man. There are accounts of this form of punishment being used in the English and French armies up to the time of World War I.

In Middle English the word "minister" meant "lowly person." It was originally adopted as a term of humility for men of the church.

The term "hooker," meaning a prostitute, originated with U.S. Army General Joseph Hooker, whose penchant for war was matched only by his predilection for paid female companionship. In New Orleans during the Civil War, Hooker spent so much time frolicking with ladies of the night that the women came to be called "Hooker's division." Eventually these specialized "troops" became known simply as "hookers."

---

The original name for the butterfly was "flutterby."

---

In the vast majority of the world's languages, the word for "mother" begins with the letter M.

---

"Facetious" and "abstemious" are the only two words in the English language that contain the vowels *a, e, i, o,* and *u* in their proper order.

---

The word "live" spelled backward is "evil."

---

Eskimos have more than twenty words to describe snow.

---

What is called a "French kiss" in England and America is known as an "English kiss" in France.

*The Kiss*, by Constantin Brancusi

The most commonly used word in English conversation is "I."

---

The act of snapping one's fingers has a name. It is called a "fillip."

---

The language of Taki, spoken in parts of French Guinea, consists of only 340 words.

---

The words CHOICE COD read the same when held in front of a mirror upside-down.

---

Words that are really words:

*bezel*—the edge of a cutting tool.

*callithump*—a loud parade.

*clerihew*—a light satirical four-line verse containing specific reference to a person, invented by E. Clerihew Bentley (1875–1956). Clerihew wrote his first clerihew while still in school:

> Sir Humphry Davy
> Abominated gravy.
> He lived in the odium
> Of having discovered sodium.

*googol*—the figure 1 followed by 100 zeros.

*haruspex*—an ancient Roman priest who practiced fortunetelling by reading entrails of sacrificed animals.

*hendecasyllabic*—an adjective applied to a line of verse of eleven syllables.

*pneumoultramicroscopicsilicovolcanoconiosis*—a disease of the lungs developed by coal miners from breathing underground fumes.

*pseudepigrapha*—spurious writings, particularly those attributed to Biblical sources.

*scop*—an Old English poet.

---

A "clue" originally meant a ball of thread. This is why one is said to "unravel" the clues of a mystery.

---

The ampersand (&) was once a letter of the English alphabet.

The word "gas," coined by the chemist J. B. van Helmont, is taken from the word *chaos,* which means "unformed" in Greek.

The words "naked" and "nude" are *not* the same. Naked implies unprotected. Nude means unclothed.

*La Grande Odalisque,* by Jean Auguste Dominique Ingres

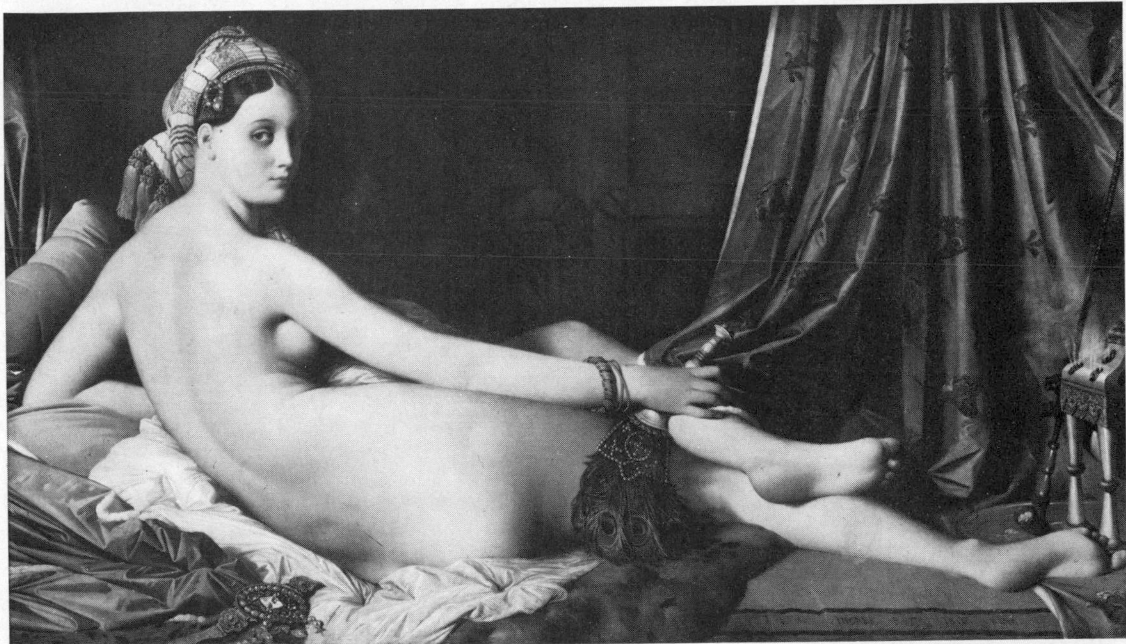

The word "geriatrics" was not coined until 1951.

In Elizabethan slang the term "to die" meant to have an orgasm. This double entendre was often used by John Donne *(The Prohibition, The Canonization),* and by Shakespeare in *King Lear.*

The word "toast," meaning a proposal of health, originated in Rome, where an actual bit of spiced, burned bread was dropped into wine to improve the drink's flavor, absorb its sediment, and thus make it more healthful.

General Jackson and His Lady sharing a toast, watercolor by H. Young

The word "turnpike" originated in the days when toll collectors were armed with pikes, long-handled weapons with sharp iron heads. They used these weapons to prevent travelers who refused to pay the tariff from using their roads.

E is the most frequently used letter in the English alphabet, Q the least.

The word "bamboo" has contributed two colloquialisms to the English language. First, we owe to it the word "joint," meaning a disreputable gathering place, a dive. This is because the pipes used in opium dens were crafted of bamboo and had many "joints." (It has been suggested that marijuana cigarettes are also known as "joints" because of their association with opium dens.) Second, there is the word "bamboozle," which means to fool or cheat. This

Opium den in New York, 1881

traces back to the Chinese custom of punishing swindlers by whacking them on the hands and back with bamboo poles. Any smart aleck so treated was a "bamboozler," that is, one worthy of being tanned with bamboo.

The word "clodhopper" originated in early England as a term of derision for the peasantry. In those days farmers traveled by foot, and had to step or jump across clods of plowed earth. Unlike the gentry, who traveled by carriage or by steed, the peasants were therefore "clodhoppers"—those who had to hop over clods.

---

The word "queue" is the only word in the English language that is still pronounced the same way when the last four letters are removed.

---

When sailors speak of sheets (as in "four sheets to the wind") they are not talking about sails. A sheet in nautical terminology is a rope or chain.

---

The jackrabbit is not a rabbit; it is a hare. A Jerusalem artichoke is not an artichoke; it is a sunflower. Arabic numerals are not Arabic; they were invented in India. India ink (sometimes called "Chinese ink") was not known until recently in either China or India.

---

The word "tip," meaning a gratuity, was originally an acronym standing for "To Insure Promptness."

---

The word "robot" was coined in 1920 in a play, *R.U.R.* (the initials stood for Rossum's Universal Robots), written by the Czech dramatist Karel Capek.

---

*Question:* What is unusual about the sentence "Jackdaws love my big sphinx of quartz"? *Answer:* It is the shortest English sentence yet devised to include all the letters of the alphabet.

---

Rhubarb is named after the Volga River. In Greek the name of the Volga is *Rha,* and *barb* means "uncultivated." Rhubarb is thus a wild plant that grows along the Volga.

---

Cinderella's slipper, many scholars believe, was made of fur, not glass. The word *verre,* or "glass," they claim, was incorrectly substituted in early versions of the story for the word *vaire.* In medieval French, *vaire* means "fur."

---

The word "toady" originally referred to a magician's assistant who literally ate toads as part of the show. Toads, at one time, were thought to be poisonous; when the "toady" recovered from eating one of them, it was considered an indication of the magician's great power.

---

The term "freelance" was invented by Sir Walter Scott to refer to itinerant mercenary soldiers who sold their abilities to the highest bidder. At first such soldiers were known as "free companions." Since they usually traveled with their own weapons, including lances, Scott dubbed them "free lancers."

---

The letter B took its present form from a symbol used in Egyptian hieroglyphics to represent a house. Its original Egyptian form looked very much like its modern one.

---

The word "Mikado" did not refer to the Japanese emperor himself but to the door of his royal chamber. In medieval Japan it was considered in bad taste to speak of this great personage directly, so instead his existence was inferred by referring to the entrance to his place of residence.

---

A fireplace is called a "mantelpiece" because at one time people hung their coats (or "mantles") over the fireplace to dry them.

---

In England, corn means wheat. In the Bible, corn means grain.

---

## Laws

Prior to the adoption of the Twelfth Amendment in 1804, the candidate who ran second in a presidential race automatically became vice-president. Thomas Jefferson became John Adams' vice-president in this way.

---

In Turkey, in the sixteenth and seventeenth centuries, anyone caught drinking coffee was put to death.

---

The United States Supreme Court once ruled Federal income tax unconstitutional. Income tax was first imposed during the Civil War as a temporary revenue-raising measure. In the late 1800's the government attempted to revive the levy again, but the Supreme Court ruled it in violation of the constitutional provision that direct taxes must be apportioned among the states according to their population. In 1913, however, Congress passed the Sixteenth Amendment, making a Federal impost legal once again.

---

It is illegal to hunt camels in the state of Arizona.

---

American Indians do not have to pay tax on their land.

---

Connecticut and Rhode Island never ratified the 18th Amendment (Prohibition).

---

In seventeenth-century Japan, no citizen was allowed to leave the country on penalty of death. Anyone caught coming or going without permission was executed on the spot.

---

Before 1941 fingerprints were not accepted as evidence in court. Up to that time it was not an established fact that no two fingerprints were alike. Today the only way in which fingerprints will *not* be allowed as evidence is if the defense can prove that there are in fact two sets of fingerprints somewhere in the world that match.

---

New York was the first state to require the licensing of motor vehicles. The law was adopted in 1901.

---

Until 1893, lynching was legal in the United States. The first antilynching law was passed in Georgia, but it only made the violation punishable by four years in prison.

---

Cattle branding in the United States did not originate in the West. It began in Connecticut in the mid-nineteenth century, when farmers were required by law to mark all their pigs.

---

During the time of Peter the Great, any Russian man who wore a beard was required to pay a special tax.

---

# Literature

Voltaire considered Shakespeare's works so deplorable that he referred to the Bard as "that drunken fool."

All the proceeds earned from James M. Barrie's book *Peter Pan* were bequeathed to the Great Ormond Street Hospital for Sick Children in London.

Marcel Proust's *Remembrance of Things Past* contains almost 1.5 million words.

Fagin, the sinister villain in Charles Dickens' *Oliver Twist,* was also the name of Dickens' best friend, Bob Fagin.

Emily Dickinson wrote more than nine hundred poems, only four of which were published during her lifetime.

Gibbon spent twenty years writing *The Decline and Fall of the Roman Empire.* Noah Webster spent thirty-six years writing his dictionary.

The Indian epic poem the *Mahabhrata* is eight times longer than the *Iliad* and the *Odyssey* combined.

There is no living descendant of William Shakespeare.

The great English poet John Keats died at the age of twenty-six.

Alfred, Lord Tennyson wrote a 6,000-word epic poem when he was twelve years old.

Robert Louis Stevenson said that he had envisioned the entire story of *Dr. Jekyll and Mr. Hyde* in a dream and simply recorded it the way he saw it. Stevenson claimed to be able to dream plots for his stories at will.

John Bunyan, author of *Pilgrim's Progress,* wrote most of

his famous book while in jail. He was imprisoned for twelve years for preaching without a license.

---

The original story of *Alice in Wonderland* was not known as *Alice in Wonderland* at all. It was called *Alice's Adventures Under Ground* and was illustrated by the author himself, Lewis Carroll—whose name was not Lewis Carroll, but Charles Lutwidge Dodgson. Dodgson was a mathematics professor at Christ's Church, Oxford.

Left: Illustration from *Alice in Wonderland*
Below: William Cullen Bryant

---

In James M. Barrie's *Peter Pan,* the place where children go with Peter Pan is not called "Never-Never Land." It is called "Neverland."

---

The fairy tales "Puss in Boots," "Little Red Ridinghood," "Cinderella," and many others were first written down by Charles Perrault, who also helped design part of the Louvre.

---

Shakespeare once wrote a play called *What You Will.* (Its alternate title: *Twelfth Night.*)

---

William Cullen Bryant, famous American critic, biographer, and civic leader, published a well-known satire on Thomas Jefferson at the age of thirteen. Before he was eighteen he had written his most famous poem, "To a Waterfowl."

---

In *Gulliver's Travels* Jonathan Swift described the two

moons of Mars, Phobos and Deimos, giving their exact size and speeds of rotation. He did this more than a hundred years before either moon was discovered.

---

Alexander Pope published "The Rape of the Lock" at age twenty-four. Browning wrote "Pauline" when he was twenty. Byron wrote "Childe Harold" at twenty-four. Keats wrote "Endymion" at twenty-three.

---

The wife of the poet Percy Bysshe Shelley was the creator of the Frankenstein story. Mary Wollstonecraft Shelley wrote the book *Frankenstein* in 1818, basing it on the writings of certain alchemists who claimed to have created a tiny human being, called a homunculus, in a test tube.

---

*Treasure Island* was created by Robert Louis Stevenson on a lark. Drawing a treasure map for his stepson on a rainy day, Stevenson was urged by the child to make up stories to go along with the drawings. Stevenson liked the stories so much he wrote them down, and these became the basis for his great novel.

Illustration from *Treasure Island,* by Howard Pyle

After completing his book on the French revolution, the great English historian Thomas Carlyle gave the manuscript to his friend John Stuart Mill to proofread. By mistake Mill's housemaid used the papers to kindle a fire and destroyed the entire manuscript. Undaunted, Carlyle sat down and, without benefit of notes (he had destroyed these himself), completely reconstructed and rewrote the book.

Thomas Carlyle

Edgar Allan Poe invented the detective story. Before he wrote "The Murders in the Rue Morgue" and "The Mystery of Marie Roget" the genre was totally unknown in English or American literature.

Samuel Taylor Coleridge wrote his famous poem "Kubla Khan" directly from a dream. Coleridge was in the midst of writing down the visions he had seen in this dream when someone knocked on the door and he rose to let him in. On returning to his work, Coleridge found that he could not remember the rest of the dream. That is why "Kubla Khan" remains unfinished.

The original title of Jane Austen's novel *Pride and Prejudice* was *First Impressions.*

# Magic & the Occult

Bobbing for apples at Halloween originated as part of a divinatory technique practiced by the Druids. Participants floated apples in a tub of water on the 31st of October (the Druid New Year's Eve) and attempted to fish them out without using their hands. Those who succeeded were guaranteed a prosperous year.

Magical symbols drawn by Roman soldiers on shields to repel the evil eye became the basis for European heraldic designs during the Middle Ages.

The Three Kings of the Nativity story were actually sorcerers. They were magicians, priests of the Zoroastrian religion of Persia. The word "magi" (as in the Three Magi) is the plural of *magus,* meaning "wizard" in Old Persian. It is from this root that the word "magic" is derived.

*Adoration of the Magi,* engraving by P. Beljembe

Some occult tongue-twisters:

*Alextoromantia:* Divination based on the direction in which a rooster turns when let loose in a circle.

*Alextryomancy:* Divination by reading the random configurations formed by scattering grains of wheat on the ground.

*Amniomancy:* Foretelling a child's future from the arrangement of the amniotic membrane at the child's birth.

*Arithomancy:* Divination by abstruse and secret numerical calculations.

*Belomancy:* Divination by reading the flight patterns of randomly shot arrows and their position when they land.

*Cereoscopy:* Interpreting the patterns made by wax melted in boiling water.

*Cledonism:* Finding omens in the first words one hears upon rising in the morning.

*Hydroscopy:* Divination by reading the ripples created by three stones tossed into a pond.

*Kieidiscopy:* Divination by reading the undulations of a key swinging on a string.

*Lycanthropy:* The study of werewolves.

*Metoposcopy:* Divination by reading the positions, shapes, and sizes of the moles or blemishes on a person's body.

*Ornithomancy:* Divination by reading the flight patterns of birds.

*Pyromancy:* Divination by reading the movements of a flame.

*Rhabdomancy:* Hunting for gold, water, or precious metals by using a hazel wand as a pointer.

*Scapulomancy:* Divination by reading the cracks and fissures in the roasted shoulder bones of a sheep.

*Screeology:* The art of reading the future in a crystal ball.

## Manners & Customs

In ancient Japan public contests were held to see who in a town could break wind loudest and longest. Winners were awarded many prizes and received great acclaim.

---

The pilgrims in Massachusetts used a special tool in church, a wooden ball attached to a long string on a stick. If anyone fell asleep during a sermon (which might go on for seven or eight hours) a specially appointed member of the clergy would hoist the pole over the reprobate's head and clop him with the wooden ball.

When ancient Egyptian priests held a banquet, a large mummy was often carried into the feast chamber and propped up at the table where all the priests could see it, a reminder that even while at pleasure, death was ever near.

The ancient Egyptians slept on pillows made of stone.

In medieval China and parts of Africa one method of enforcing chastity was to sew up a girl's vaginal labia as soon as she reached puberty. The stitches were not cut until marriage; the husband then had the option of sewing them up again if he was called to war or on a long journey.

In Elizabethan England the spoon was such a novelty, such a prized rarity, that people carried their own folding spoons to banquets.

Tibetans drink tea made of salt and rancid yak butter. Tibetan women carry a special instrument with metal blades for cleaning their ears and picking their nose.

Date-palm trees in Iraq are passed down through generations as part of family legacies. The trees are given individual names, have carefully recorded personal histories, and are considered a basic part of family wealth.

The champagne used to christen a ship is a substitute for human blood. In bygone times the Vikings and various South Sea tribes sacrificed human beings on the prows of their ships so that the spirits of the murdered victims would guard the craft. Later wine was substituted for blood, and, in our day, champagne for wine.

During the Middle Ages German men went to the barber to take a bath as well as to get a shave.

At Versailles, during the reign of Louis XIV, it was considered gauche to knock on a door with the knuckles. Instead one scratched with the little finger of the left hand,

and for this purpose courtiers let that particular nail grow long.

---

America in the year 1800:

There was no public library.

Crockery plates were objected to because they dulled knives.

Over one-fifth of the country's population lived in the state of Virginia.

Men and women spat on the floors of their own homes and bathed only once a week.

When someone was finished with dinner he placed his spoon across his cup to show that he wanted no more food.

Gentlemen wore wigs and powdered their hair.

---

When gentlemen in medieval Japan wished to seal an agreement, they urinated together, crisscrossing their streams of urine.

---

Among the Betsileo natives of Madagascar, in the eighteenth century, there was a caste of servants known as the *ramanga* who were made to eat all nail parings and blood lost by members of the upper classes. If the nail parings were too long or jagged they were minced up before being gobbled down. If a noble cut himself or was wounded in battle a *ramanga* would lick his wounds. Those of high rank rarely went anywhere without these attendants, and if by chance a nail broke or blood flowed when the aristocrat was alone he would preserve the residues and later give them to a *ramanga,* who obediently swallowed them.

---

In medieval Japan, a woman who was caught alone in a room with a man other than her husband was immediately put to death, even if the meeting was completely innocent.

---

The Tasaday tribe recently discovered in the Philippine Islands has no known enemies, no weapons of war, no words in their language for hate, war or dislike. They neither hunt nor cultivate.

---

In medieval Spain it was customary to clean the teeth with

stale urine. The theory behind this strange practice was that the urine would render the teeth especially bright and keep them firmly fixed in the gums.

## Marriage & Divorce

According to the Population Council, people overwhelmingly tend to marry partners who live near them.

It takes one day to get a divorce in the Dominican Republic.

## Mathematics & Numbers

George Parker Bidder, builder of London's Victoria docks in the nineteenth century, could figure problems like "How many times does 15,228 go into the cube of 36" in four seconds. Bidder's brother memorized the entire Bible and could remember every date he ever read. George Bidder's eldest son, George Bidder Jr., was able to multiply a fifteen-digit number by another fifteen-digit number mentally in less than a minute.

Oscar Verhaeghe of Uccle, Belgium, can multiply four-digit numbers by two-digit numbers in fifteen seconds without pencil and paper. Verhaeghe can give square roots, cube enormous numbers, and square large sums in less than half a minute. Once, under test conditions, he calculated the square of 888,888,888,888,888 in forty seconds (the answer is 790,123,426,790,121,876,543,209,876,544). Except for his mathematical ability, Verhaeghe, now well on in years, has the mental capacity of a child.

The Babylonians developed a series of advanced quadratic equations centuries before the birth of Christ.

When one adds up the number of letters in the names of the playing cards—ace (3), two (3), three (5), four (4), five (4), six (3), seven (5), eight (5), nine (4), ten (3), jack (4), queen (5), king (4)—the total comes to 52, the precise number of cards in a deck.

---

According to modern theories of higher mathematics:

If a person approached the speed of light he would shrink to a tiny size.

If a person surpassed the speed of light he would start moving backward in time.

The shortest distance between two points is a curve, not a line.

Parallel lines eventually meet.

Time is a curve.

Space is, paradoxically, at the same time both infinite and bounded.

There is no such thing as a straight line in the universe.

The faster an object moves in space the heavier it becomes—but at the same time, the smaller it becomes as well.

---

If one started counting the moment he or she was born and continued counting without stopping until he or she reached the age of sixty-five, that person still would not have counted to a billion.

---

If at the birth of Christ someone began to spend a dollar every second and continued spending up to the present time, that person would have spent less than $62 billion.

---

If you are thirty-five years old you have lived approximately 12,800 days. If you are fifty you have lived 18,300 days. If sixty, 21,900 days; if seventy-five, 27,400.

---

If a person places a single coin on the first square of a chessboard, then places twice this number, or two coins, on the second square, twice this number again, or four coins, on the third, and so on until all sixty-four squares are covered, exactly 18,446,744,973,709,551,661 coins will be required to do the job—more than have been minted in the world since the beginning of recorded civilization.

---

If one counted twenty-four hours a day, it would take 31,688 years to count to a trillion. If a trillion dollar bills were stacked one on top of the other the stack would be twice as high as Mount Everest. A trillion dollar bills laid end to end would circle the world 3,882 times.

## Medicine

Twenty minutes before the pain of a migraine headache begins, many sufferers experience a phenomenon called the aura. During this time the sufferer may see intense colors, flashing lights, even monsters and apparitions. Lewis Carroll, a migraine victim most of his life, is supposed to have taken some of his characters for *Alice in Wonderland* from the apparitions he saw before attacks.

In 1374 at Aix-la-Chapelle during the siege of the Black Death, a thousand men, women, and children lost all control, joined hands, and danced in the streets, shrieking and maiming each other until they all died of wounds or fatigue.

According to the American Society for the Study of Headaches 80 percent of migraine sufferers are women.

The Black Plague destroyed half the population of Europe in the fourteenth century.

English townspeople fleeing to the country to escape the Plague

The mortality rate for infectious diseases is lowest between the ages of five and fifteen. After twenty-five the body is much more susceptible to disease.

There is a disease called ichthyosis that turns the skin scaly like a fish.

Humans are susceptible to a disease called the "laughing sickness." People stricken with this disease literally laugh themselves to death. The disease is known in only one place in the world, among the Kuru tribe of New Guinea.

According to the National Health Foundation, after suffering a cold one should wait at least six days before kissing someone.

People recovering from a cold may find rubbing noses less risky than kissing. Sculpture by Gustav Vigeland in the Vigeland Museum, Oslo.

Dr. John Cohausen wrote a book in 1743 "proving" that one could live to be 115 years old by inhaling the breath of little girls. In his book, *Hermippus Redivivus,* Dr. Cohausen gave the following prescription: take 1 pound of gum olibani, 2 ounces of styrae, myrrh, and several other herbs, mix, burn, and inhale while at the same time imbibing the exhalations of the nearest little girl.

The primary source of physical discomfort among Americans is back pain.

Wyoming has fewer than 1,000 cases of cancer each year. New York State has the highest incidence, with more than 70,000 cancer victims each year.

Statistics indicate that girls who have intercourse early in life, particularly before the age of sixteen, are twice as likely to develop cancer of the cervix as those who do not begin having intercourse until they are in their twenties.

According to the American Heart Association, although people on a low-saturated-fat diet have a 20 percent lower death rate from heart disease than people on a normal diet, they have a 30 percent higher death rate from cancer.

---

According to scientists from Harvard, Western Reserve, and New Mexico universities, the death rate from coronary heart disease is 28 percent lower among males who live above 7,000 feet than it is among those who live at altitudes between 3,000 and 4,000 feet.

---

Women who work have fewer heart problems than men who work. Women in general have remarkably fewer heart attacks than men.

---

One out of every four Americans will get cancer. Cancer causes one death in the United States every 90 seconds.

---

The average waiting time in a doctor's office, the American Medical Association reports, is twenty minutes. If the doctor is a family physician, the average waiting time can be as long as half an hour. Waiting time for a psychiatrist, however, is usually less than five minutes.

---

In ancient China doctors were paid when their patients were kept well, not when they were sick. Believing that it was the doctor's job to prevent disease, Chinese doctors often paid the patient if the patient lost his health. Further, if a patient died, a special lantern was hung outside the doctor's house. At eaoh death another lantern was added. Too many of these lanterns were certain to ensure a slow trade.

---

More than half a million Americans died during the influenza epidemic of 1918.

---

According to Planned Parenthood, the number of legal abortions in the United States has increased by 20 percent each year since 1974. Legal abortions, says the organization, are now the second most common surgical operation in the United States, second only to tonsillectomies.

---

The jaws of African fire ants are used as sutures for wounds in Kenya, Uganda, and parts of South Africa. After an operation is performed, an ant is allowed to bite into the two flaps of skin along the line of the incision. The ant's body is then twisted off, leaving the head with its mandibles locked into the skin like a stitch. A number of these miniature "stitches" are placed along a wound. During the healing process, they closely resemble modern surgical stitching.

---

Pirates believed that piercing the ears and wearing an earring improved eyesight. This idea, scoffed at for centuries, has been reevaluated in light of acupuncture theory. The point on the lobe where the ear was pierced corresponds to the auricular acupuncture point controlling the eyes.

Pirate's earring may have improved his eyesight. Illustration by Howard Pyle from *The Book of Pirates*.

# Minerals & Precious Metals

Most precious gems are actually colorless. Their color comes from impurities in the stone that act as pigmenting agents.

Sterling silver is not pure silver. Because pure silver is too soft to be used in most tableware it is mixed with copper in the proportion of 92.5 percent silver to 7.5 percent copper.

Twenty-four-karat gold is not pure gold; there is a small amount of copper in it. Absolutely pure gold is so soft that it can be molded with the hands.

The best diamonds are colored blue-white.

Some of the world's most celebrated diamonds, including the Hope (bottom row, 2nd from right) and the Kohinoor (2nd row from bottom, far right)

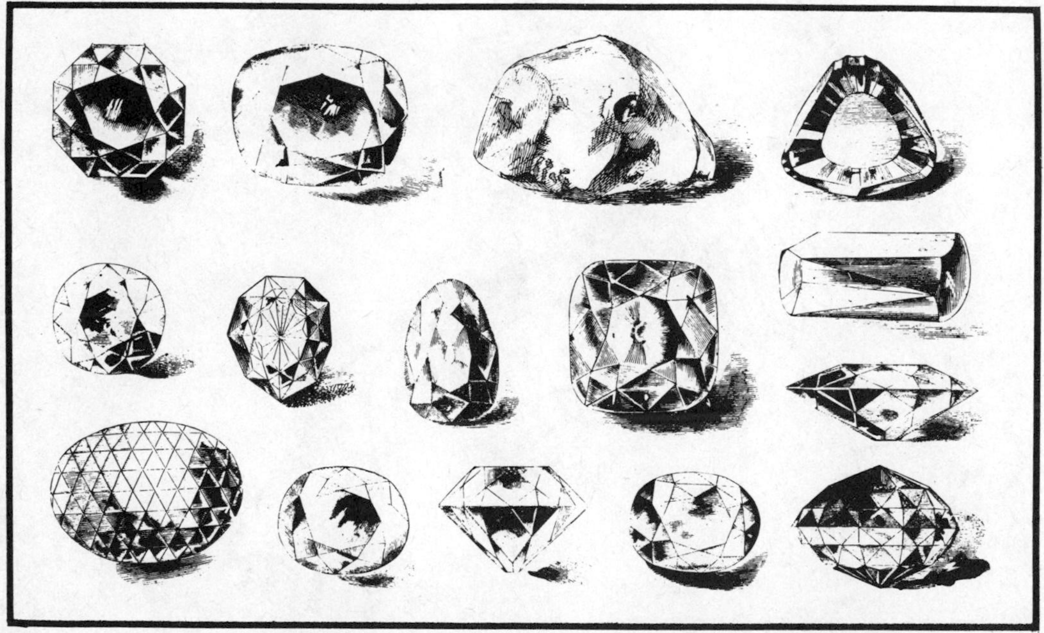

The ruby, sapphire, and emerald are not specific minerals. A ruby is the red, a sapphire the blue, variety of corundum. An emerald is the green, an aquamarine the blue, variety of beryl.

The term "magnetism" is derived from the region of Magnesia in Asia Minor, where a black mineral known as the lodestone is mined. Because of its magnetic properties, the lodestone was used by ancient seamen to navigate their ships, as a compass is used today.

Crystals grow by reproducing themselves. They come nearest to being "alive" of all members of the mineral kingdom.

## Money

The first coin minted in the United States was a silver dollar. It was issued on October 15, 1794.

On March 16, 1970, a bidder at Sotheby & Company in London paid $20,000 for one glass paperweight.

During the American revolution, inflation was so great that the price of corn rose 10,000 percent, the price of wheat 14,000 percent, the price of flour 15,000 percent, and the price of beef 33,000 percent.

A quarter has 119 grooves on its circumference. A dime has one less.

Assuming that each fold neatly overlaps its opposite side, a dollar bill can be folded only six times—seven if put into a vise. (Try it.)

In 1915 the average annual family income in the United States was $687 a year.

In 1975 a birdhouse costing $10,000 was built in Quebec by the city fathers.

As of 1976 there was $77 billion worth of paper currency in circulation in the United States.

In 1060 a coin was minted in England shaped like a clover. The user could break off any of the four leaves and use them as separate pieces of currency.

During the early boom days of the Gold Rush in San Francisco a glass of whiskey could cost as much as $7.

Gold mine in California, 1854

Until the twentieth century dogs' teeth were used as money by Solomon Island natives.

In 1973 the United States Customs Service in New York City collected more than $1.3 billion in import duties.

---

According to the Nielson Clearing House in Clinton, Iowa, so many advertiser and manufacturer coupons are redeemed in America each year that if their value were averaged out per capita, every person in the United States would receive $1.25 in cash—this though the average coupon is worth only 14 cents.

---

More than a million dollars belonging to Adolf Hitler and other prominent Nazis is still unclaimed in American banks. The money was deposited several years before America entered World War II and no one knows what to do with it today.

---

One-fourth of the world's population lives on less than $200 a year. Ninety million people survive on less than $75 a year.

---

During the early 1920's, at the height of the inflation in the German Weimar Republic, one American dollar was equal to 4 trillion German marks.

---

In 1965, a collection of eight bottles of Château Lafite Rothschild was sold at auction for $2,200.

---

The percentage of income tax paid by the average American family has more than doubled since 1953. In 1953 the average family paid 11 percent of its income out in taxes. In 1976 it paid 23 percent.

---

The amount of play money printed each year for use in the Parker Brothers game *Monopoly* totals more than the amount of real currency issued annually by the United States Government. As of 1974, according to Parker Brothers, almost 70 million *Monopoly* sets had been sold throughout the world.

---

It costs more to buy a new car today in the United States than it cost Christopher Columbus to equip and undertake three voyages to and from the New World.

---

Until the nineteenth century, solid blocks of tea were used as money in Siberia.

---

America once issued a 5-cent bill.

In 1776 a man who made $4,000 a year was considered wealthy.

As of 1976 there were approximately 375 ten-thousand-dollar bills in circulation in the United States.

There are six coins currently minted by the United States Treasury: the silver dollar, the 50-cent piece, the quarter, the dime, the nickel, and the penny. The faces on all these coins look to the left with one exception. Which one? The penny.

The Yap islanders in the South Pacific use 18-foot-high stone rings as money. The stones sometimes weigh as much as 15 tons, which means that when someone is paid in such currency, he goes to where the money is, not vice-versa.

## Movies & Movie Stars

The cowboy movie star Tom Mix drove a Rolls-Royce that had a pair of antlers as a radiator cap. Mix once ordered tires for his limousine with his initials printed in relief. At that time Hollywood was connected by a network of dirt roads; whenever Mix drove along one of these roads he would leave a long trail of "TM"s imprinted in the dust.

Grace Kelly was the first motion-picture actress to appear on a postage stamp. In April, 1956, she was featured with her husband, Prince Rainier III of Monaco, on a stamp that commemorated their wedding.

Alfred Hitchcock directed the first talking film ever made in England. It was called *Blackmail* and was made in 1931.

In 1939, Hollywood film companies produced an average of two motion pictures every day.

The figure of King Kong seen in the original movie of the same name was actually a model 18 inches high.

Scene from original
movie version
of *King Kong*, 1937

Vivien Leigh as Scarlett O'Hara and Leslie Howard as Ashley Wilkes in a scene from *Gone with the Wind*

During the casting of the film *Gone with the Wind,* more than 1,400 candidates were interviewed for the part of Scarlett O'Hara, and more than $92,000 was spent in the search.

---

The film *Quo Vadis* used 30,000 extras (and 63 lions).

---

# Museums & Libraries

---

Wonalancet, New Hampshire, boasts the world's only Antarctic dog museum, the Byrd Antarctic Dog Memorial Museum.

---

The work of an artist cannot be exhibited in the Louvre until he has been dead for at least sixty years. The only exception ever made to this rule was Georges Braque.

---

James Smithson, English scientist and founder of the Smithsonian Institution, never once set foot in America. The Institution was established in 1846 with funds from his estate which he left for "the increase and diffusion of knowledge among men."

---

The Library of Congress has 327 miles of bookshelves.

---

Old Lyme, Connecticut has the world's only museum dedicated to nuts. The world's largest nutcracker, 8 feet long, hangs outside on a tree.

The Smithsonian Institution has over 30 million fossils in its paleontology collection and more than 24 million insect specimens.

## Music & Musicians

Mozart wrote the opera *Don Giovanni* at one sitting. It was played without rehearsal the day after it was written.

Haydn could write music only on clean white paper. Mozart composed while playing billiards. Christoph Gluck would write only when seated in the middle of a field. Rossini composed most of his music when he was drunk. Wagner found it easiest to compose when he was dressed up in historical costumes. Haydn believed he could not compose well unless he was wearing a ring given to him by Frederick the Great.

Richard Wagner

The famous Russian composer Alexander Borodin was a professor of chemistry at the Academy of Medicine in St. Petersburg. Borodin always referred to himself as a "musical amateur."

The song most frequently sung in the western world is "Happy Birthday to You." The song was written in 1936 by Mildred and Patty Hill, and their estate still collects royalties on it.

Fifty-three operas have been written about Faust.

The oboe is considered the most difficult of all woodwind instruments to play correctly.

Wooden clarinets are always made of wood from the granadilla tree.

Felix Mendelssohn wrote his most famous overture, *A Midsummer Night's Dream,* when he was seventeen.

Lewis H. Dedner, composer of the music to "O Little Town of Bethlehem," claimed that the hymn's melody came to him in a dream on Christmas Eve. Charles Wesley, author of "Hark, the Herald Angels Sing" (written in 1730), wrote a total of 6,000 hymns. He was inspired to write "Hark" while listening to the pealing of bells as he walked to church one Christmas morning.

Beethoven was totally deaf when he composed his Ninth Symphony.

Ludwig van Beethoven

Ignace Paderewski, one of the greatest concert pianists of all time, was also premier of Poland.

Cello and saxophone players, as of 1975, could join the Marine Corps and play in the band without taking basic training.

Verdi wrote the opera *Aida* at the request of the khedive of Egypt to commemorate the opening of the Suez Canal.

"The Washington Post March" by John Philip Sousa was named after a newspaper, the Washington *Post*.

Franz Liszt was Richard Wagner's father-in-law. Arturo Toscanini was Vladimir Horowitz's father-in-law.

More than 100 descendants of Johann Sebastian Bach have been cathedral organists.

The oldest piano still in existence was built in 1720.

Piano built by Bartolomeo Cristofori in Florence, 1720

No one knows where Mozart is buried.

The cello's real name is the violoncello. The full name of the piano is the pianoforte.

Wolfgang Amadeus Mozart

The Greek national anthem has 158 verses.

Dr. Friederich Mesmer, Austrian physician and the inventor of mesmerism, a forerunner of hypnosis, introduced the harmonica to France.

Franz Schubert's masterpiece, his Sixth Symphony, was turned down by the Paris Symphony Orchestra. The London Philharmonic laughed at it, and its conductor withdrew it from rehearsal. The piece was not played publicly until thirty years after it was written.

## Names: People, Places, & Things

What have the following towns in common: Dayton, Atlanta, Cleveland, Philadelphia, Jacksonville, Norfolk, Bangor, Hartford, New Haven, Phoenix, Stamford, Urbana, and Newark? They are all towns in New York State.

The initials BVD, which have come to stand for men's underwear in general, stand for the names of the three men who originally manufactured BVDs—Bradley, Voorhies, and Day.

The town of Modesto, California, was named in honor of its founders, who were too "modest" to name it after themselves. The town of Tarzana, California, is named for the fictional character Tarzan, having been the home for many years of Edgar Rice Burroughs, creator of the Tarzan saga.

The official name of India is not India. It is Bharat.

The first letter of every continent's name is the same as the last: AmericA, AntarcticA, EuropE, AsiA, AustraliA, AfricA.

Muhammad is the most common name in the world.

The word "Nazi" was actually an abbreviation. The party's full name was the *Nazionalsozialistische Deutsche Arbeiterpartei.*

Cotton Mather, famous American clergyman, had an odd first name. His father had an even odder one: Increase.

---

Maine is the only state in the United States whose name has one syllable.

---

Battleships are always named after states, submarines after fish, cruisers after cities, and destroyers after naval heroes.

---

Until 1796, there was a state in the United States called Franklin. Today it is known as Tennessee.

---

There were 2,282 people named Smith in the 1975 Manhattan telephone directory.

---

Their real names:

Hieronymus Bosch—Hieronymus van Aken
Sandro Botticelli—Alessandro di Mariano dei Filipepi
Anthony Burgess—John Wilson
El Cid—Rodrigo Díaz de Bivar
Joseph Conrad—Teodor Korzeniowski
Le Corbusier—Charles Edouard Jeanneret
Marie Corelli—Mary Mackay
Donatello—Donato di Niccolò di Betto Bardi
George Eliot—Mary Ann Evans
Anatole France—Jacques Thibault
Maxim Gorky—Alexey Peshkov
Lenin—Vladimir Ulyanov
"Baby Face" Nelson—Lester Gillis
George Orwell—Eric Blair
Ellery Queen—Frederic Dunnay and Manfred B. Lee
George Sand—Amandine Aurore Lucie Dupin, Baronne Dudevant
"Dutch" Schultz—Arthur Flegenheimer
Josef Stalin—Josef Dzhugashvili
Emanuel Swedenborg—Emanuel Swedberg
Tintoretto—Jacopo Robusti
Jules Verne—L. M. Olehewitz
Voltaire—Francois Marie Arouet

---

The blazer jacket is named for a British ship, H.M.S. *Blazer*. The ship's captain insisted that his crew always wear blue jackets with metal buttons, even for casual duty.

Benito Mussolini was named after a Mexican revolutionary and liberal statesman, Benito Juárez.

Benito Mussolini

The name "pumpernickel" was coined by Napoleon's troops during the Napoleonic Wars. His men complained that although they were often poorly fed, there was always bread for Napoleon's favorite horse, Nicoll. Thus the word "pumpernickel" was coined—*pain* (bread) *pour* (for) Nicoll.

The following are all names of men who have played major-league baseball:

Eli Grba, Malachi Kittredge, Tacks Neuer, Prince Oana, Orval Overall, Ty Pickup, Squiz Pillon, Shadow Pyle, Ossie Schreckengost, Tony Suck, Clay Touchstone, Coot Veal, Yats Wuestling, Ad Yale.

When the planet Uranus was discovered by Sir William Herschel in 1781 it was named "Georgium Sidium" in honor of King George III of England. For many years the planet was known as the "Georgian." Not until 1850 was it christened

Uranus in accordance with the tradition of naming planets for Roman gods.

---

Named after:

*Bloomers* were the brainstorm of Amelia Bloomer, who caused a scandal by wearing trousers that exposed two inches of her ankles.

The *braille* reading system is named for Louis Braille. Blinded in an accident at age three, Braille became one of the most brilliant prodigies of his time and invented his famous reading method while still in his twenties.

The *chesterfield* settee is named after a nineteenth-century Earl of Chesterfield.

The *derrick* is named after Thomas Derrick, a seventeenth-century English executioner-hangman whose association with the gallows gave his name to the crane.

The *doily* is named after a Mr. Doiley, a seventeenth-century linendraper in London.

The *guillotine* is named after Dr. Joseph Guillotin. Guillotin did not invent the deadly mechanism—it had been in use for centuries before his time—but suggested it in the eighteenth century as a humane method of execution.

Above: Amelia Bloomer wearing the garment she attempted to popularize
Left: Execution by guillotine during the French revolution

The *Norfolk jacket* is named for a nineteenth-century Duke of Norfolk.

The *Oscar* film trophy is named after Oscar Pierce, a wealthy Texas farmer. Before the trophy had any name at all, Pierce's niece, then serving as librarian for the

Academy of Motion Picture Arts and Sciences, commented that the statue reminded her of her Uncle Oscar. A newspaper columnist overheard the chance remark and subsequently wrote that "employees have affectionately dubbed their famous statuette 'Oscar.' " The name stuck.

The *peach Melba* is named after Dame Nellie Melba, an Australian operatic soprano, for whom the dish was first created.

The *saxophone* is named after Antoine Sax. Born in Belgium, Sax invented a number of unusual-sounding brass instruments, all of which he named after himself. Besides the saxophone he created the saxhorn and the saxotromba.

The *silhouette* is named after Etienne de Silhouette, a French author and statesman who reputedly was highly skilled at the art of cutting profiles out of paper.

The *tam o' shanter* is named for the hero of Robert Burns's poem of the same name.

*Wellington boots* were the invention of Arthur Wellesley, first Duke of Wellington.

---

## Natural Phenomena

When the volcano Krakatoa erupted in the Dutch East Indies in 1883, the sound was heard in Bangkok, 3,000 miles away. At Batavia, 100 miles away, the sky was so darkened that people had to light their lamps during the day. The fine particles ejected by the blast covered almost every part of the world, and for the next two years a thin haze of these particles could be seen in the sky each night as far away as London.

---

There are more than 50,000 earthquakes throughout the world every year.

---

More than 71 million gallons of water pass over Victoria Falls in Africa every minute.

---

Venezuela's Angel Falls are a mile high.

---

One can see the stars during the day from the bottom of a well.

The Niagara Falls have eroded their way 10 miles upstream since they were first formed some 10,000 years ago. The tremendous amount of water tends to eat through its limestone base relatively rapidly, and if erosion continues at its present rate, geologists estimate that the falls will disappear completely in 22,000 years.

Still majestic, Niagara Falls may be slowly disappearing.

Old Faithful in Yellowstone National Park, Wyoming, is *not* the highest natural geyser in the United States. Its neighbor, the Beehive Geyser, spouts well over 200 feet of water, compared with Old Faithful's 160. The Beehive, however, performs its majestic ejections at infrequent and unpredictable intervals.

# People

Thomas Edison was deaf from the time he was twelve years old. The malady was caused while Edison was trying to board a train at Frazer Station, Michigan. A conductor took hold of his ears to help pull him aboard. "I felt something snap inside my head," Edison later said. "My deafness

Thomas Edison's impaired hearing did not impede his brilliance as an inventor.

started from that time and has progressed ever since." Edison never went to school—his formal education consisted of three months' attendance at a public school in Port Huron, Michigan.

---

Faust, the protagonist of works by Christopher Marlowe, Goethe, and dozens of other writers, was an actual person. Johann Faust was a sixteenth-century doctor of theology at the University of Wittenberg in Germany. Many stories were told about him during his lifetime, including one in which he sold his soul to the devil in exchange for eternal youth and wisdom. The tale captured the imagination of authors for centuries afterward.

---

Napoleon had conquered Italy by the time he was twenty-six.

---

Arthur Conan Doyle, author of the Sherlock Holmes stories, was an ophthalmologist by profession.

Christopher Columbus had blond hair.

Karl Marx once served as a reporter on the New York *Herald Tribune* (the paper was then known as the New York *Tribune*). In 1848 he worked in the London office of the *Tribune,* and his boss, the managing editor, was Richard Henry Dana, who himself became world-famous as author of *Two Years Before the Mast.*

Sir Christopher Wren, designer of St. Paul's Cathedral in London, was not an architect. He was a mathematician and an astronomer. Wren was in fact a great astronomer, having developed a method for computing eclipses and another for measuring the rings of Saturn.

The longest biographical entry in the 1975 edition of *Who's Who* is that of Buckminster Fuller, the well-known American architect, engineer, and designer.

Casanova, the greatest adventurer and lover of his time, ended his life as a librarian. From 1785 to 1798 he lived in Bohemia, semiretired, working as librarian for Count von Waldstein in the Château de Dux. He died quietly at the job.

Giovanni Jacopo Casanova

Lord Byron had four pet geese that he brought everywhere with him, even to social gatherings. Byron, though considered one of the most dashing and attractive men of his time, was fat and had a club foot.

Romantic portrait of George Gordon, Lord Byron, by Vincenzo Camuccini

Julius Caesar, Alexander the Great, and Dostoyevsky were all epileptics.

Alexandre Dumas *père* was one-quarter black.

There is absolutely no documented proof that Betsy Ross designed the American flag.

Attila the Hun was a dwarf. Pepin the Short, Aesop, Gregory of Tours, Charles III of Naples, and the Pasha Hussain were all less than 3½ feet tall.

Rudyard Kipling would only write when he had black ink in his pen. Beethoven poured ice water over his head when he sat down to create music, believing it stimulated his brain. Dickens wrote (and slept) facing north, aligning himself with the poles of the earth. Rossini covered himself with blankets when he composed. Proust worked in bed, and only in a soundproof room.

---

In 1898 P. T. Barnum's side show included a man who looked like a Skye terrier; a woman with a goatee; a woman with scaly alligatorlike skin; a blue man (he had permanently dyed himself by accident with silver nitrate); the most tattooed woman in the world (she claimed to have been stabbed by the tattooer's needle 100 million times); a Ubangi with saucers in both lips; an "India-rubber man" who could pull the skin several inches off his cheeks; a woman whom no one could make laugh (her facial muscles were paralyzed); a "hardheaded man" (people could break blocks of granite over his skull. A doctor once examined him and found his skull to be 2 inches thick); an ossified man (his flesh had completely hardened and crystallized before he died); a "living skeleton" (6 feet tall and 70 pounds); a "gorilla girl" (billed as the ugliest woman in the world); and "What Is It," a congenital idiot so misshapen and retarded that some people believed him to be an unknown species of monkey.

---

One of Napoleon's drinking cups was made from the skull of the famous Italian adventurer Cagliostro.

---

Henry Wadsworth Longfellow, who made John and Priscilla Alden famous in his poem "The Courtship of Miles Standish," was related to both these actual historical personages.

---

Tom Fuller, a slave brought to America when he was fourteen years old, could tell the exact number of seconds in any given length of time. Once, when asked to give the precise number of seconds in seventy years, he obliged in less than one and a half minutes. Yet Fuller could neither read nor write.

---

Lafayette was a major general in the United States at the age of nineteen. Lafayette's whole name takes up an entire line on a page: Marie Joseph Paul Yves Roch Gilbert du Motier, Marquis de Lafayette.

Lafayette conferring with George Washington at Mount Vernon, detail of a painting by Horace K. Turner after Thomas Rossiter

---

An eighteenth-century German named Matthew Birchinger, known as "the little man of Nuremberg," played four musical instruments including the bagpipes, was an expert calligrapher, and was the most famous stage magician of his

The "little man of Nuremberg"

day. He performed tricks with the cup and balls that have never been explained. Yet Birchinger had no hands, legs, or thighs, and was less than 29 inches tall.

---

There is absolutely no evidence that Adolf Hitler was a paperhanger.

---

The African country of Rhodesia is named after an English entrepreneur, Cecil Rhodes. Rhodes, prime minister of Cape Colony in South Africa in the late nineteenth century and creator of the South Africa diamond syndicate, at one time controlled 90 percent of the world's supply of diamonds. When he died, in 1902, his will stipulated that a great part of his fortune was to be used for the establishment of a foundation for the furtherance of higher education, which today grants the Rhodes Scholarship.

---

Nobody knows where the body of Voltaire is. It was stolen from its tomb in the nineteenth century and has never been recovered. The theft was discovered in 1864, when the tomb was opened and found empty.

---

The Mongol conqueror Timur the Lame (1336–1405), whom Christopher Marlowe called Tamburlaine, played polo with the skulls of those he had killed in battle. Timur left records of his victories by erecting 30-foot-high pyramids made of the severed heads of his victims.

---

There are a number of Americans who are related to Napoleon Bonaparte. Napoleon's youngest brother, Jerome, married an American.

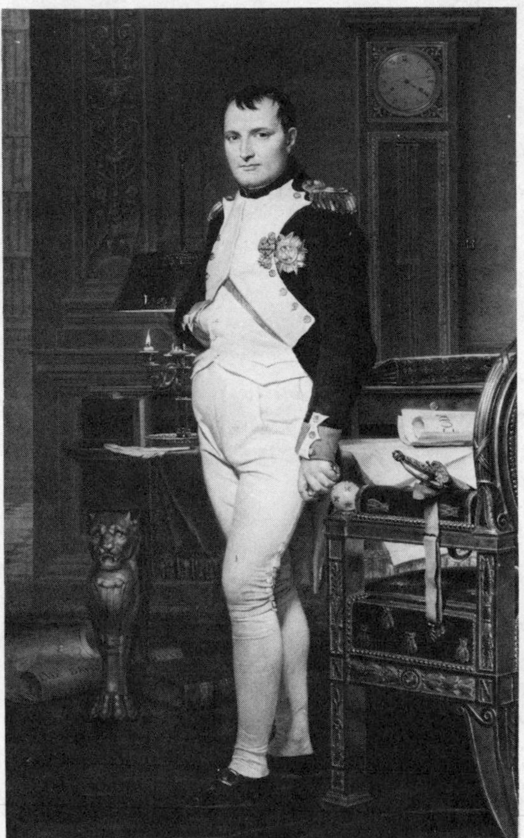

*Napoleon in His Study,* by Jacques Louis David

The famous nineteenth-century bullfighter Lagartijo (born Rafael Molina) killed 4,867 bulls.

The Graham cracker was named after Sylvester Graham (1794–1851). A New England minister, Graham not only invented the cracker but also published a journal in Boston that took a rabid stand against tea, coffee, feather beds, and women's corsets.

Alexandre Gustave Eiffel, the man who designed the Eiffel Tower, also designed the inner structure of the Statue of Liberty in New York Harbor.

James A. Garfield

President James Garfield could write Latin with one hand and Greek with the other—simultaneously! Leonardo da Vinci could draw with one hand and write with the other, also simultaneously.

The Second Marquess of Ripon, a well-known British sportsman, killed a total of 556,000 gamebirds in his life. The Marquess dropped dead on a grouse hunt in 1923, after having bagged 52 birds that morning.

Irénée Du Pont, onetime president of E. I. Du Pont de Nemours and Company, kept pet iguanas on his estate in Cuba. Mr. Du Pont spent many hours training these pets and succeeded in teaching them to stand at attention and to come when called.

---

Pierre Beaumarchais, one of the leading French dramatists of the eighteenth century, invented a device called the escapement, without which modern wristwatches would have been impossible. Beaumarchais was one of the most important Frenchmen to fight on the side of the colonies in the American revolution, was a secret agent for Louis XVI and gave harp lessons to the King's daughter, instituted in France the practice of paying playwrights royalties for their performed works, spent several years in jail for bank fraud and treason and pleaded his own case in court several times, edited the works of Voltaire, and wrote the operas *The Barber of Seville* and *The Marriage of Figaro.*

---

David Kennison, born in 1736, lived to 115 and was the longest-surviving participant in the Boston Tea Party. He served in both the American revolution and the War of 1812. He served in the latter at the age of seventy-six, and had his hand shot off at Sackett's Harbor. Several years later, his skull was fractured when a tree fell on his head, and several years after that, while he was training for a militia drill, a premature explosion from a cannon shattered both his legs. When he recovered from the injury, his legs became covered with sores that never healed, and he was stricken with rheumatism. Some time later, his face was mutilated when he was kicked by a horse. He finally died a quiet death in Illinois in 1851.

---

After Sir Isaac Newton died, a sealed trunk was found among his belongings containing nearly 100,000 pages he had written on the subjects of alchemy, astrology, and the occult.

---

Sir Richard Burton (1821–1890), the English explorer and the first westerner ever to enter the sacred Moslem city of

Mecca, spoke twenty languages, almost discovered the source of the Nile, fought Indians with Kit Carson, was a close friend of Brigham Young, was one of the first white men to sail down the Amazon, and wrote the first western translation of *The Arabian Nights.*

Sir Richard Burton in 1857

---

Charles Carroll, one of the signers of the Declaration of Independence, lived long enough to help lay the cornerstone of the Baltimore & Ohio Railroad in 1828. Carroll, the longest-lived of all the signers, died in 1832 at the age of ninety-five.

---

When the circus dwarf Lavinia Bump married the circus dwarf Tom Thumb, more than 2,000 guests attended their

Wedding portrait of Mr. and Mrs. Tom Thumb

wedding, including President and Mrs. Abraham Lincoln and the entire United States Cabinet. The famous ceremony was dubbed "The Fairy Wedding."

Charles Lindbergh was instrumental in the development of a method for preserving human tissue outside the body. He coauthored a book on the subject, *The Culture of Organs,* with the French scientist Alexis Carrel. Lindbergh was also among the first to perfect a mechanical heart, a pumping apparatus that supplied blood to organs to keep them alive outside the body.

---

Both Josef Stalin and Kaiser Wilhelm had crippled left arms. Stalin, despite his popular image, was not a pipe smoker. He used the pipe only for effect at conferences and public appearances. In private he chain-smoked cigarettes.

---

When he was a child, Blaise Pascal once locked himself in his room for several days and would not allow anyone to enter. When he emerged, he had figured out all of Euclid's geometrical propositions totally on his own.

---

Edgar Allan Poe and James Abbott McNeill Whistler both went to West Point.

---

The English poet Thomas Chatterton died at seventeen. Mozart died at thirty-six, Raphael died at thirty-seven, Aubrey Beardsley died at twenty-six, and the painter Masaccio died at twenty-seven.

*The Death of Chatterton,* by H. Wallis

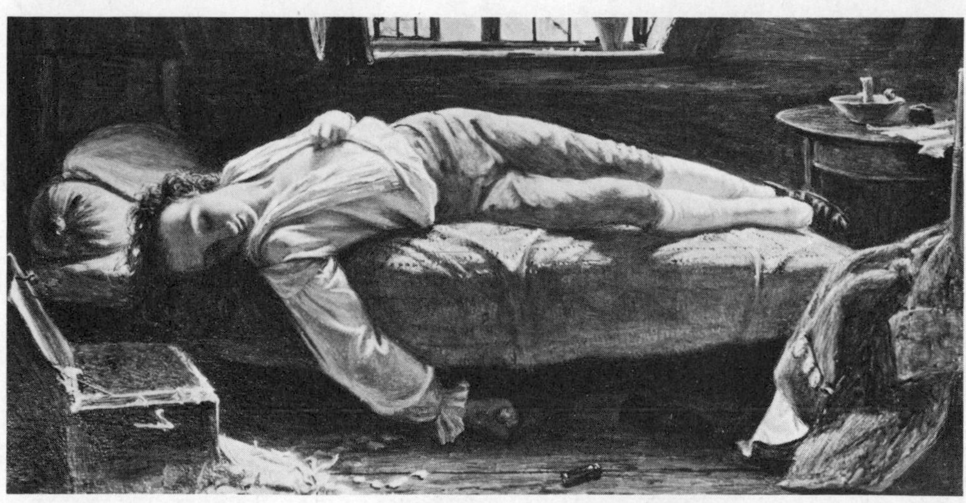

The famous Swedish astronomer Tycho Brahe had a nose made of gold. It was a replacement for his own, which he lost in a duel with a Danish nobleman in 1566.

Geoffry Hudson, a famous dwarf at the seventeenth-century court of Charles II of England, stood 3 feet high and enjoyed entertaining the king by popping out of large pastries. Hudson once fought a duel against a full-sized man for a full-sized woman and won.

Edward Hyde, Viscount Cornbury, colonial governor of New York and New Jersey from 1702 to 1708, was a professed transvestite. He commonly robed himself in women's outfits, rouged and powdered his face, and promenaded through the town in drag. He was once arrested on a morals charge. For his official portrait Viscount Cornbury posed in a low-cut evening gown holding a fan and wearing a sprig of lace in his hair. He was fired in 1708—not for his outrageous behavior, but for taking bribes.

# Physics

An ice cube in a glass of water will not raise the water level when it melts. The amount of space it displaces as a cube is equal to the amount it takes up when liquefied.

All snow crystals are hexagonal.

No one can drown in the Dead Sea. It is 25 percent salt, which makes the water very heavy. This property makes a body extremely buoyant on the Dead Sea, so that it is almost impossible to remain submerged.

A ball of glass will bounce higher than a ball made of rubber. A ball of solid steel will bounce higher than one made entirely of glass.

In one second 6,242,000,000,000,000,000 electrons pass any given point in an electrical current.

Dry ice does not melt. It evaporates.

When glass breaks the cracks move faster than 3,000 miles per hour. To photograph the event a camera must shoot at a millionth of a second.

Where there is fire there is not always smoke. Smoke simply means that a fire is not burning properly and that bits of unburned materials are escaping. A perfectly clean fire produces almost no smoke.

If hot water is suddenly poured into a glass the glass is more apt to break if it is thick than if it is thin. This is why test tubes are made of thin glass.

A bubble is round because the air within it presses equally against all its parts, thus causing all surfaces to be equidistant from its center.

Nothing can be burned again that has already been burned once.

The color black absorbs heat. White reflects it.

A whip makes a cracking sound because its tip moves faster than the speed of sound (760 miles per hour).

Gasoline has no specific freezing point—it freezes at any temperature between -180° and -240° F (-118° to -151° C). When it does freeze it never solidifies totally, but resembles gum or wax.

An egg will float if placed in water to which sugar has been added.

It takes as much heat to turn one ounce of snow to water as it does to make an ounce of soup boil at room temperature.

Dirty snow melts faster than clean.

Granite conducts sound ten times faster than air.

Water has a greater molecular density in liquid form than as a solid. This is why ice floats.

If a glass of water were magnified to the size of the earth, the molecules comprising it would be about as big as a large orange.

Hot water weighs more than cold.

## Predictions

Roger Bacon, a thirteenth-century Franciscan monk, predicted the following things in his *Communia Mathematica:*

*High-speed sea travel.* "It is possible to make machines of navigation," wrote the erudite monk, "which need no man to navigate them, so that very large seagoing ships may go along with one man to steer, and at a greater speed than if they were full of men working them."

*The automobile.* "Cars could be made which move at inestimable speed without animals to draw them as if they were the chariots in which men fought of old."

*The airplane.* "Flying machines can be built so that a man sitting in the middle of the machine may turn an instrument by which wings artificially made will beat the air, like a bird flying."

First airplane flight, December 17, 1903. Pilot was Orville Wright.

*The microscope and telescope.* "Instruments can be designed so that enormous things will appear very small, and contrariwise . . ."

*Gunpowder and bombs.* "Sounds like thunder can be made in the air but more terrifying than those which occur in nature; for an appropriate material in moderate quantity, as big as a man's thumb, makes a horrible noise and shows a violent flash; and this can be done in many ways by which a whole town or army may be destroyed."

## Presidents

Franklin D. Roosevelt's birthday is a legal holiday in the Virgin Islands.

The teddy bear was named for Theodore Roosevelt. When presented with a koala from Australia, Roosevelt, whose fondness for animals was well known, so praised the creature that a copy of it was made for children. Called the "teddy bear" in the President's honor, the toy soon caught on and became a standard item on every child's shelf.

Grover Cleveland is the only United States president to have been married in the White House.

President and
Mrs. Grover Cleveland

James Madison, 5 feet, 4 inches tall, was the shortest president of the United States. Abraham Lincoln was the tallest at 6 feet, 4 inches.

James Madison

During World War I, Woodrow Wilson's wife grazed sheep on the front lawn of the White House.

President Taft weighed 352 pounds.

Thomas Jefferson, John Adams, and James Monroe all died on July 4th. Jefferson and Adams died at practically the same minute of the same day.

Martin Van Buren, eighth president of the United States, was the first to be born a citizen of the United States. He was born in 1782, six years after the signing of the Constitution.

Martin Van Buren

In 1824, Andrew Jackson received more popular votes than John Adams, yet lost the election. The vote was so close that neither candidate received a majority of the electoral votes. The decision then went to the House of Representatives, which elected Adams.

President Grover Cleveland was a draft dodger. He hired someone to enter the service in his place, for which he was ridiculed by his political opponent, James G. Blaine. It was soon discovered, however, that Blaine had done the same thing himself.

For his entire forty-seven years in government, Herbert Hoover turned over each of his Federal salary checks to charity. He had become independently wealthy before entering politics.

George Washington's face was badly scarred from smallpox.

Theodore Roosevelt became president at the age of forty-two. He was the youngest president ever to hold office.

Theodore Roosevelt

William Howard Taft is the only man ever to have been both chief justice and president of the United States.

In 1920 Socialist Eugene Debs received 920,000 votes for president of the United States. Yet he ran his entire campaign while in jail.

In 1976 President Gerald R. Ford sent out 40,000 Christmas cards.

Theodore Roosevelt was Eleanor Roosevelt's uncle.

President John Tyler had fifteen children.

At the inauguration of Abraham Lincoln in 1860 four future presidents were in attendance: Benjamin Harrison, Chester Alan Arthur, Rutherford B. Hayes, and James A. Garfield.

Zachary Taylor, twelfth president of the United States, did not vote until he was sixty-two. He did not even vote in his own election. Taylor, a professional soldier, lived in so many places during his life that he was unable to establish a legal residence until he retired.

Zachary Taylor

Gerald Ford was one of the members of the Warren Commission appointed to study the assassination of President John F. Kennedy.

Theodore Roosevelt's wife and mother both died on the same day.

James Buchanan was the only United States president never to marry. During his term in office, his niece Harriet Lane played the role of First Lady.

James Buchanan

George Washington left no direct descendants. Though his wife Martha had four children by a previous marriage, Washington never sired a child to continue his line.

Franklin D. Roosevelt, the most popular president ever to hold office in the United States, did not carry his home county of Dutchess, New York, in any of his four elections.

John F. Kennedy and Warren Harding were the only United States presidents to be survived by their fathers.

George Washington was *not* the first president of the United States. The first president was John Hanson, Maryland's representative at the Continental Congress. On November 5, 1781, Hanson was elected by the Constitutional Congress to the office of "President of the United States in Congress Assembled." He served for one year.

A man named David Rice Atchison was president of the United States for one day and didn't know it. According to a nineteenth-century law, if neither the president nor the vice-president was in office, the president pro tem of the Senate became chief executive. On March 4, 1849, President James Knox Polk's term had lapsed, and the newly elected Zachary Taylor could not yet be sworn in (it was a Sunday). So for one day Atchison was president. It was not until several months later that Atchison learned of this, as the law was then an obscure one. It has since been changed.

When Abraham Lincoln's funeral procession passed Ford's Theater, where Lincoln had been shot, one of the cornices fell off the building. When John Wilkes Booth leaped onto the stage after shooting the President, he tripped—on the American flag. A short time before his assassination Lincoln dreamed he was going to die, and he related his dream to the Senate.

On New Year's Day, 1907, Theodore Roosevelt shook hands with 8,513 people.

President Ulysses S. Grant was once arrested during his term of office. He was convicted of exceeding the Washington speed limit on his horse and was fined $20. President Franklin Pierce was arrested while in office for running over an old woman with his horse, but the case was dropped for insufficient evidence in 1853.

Ulysses S. Grant

Norfolk County, Massachusetts, is the birthplace of three United States presidents: John Adams, John Quincy Adams, and John F. Kennedy.

Robert Todd Lincoln, son of Abraham Lincoln, was present at the assassinations of three presidents: his father's, President Garfield's, and President McKinley's. After the last shooting, he refused ever to attend a state affair again.

Assassination of President James Garfield by Charles Guiteau, 1881

## Psychology

There is no one who does not dream. Those who claim to have no dreams, laboratory tests have determined, simply forget their dreams more easily than others.

The color combination with the strongest visual impact is black on yellow. Next follow black on white, yellow on black, white on black, dark blue on white, and white on dark blue.

The Psychology Department of Dayton University reports that loud talk can be ten times more distracting than the sound of a jackhammer. Loud, incessant chatter can make a listener nervous and irritable, say the findings, and even start him on the road to insanity.

---

The short-term memory capacity for most people is between five and nine items or digits. This is one reason that phone numbers are seven digits long.

---

Studies done by the Psychology Department of DePauw University show that the principal reason people lie is to avoid punishment.

---

Man is the only animal that cries.

---

Men laugh longer, more loudly, and more often than women.

---

A list of odd phobias:

*Ailurophobia*—fear of cats.
*Androphobia*—fear of men.
*Apiphobia*—fear of bees.
*Astraphobia*—fear of storms.
*Aviophobia*—fear of flying.
*Baccilophobia*—fear of microbes.
*Ballistophobia*—fear of bullets.
*Belonephobia*—fear of needles and sharp, pointed objects.
*Clinophobia*—fear of beds.
*Gephydrophobia*—fear of crossing bridges.
*Iatrophobia*—fear of doctors.
*Nyctophobia*—fear of night.
*Ombrophobia*—fear of rain.
*Otophobia*—fear of opening one's eyes.
*Peccatophobia*—fear of sinning.
*Sitophobia*—fear of food.
*Taphephobia*—fear of being buried alive.
*Thalassophobia*—fear of the ocean.
*Trichophobia*—fear of hair.
*Vestiphobia*—fear of clothing.

---

The term "doing one's own thing" was coined by the Gestalt psychologist Fritz Perls. His "Gestalt Prayer" reads:

"I do my thing and you do your thing. I am not in this world to live up to your expectations and you are not in this world to live up to mine. You are you and I am I, and if by chance we find each other, it's beautiful. If not, it can't be helped."

## Records

Babe Ruth, besides holding the world lifetime record for home runs up to the 1970's, holds the world record for strikeouts as well.

Babe Ruth in the 1920's

Harry Drake of Lakeside, California, competing in a foot-bow archery contest at Ivanpah Dry Lake, California, in October, 1970, shot an arrow that traveled 1 mile, 101 yards, and 21 inches. A foot bow is fired by lying on one's back, stringing the bow, and pushing out the wooden part of the bow with one's feet.

The record for traveling from New York to Los Angeles by motorcycle is 45 hours, 41 minutes. It was set in 1968 by Tibor Sarossy, riding a BMW Model R69S. Sarossy made four fuel stops, never slept, fainted twice, and averaged 58.7 miles per hour all the way across.

In June, 1963, in Britain, the British tennis player Michael Sangster served a ball that was clocked at 154 miles per hour. This is the fastest tennis serve ever recorded.

The best-selling nonfiction book of all time is Benjamin Spock's *Common Sense Book of Baby and Child Care.*

## Religion

Throughout history, nearly all religions of the world have had a celebration that falls close to Christmas. In Judaism it is Hanukkah, the Festival of Lights. Pre-Christian Scandinavians enjoyed the Feast of the Frost King. In Rome there was the Saturnalia, in Egypt the midwinter festival in honor of the god Horus. The Druids had an annual mistletoe-cutting ceremony. Mithraists celebrated the feast of Sol Invictus, representing the victory of light over darkness. In Hinduism the feasts of Diwali and Taipongal are observed close to the Christmas season. Many other civilizations have similar festivals.

In the year 632, when the prophet Muhammad died, the Islamic empire comprised only an insignificant corner of Arabia. A little more than a hundred years later the Moslem religion had spread to Persia, Egypt, Syria, India, Central Asia, parts of northern Africa, and into southern Africa. In a century's time Islam had converted one-third of the world.

---

The toe of the metal statue of St. Peter in St. Peter's Cathedral, Rome, is worn down almost to a nub by the great number of pilgrims who have kissed it through the centuries.

---

The Roman Catholic population of the world is larger than that of all other Christian sects combined.

---

Hairs from the tail of a mule ridden by the crusader Peter the Hermit brought high prices as sacred relics throughout Europe in the fourteenth century.

---

Before the Chinese takeover of Tibet in 1952, 25 percent of the males in the country were Buddhist monks.

---

On the stone temples of Madura in southern India, there are more than 30 million carved images of gods and goddesses.

---

There have been 262 popes since Saint Peter.

---

Christianity has a billion followers. Islam is next in representation with half this number.

---

In the Greek monastery of Mount Athos *nothing* female is allowed. Men can enter but not women; roosters but no hens; horses but no mares; bulls but no cows. The border is patrolled by armed guards to ensure that nothing feminine passes the gates. It has been this way for more than 700 years.

---

Tibetan monks and Inca priests both practiced a brain operation called "trepanation," in which a small hole was drilled through the skull of a living person, right between the eyes. Its purpose was to stimulate the pineal gland and thereby induce a mystical state of consciousness. The operation is occasionally still practiced today.

---

Hugnes was archbishop of Reims in the tenth century when he was five years old. In the eleventh century Benedict IX was Pope at eleven years old.

---

The Puritans forbade the singing of Christmas carols.

---

Priests in ancient Egyptian temples plucked every hair from their bodies, including their eyebrows and eyelashes.

Ancient Egyptian priest, accompanied by a sacred scribe

# Royalty

The Japanese emperor Hirohito is the 124th holder of his title. The same family has held the throne in Japan since the sixth century A.D. Hirohito has published several books on ichthyology (the study of fish) and is considered an expert on the subject.

Cleopatra was married to her own brother, Ptolemy.

Henry VIII's second wife, Anne Boleyn, had six fingers on one hand. She wore special gloves all her life to hide her deformity.

Louis XIV owned 413 beds.

Every queen named Jane has either been murdered, imprisoned, gone mad, died young, or been dethroned.

At the court of Louis XIV, prestige was measured by the height of the chair one was allowed to sit in. Only the King and Queen could sit in chairs with arms.

King George I of England couldn't speak a word of English. His native tongue was German (he came from Hanover, Germany); he communicated with his cabinet in French.

John Hancock signed his name in extra-large letters on the Declaration of Independence not out of self-esteem but so that King George III, notoriously poor-sighted, could read it without the aid of spectacles.

Louis XIV of France, the Sun King, had Jewish blood. It came to him through the bloodline of the Aragons of Spain, to whom he was related.

When Louis XIV and Marie-Thérèse were awakened in the morning, if the Queen sat up after the curtains had been parted and clapped her hands, the servants knew that the King had performed his royal duty the night before—intercourse with the Queen.

Berengaria, Queen of England and wife of Richard the Lionhearted, never set foot in England. She lived in Italy most of her life while her husband was off on adventures and crusades.

Jahangir, a seventeenth-century Indian Mughal ruler, had 5,000 women in his harem and 1,000 young boys. He also owned 12,000 elephants.

*The Emperor Jahangir Viewing Fighting Elephants,* 17th-century Indian manuscript illustration

The longest indoor corridor in the world is the *Grande Galerie* in the Louvre, built in 1607 by Henry IV of France. On rainy days the King would clear the entire passageway, move trees, rocks, and grass turf inside, and stage a fox hunt with his entire court down the middle of the corridor.

The Pekingese dog was considered sacred among Chinese royalty. At the court of Li Hsui, one of the last Manchu queens, all court Pekingese had human wet nurses. Each dog had its own eunuch to protect it from other dogs; some even had private palaces, complete with servants.

An elevator was installed in the palace of Versailles in 1743. Run by a series of hand-operated weights, gears, and pulleys, it was used by Louis XV to go from his own apartments to those of his mistress, Madame de Châteauroux, on the floor above him.

An average dinner eaten by King Louis XIV of France: four plates of soup, a whole pheasant, a whole partridge, two slices of ham, a salad, mutton with garlic, pastry, fruit, and hardboiled eggs. At his death it was discovered that the King's stomach was twice the size of a normal stomach.

Cleopatra tested the efficacy of her poisons by giving them to slaves.

In the harem of Mughal kings in India, ladies of royal blood changed their garments several times a day and never put them on again. The once-used costumes were given to slaves.

Queen Elizabeth I of England was completely bald. She lost her hair after suffering smallpox at the age of twenty-nine. To disguise her loss she always wore a wig, thus creating a vogue for wigs in Europe that lasted several hundred years.

Elizabeth I of England owned 3,000 gowns.

The sixteenth-century Indian emperor Akbar often used real dancing girls as chess pieces and an entire garden as a chessboard. Akbar sat high in a marble tower calling each move from his throne and watching the beautiful living pieces whirl from square to square. Two centuries later, in Madras, India, visitors witnessed an equally remarkable sight in the court of the maharajah—chessmen over 25 feet tall, mounted on wheeled platforms and pulled across a giant chessboard by teams of fifty men.

---

Peter the Great of Russia was almost 7 feet tall.

## Safety

There were 24,887,000 automobile accidents in the United States in 1975. In these accidents 46,000 people were killed.

---

More Americans have died in automobile accidents than have died in all the wars ever fought by the United States.

---

The death rate for accidents of all kinds is twice as high for males as it is for females in the United States.

---

Natural gas has no smell. The odor is artificially added so that people will be able to identify leaks and take measures to stop them.

---

According to the Health Insurance Institute, a person who suffers an accident on a motorcycle has a 90 percent chance of injury or death. A person involved in an automobile crash has only a 10 percent chance of the same. Motorcycles account for 4 percent of all licensed vehicles in America yet are involved in 8 percent of all accidents.

---

According to the Health Insurance Institute, drivers with the highest mortality rate are those between twenty and twenty-four years old. (Twenty percent of the people killed in automobile crashes in 1975 were between nineteen and twenty-five.) The age group with the lowest mortality rate in car accidents is the seventy-and-over bracket.

---

The National Safety Council reports that seventy people a day die in home accidents in the United States. Falls account for the greatest number of deaths. Next in frequency are fire, poisoning, electrocution, and choking on food. Most of the people who die from falls are over sixty-five. Middle-aged people and infants die most often in fires. Teen-agers succumb primarily to poison and drugs.

---

Firemen have the most dangerous job in America.

---

According to the National Safety Council, ingesting home chemicals such as detergents, solvents, and paint is *not* the major cause of poisoning among children. Children are poisoned most frequently by eating deadly plants.

---

According to the National Safety Council, a toothpick is the object most often choked on by Americans.

---

One million people each year are bitten by animals in the United States. Seventy-five percent of these bites are inflicted by wild animals. Approximately 30,000 of the victims must be treated for rabies.

---

The number of automobile accidents in the United States has been *declining* since 1969.

---

Motor-vehicle accidents account for 50 percent of all accidental deaths in the United States.

---

The National Safety Council reports that bicycles, stairs, and doors, in that order, cause more accidents in the home than any other objects.

---

Two-thirds of all people in the United States who choke to death are under four years of age, according to the National Safety Council.

---

If a car is moving at 55 miles per hour it will travel 56 feet before the driver can shift his foot from the accelerator to the brake.

---

Every 45 seconds a house catches fire in the United States.

---

The Insurance Information Institute reports that there is a motor-vehicle accident in the United States once every eighteen seconds. Deaths in motor-vehicle accidents occur on the average of once every eleven minutes.

---

According to the National Safety Council, there is one accidental death every five minutes in the United States. There is a major injury every three seconds.

---

# The Sea

When a tidal wave is about to hit a coastline the water first recedes all the way to the horizon. If a person were foolish enough to do so, he could walk out several miles before the wave came smashing ashore.

*The Great Wave at Kanagawa,* by Hokusai

---

The Amazon River discharges 4.2 million cubic feet of water per second in the Atlantic Ocean.

---

The Pacific Ocean encloses an area larger than all the land surfaces of the earth put together.

---

Ninety-seven percent of the world's water is in the ocean.

---

If the ice floes of Antarctica were to melt, they would raise the ocean level by 240 feet, submerging a quarter of the world.

---

# Smoking

Tobacco is a food. Though hazardous if smoked, its leaves contain a number of nutritional substances that can sustain life for a time if no other food is available.

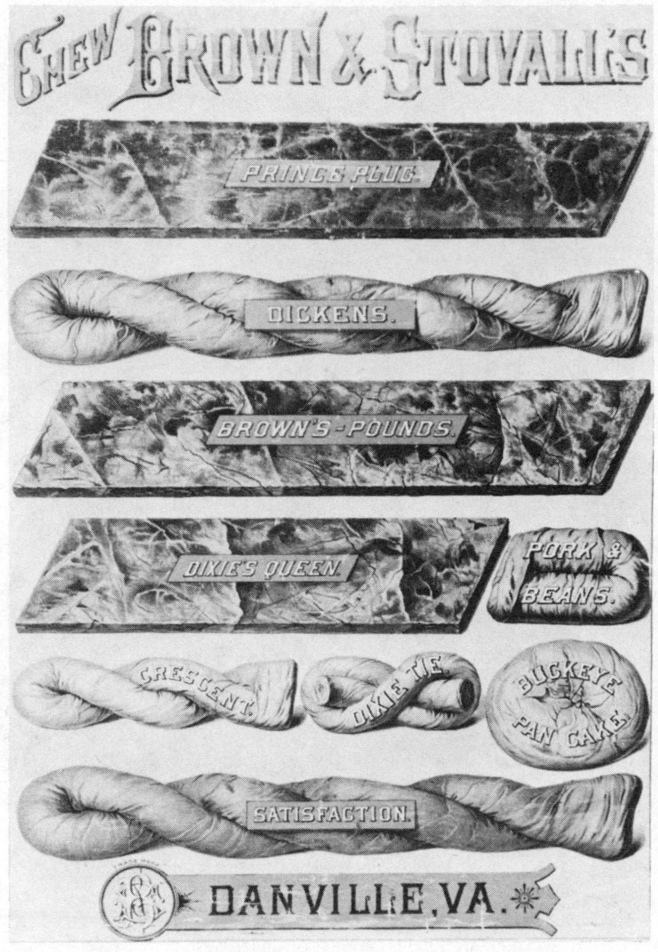


19th-century poster advertising chewing tobacco

In the United States there are 4 pipe smokers, 3 cigar smokers, 3 tobacco chewers, and 1 snuff taker for every 17 cigarette smokers.

Every year, 3 million Americans become cigarette smokers.

Tobacco was originally smoked through the nose. American Indians fashioned a special pipe with a forked end, designed to fit into the nostrils. The smoke was then inhaled through these ends by short, violent snorts. The name of this pipe was a *tubak*—and thus our word "tobacco."

18th-century engraving of pipe-smoking Indian next to tobacco plant

Americans are the heaviest smokers in the world. If the number of cigarettes smoked per day were averaged out individually among the entire population, every man, woman, and child in the United States would smoke an average of two cigarettes a day.

Since 1971, more than 105 new brands of cigarettes have been introduced into the United States.

The average smoker—the smoker who inhales one and a half packs of cigarettes a day—smokes 10,950 cigarettes a year. A heavy smoker may smoke as many as 30,000 cigarettes a year, a nonstop chain smoker as many as 40,000.

A person who smokes one pack of cigarettes a day inhales a half-cup of tar every year.

# Sports

Seven thousand years ago, the ancient Egyptians bowled on alleys not unlike our own.

Babe Ruth, one of the greatest hitters in baseball history, began his career as a pitcher.

Volleyball was invented in a Holyoke, Massachusetts, YMCA in 1895. Its inventor was William George Morgan. The game was first called "mintonette" and was played by hitting a basketball over a rope.

Volleyball game in the gymnasium of a New York City school

Runner about to be tagged out in an 1886 baseball game. Contrary to popular belief, Abner Doubleday did not invent baseball.

Abner Doubleday did not invent baseball. Publications about the game were issued as early as 1835, when Doubleday was only sixteen. Further, though he is credited with inventing baseball in Cooperstown, New York, in 1839, it is known that Doubleday was enrolled at West Point from 1838 to 1842. At that time a West Point cadet was not allowed to leave campus until his last years in school; thus it was impossible for Doubleday even to have visited Cooperstown before 1841. Doubleday was, however, distinguished in other ways. He was a Union general during the Civil War and played a leading part in the Battle of Gettysburg.

The Cleveland Indians were named in honor of Louis Sockolexis, a native Maine Indian who was the first American Indian to play professional baseball. Before it became the Indians, the Cleveland team was known as the Spiders.

An expert fly fisherman may have as many as 10,000 flies in his collection.

Fly-casting tournament, late 19th century

A total of 63 errors were made in the 1886 World Series.

In ancient Greece a boxing match began with two boxers standing face to face, their noses touching. Greek boxers wore leather thongs embedded with metal studs strapped on their wrists. At one time metal spikes were added, too.

In the early days of baseball, between 1840 and 1850, a fielder put a runner out by hitting him with the ball. Home base and the batter's plate were two separate spots (and thus the lineup included a fourth baseman), and there was no distinction between fair and foul balls.

19th-century lacrosse match

The game of lacrosse was invented by American Indians.

---

Before 1859 baseball umpires sat in a padded rocking chair behind the catcher.

---

In the 1936 Swaythling Cup Match in table tennis, Alex Ehrlich of Poland and Paneth Farcas of Rumania volleyed for 2 hours and 12 minutes on the opening serve.

---

The St. Sylvester Road Race in Brazil is witnessed by 1 million people every year.

---

In the early days of boxing, when a boxer was getting throttled and wished to end the bout, he would take his sponge and toss it in the middle of the ring. Thus originated the phrase "to throw in the sponge."

Detail of *Bare Knuckles*, by George A. Hayes, which depicts boxing in its early days in the U.S.

## Survival

A person who is lost in the woods and starving can obtain nourishment by chewing on his shoes. Leather has enough nutritional value to sustain life for a short time.

---

The average person can live for eleven days without water, assuming a mean temperature of 60° F.

---

More than 50 percent of the people who are bitten by poisonous snakes in the United States and who go untreated still survive.

---

According to *Time* magazine (August 6, 1951), the following rule of thumb can be used to determine whether victims of radiation poisoning will live or die:

1. All those who do not vomit after contamination will live.
2. Those who vomit for an extended period of time will probably die.
3. Half of those who stop vomiting within a few hours will probably live.

## Theater

Noel Coward wrote *Private Lives* in two weeks.

---

Toward the end of her life, Sarah Bernhardt had a wooden leg and often wore it on stage. The "Divine Sarah" slept in a coffin, owned her own railroad car, and played Juliet when she was seventy.

---

James O'Neill, father of the playwright Eugene O'Neill, acted in the play *The Count of Monte Cristo* no less than 5,352 times—an average of one performance a day every day for fourteen years. "I believe," O'Neill once said, "that I should have lost my memory and mind altogether had I continued to keep up the strain."

Slapstick comedy is named after an actual slapping stick. The stick, which came to be equated with broad farce in the sixteenth century as part of the Italian commedia dell'arte, was used by the comic hero Harlequin to whack the rumps of artless stooges. It was made of two pieces of wood joined together to make a slapping sound when it hit.

John Rich, famous English Harlequin of the 18th century, still used slapping stick that originated with 16th-century commedia dell'arte.

John Wilkes Booth was the greatest matinee idol of his era. Though history books rarely mention it, the man who shot Lincoln was beloved and familiar to thousands of theatergoers and was especially popular with women, from whom he received a hundred fan letters a week. In fact, it was Booth's familiarity with the layout of Ford's Theater—he had played there many times—and his friendliness with the stagehands that allowed him to penetrate the security guard so easily the night of the shooting.

Stage bows were originally devised as a way for actors to thank the audience. The audience would or would not acknowledge each of the actors in turn, depending on how much they enjoyed the performances.

Edwin Booth is the only actor in the American Hall of Fame.

Edwin Booth as Iago.
Painting by Thomas Hicks, 1863.

# Transportation & Travel

Most automobile trips in the United Sates are under 5 miles.

The first railroad in America had wooden tracks. It was built by Thomas Leiper in 1809 in Crown Creek, Pennsylvania.

To establish how fast a railroad train moves, count the number of clicks heard in twenty seconds. This figure is roughly equal to the number of miles per hour the train is moving.

There is 1 mile of railroad track in Belgium for every 1½ square miles of land.

In 1928 E. Romer of Germany crossed the Atlantic Ocean from Lisbon, Portugal, to the West Indies in a kayak. The trip took him fifty-eight days.

Kayak similar to the one used by E. Romer to travel from Portugal to the West Indies

One method of crossing great expanses of waterless desert used by traders and merchants in the Middle East is as follows: setting out on horseback with their wares, the merchants bring a large number of well-watered camels, which they use as pack animals. At various intervals along

19th-century engraving of Middle Eastern merchants loading their camels

the way they stop the caravan and slaughter several of the camels. Then they remove the camel's stomach and give the large amounts of water stored within it to the horses. This water thus sustains their own mounts all the way across the desert and at the same time makes it unnecessary to bring extra stores of water.

# The Universe: Stars, Planets, Space

If one were to capture and bottle a comet's 10,000-mile vapor trail, the amount of vapor actually present in the bottle would take up less than 1 cubic inch of space.

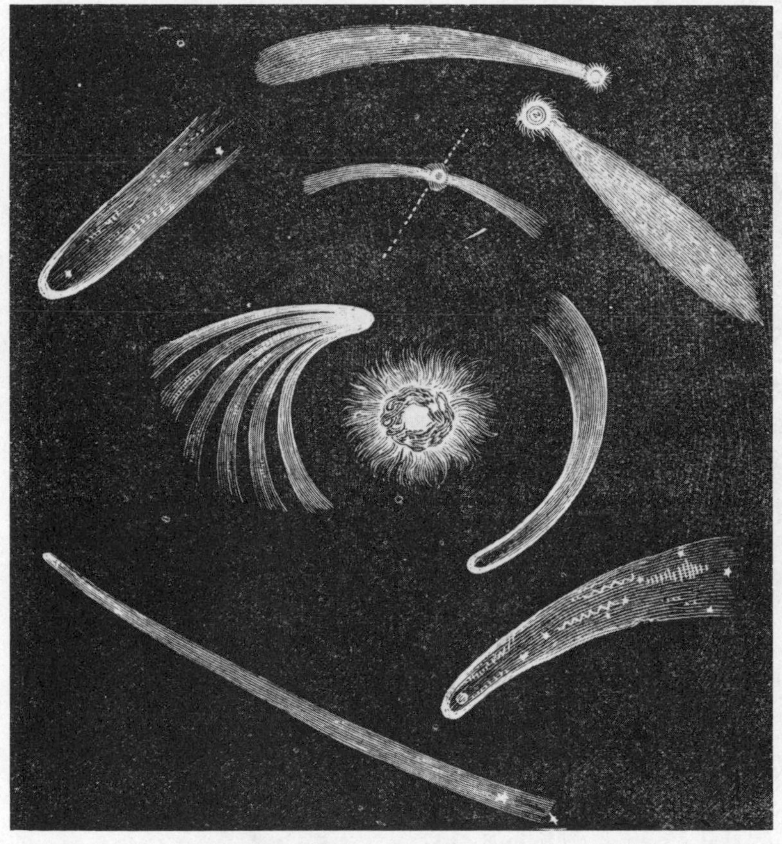

Some of the comets that have appeared over the last four centuries

Members of the Dogon tribe in Mali, Africa, for many centuries worshiped a star known today by astronomers as Sirius B. The Dogon people knew its precise elliptical orbit, knew how long it took to revolve around its parent star, Sirius, and were aware that it was made up of materials not found on earth—all this centuries before modern astronomers had even discovered that Sirius B existed.

Deimos, one of the moons of Mars, rises and sets twice a day.

To an observer standing on Pluto, the sun would appear no brighter than Venus appears in our evening sky.

Saturn's rings are 500,000 miles in circumference but only about a foot thick.

As of 1973 there were more than 5,000 man-made objects flying in space.

It is estimated by scientists that the universe as a whole contains .000000000000000000000000000001 grams of matter per cubic centimeter of space. It is also estimated that the universe is 35 billion light years in size, or 210,000,000,000,000,000,000,000 miles.

Five times as many meteors can be seen after midnight as can be seen before.

The star Zeta Thauri, a supernova, was so bright when it exploded in 1054 that it could be seen during the day.

The star Antares is 60,000 times larger than our sun. If our sun were the size of a softball, the star Antares would be as large as a house.

---

When we look at the farthest visible star we are looking 4 billion years into the past—the light from that star, traveling at 186,000 miles a second, has taken that many years to reach us.

---

The telescope on Mount Palomar, California, can see a distance of 7,038,835,200,000,000,000,000 miles.

Hale telescope, Mount Palomar

The sun is 3 million miles closer to the earth during winter than summer.

The diameter of the star Betelgeuse is more than a quarter the size of our entire solar system.

The sun is 330,330 times larger than the earth.

The earth moves in its 585-million-mile orbit around the sun approximately eight times faster than a bullet travels.

It is estimated that within the entire universe there are more than a trillion galaxies (the Milky Way itself contains 100 billion stars). This means that there are probably about $10^{22}$ stars in the entire cosmos.

Traveling at a speed of 186,000 miles per second, light takes 6 hours to travel from Pluto to the earth.

The sun burns 9 million tons of gas a second. At this rate, it has been estimated, it will burn out in another 10 billion years.

If the sun were the size of a beachball, 21 inches in diameter, and were placed atop the Empire State Building, the nearest group of stars, the Triple Centauri system, would be somewhere in Australia, more than 10,000 miles away. The next "closest" star would be so distant that it would be off the surface of the earth.

When astronauts first shaved in space, their weightless whiskers floated up to the ceiling. A special razor had to be developed which drew the whiskers in like a vacuum cleaner.

A sunbeam setting out through space at the rate of 186,000 miles a second would describe a gigantic circle and return to its origins after about 200 billion years.

The star known as LP 327-186, a so-called white dwarf, is

smaller than the state of Texas yet so dense that if a cubic inch of it were brought to earth it would weigh more than 1.5 million tons.

---

All the planets in our solar system could be placed inside the planet Jupiter.

---

Because of the speed at which the sun moves, it is impossible for a solar eclipse to last more than 7 minutes and 58 seconds.

Solar eclipse

Four million tons of hydrogen dust are destroyed on the sun every second.

When the Apollo 12 astronauts landed on the moon, the impact caused the moon's surface to vibrate for fifty-five minutes. The vibrations were picked up by laboratory instruments, leading geologists to theorize that the moon's surface is composed of many fragile layers of rocks.

Apollo 12 astronaut holding container of lunar soil during exploration of the surface of the moon, 1969

If a baseball-sized piece of a supernova star (known to astronomers as a pulsar) were brought to earth, it would weigh more than the Empire State Building.

Phobos, one of the moons of Mars, is so close to its parent planet that it could not be seen by an observer standing at either of Mars's poles. Phobos makes three complete orbits around Mars every day.

A day on the planet Mercury is twice as long as its year. Mercury rotates very slowly but revolves around the sun in slightly less than eighty-eight days.

Statistically, UFO sightings are at their greatest number during those times when Mars is closest to Earth.

According to Professor David Saunders of the Psychology Department of the University of Chicago, abnormally large numbers of UFO sightings occur every sixty-one months, usually at distances from 1,500 to 2,000 miles apart.

## U.S. History

During the American revolution, more inhabitants of the American colonies fought for the British than for the Continental Army.

The area sold by France to the United States in the Louisiana Purchase was first offered to England, who refused it. The price paid by the United States for the land, some 100 million acres, averaged out to 4 cents an acre.

The Americans *lost* the Battle of Bunker Hill. They ran out of gunpowder and had to retreat. Further, the Battle of

Battle of Bunker Hill, June 17, 1775

Bunker Hill was not fought at Bunker Hill at all. The actual skirmish took place at Breed's Hill in Charlestown, Massachusetts.

America purchased Alaska from Russia for $7,200,000—about 2 cents an acre.

In the Declaration of Independence as first written by Thomas Jefferson, there was a clause abolishing slavery. Because of popular pressures, however, Jefferson deleted the clause.

Drafting the Declaration of Independence. Thomas Jefferson is 2nd from left.

The Declaration of Independence was *not* signed on July 4th. It was signed in Philadelphia on July 8th, and was first read before Washington's army the following day. Nor did all the delegates sign the document in 1776. Thomas McKean of Delaware did not add his name until 1777. After its ratification, the Declaration of Independence was moved about from place to place, finding shelter in ten different cities and five different states between 1776 and 1951. During this time it twice escaped destruction by fire and was almost captured by the British in both the revolution and the War of 1812. Since 1952 the document has been kept in the National Archives in Washington, D.C.

# War & Weapons

Before World War II blacks were not allowed to enlist in the United States Navy.

During World War I the punishment for homosexuality in the French army was execution. If the offender was an officer he was allowed a final charge against the enemy on the understanding that he would get himself shot.

Alexander the Great ordered his entire army to shave their faces and heads. He believed that beards and long hair were too easy for an enemy to grab preparatory to cutting off the head.

At the outbreak of World War I the American air force consisted of only fifty men.

One out of every three English males between the ages of seventeen and thirty-five was killed in World War I.

Only eight men were killed in the Battle of Lexington.

Only 16 percent of the able-bodied males in the American colonies participated in the Revolutionary War.

Battle of Lexington, April 19, 1775

George Custer was the youngest American officer ever to become a general in the United States Army. He made his rank at age twenty-three.

Robert E. Lee

During the Civil War, Robert E. Lee was offered command of the Union Army before he accepted his post with the Confederacy.

---

In 1221, Genghis Khan killed 1,748,000 people at Nishapur in one hour.

---

Soldiers in Genghis Khan's army were made into executioners after every battle. The inhabitants of a defeated town were ordered to assemble outside the walls of the town, and each Mongol soldier, armed with a battle axe, was assigned to kill as many as fifty of the captives. As proof that they had carried out their orders, the soldiers were obliged to cut an ear off every victim, collect the ears in sacks, and bring them to their officers to be counted.

---

The Hessian soldiers hired by the British to fight the colonists during the Revolutionary War were paid about 25 cents a day.

---

In feudal Japan the Imperial Army had special soldiers whose only duty was to count the number of severed enemy heads after each battle.

---

During the American revolution soldiers in General John Burgoyne's regiment who misbehaved were not flogged or imprisoned. They were simply made to wear their coats inside-out. Yet so much respect did Burgoyne's men have for their general that his troops had the lowest disobedience record of any soldiers in the war.

---

The Marine Corps was originally a branch of the British army in the American colonies. The corps was organized in 1740 in New York and was incorporated into the United States military after the revolution.

---

In Japan there is a deadly martial art, called *tessenjutsu,* based solely on the use of a fan.

---

Conquering Arab armies in the tenth century used a primitive form of flame thrower and hand grenade. The flame thrower spurted flames of niter and sulphur through copper tubes. Grenades were made of terra cotta shaped to fit the contours of the hand, filled with inflammable naphtha, and covered with relief designs to prevent them from slipping when being thrown.

---

The Yo-Yo originated as a weapon in the Philippine Islands in the sixteenth century. It weighed 4 pounds and had a 20-foot cord. Louis Marx, the toymaker, introduced it to America in 1929.

---

Karate, generally considered a Japanese martial art, did not come to Japan until 1916. Prior to this time it was practiced solely by the Okinawa islanders, who had developed it centuries earlier as a means of weaponless defense *against* the Japanese.

---

The 1905 peace treaty ending the Russo-Japanese War was signed in Portsmouth, New Hampshire. Though the United States had nothing to do with the war, the treaty was arranged and negotiated by United States President Theodore Roosevelt.

---

## Weather

---

No one has ever discovered two snowflakes with exactly the same crystal pattern.

---

A thousand tons of meteor dust fall to earth every day.

---

During the heating months of winter, the relative humidity of the average American home is only 13 percent, nearly twice as dry as the Sahara Desert.

---

According to Professor Walter Connor of the University of Michigan, men are six times more likely than women to be struck by lightning.

---

Studies in modern China have found that one can predict

weather with 80 percent accuracy by monitoring the croaking of frogs. A peasant named Chang Chi-tsai devised the following formula, which has been adopted by millions of Chinese farmers and peasants: "If frogs croak on a fine day it will rain in two days. If frogs croak after rain, there will be fine weather. It will continue to rain if frogs do not croak after successive overcast days."

---

The town of Tidikelt in the Sahara Desert once went ten years without a rainfall.

---

A bolt of lightning can strike the earth with a force as great as 100 million volts.

18th-century painting showing house being hit by lightning

During a severe windstorm or rainstorm the Empire State Building may sway several feet to either side.

---

It snows more in the Grand Canyon than it does in Minneapolis, Minnesota.

---

Lightning puts 10 million tons of nitrogen into the earth each year.

Electrical storm over New York City

In Calama, a town in the Atacama Desert of Chile, it has never rained.

Moist air holds heat better than dry, which is why nights in the desert are cool while nights in the humid tropics are torrid.

The outdoor temperature can be estimated to within several degrees by timing the chirps of a cricket. It is done this way: count the number of chirps in a 15-second period, and add 37 to the total. The result will be very close to the actual Fahrenheit temperature. This formula, however, only works in warm weather.

In 1816 there were frosts and snow in the northeastern United States in every month of the year. Similar weather conditions prevailed in France, Italy, and Spain. The year 1816 became known throughout Europe and the United States as "the year without a summer."

Clouds fly higher during the day than during the night.

We are in the middle of an ice age. Ice ages include both cold and warm periods; at the moment we are experiencing a relatively warm span of time known as an "interglacial period." Geologists believe that the warmest part of this period occurred from 1890 through 1945 and that since 1945 things have slowly begun freezing up again.

At any given time, there are 1,800 thunderstorms in progress over the earth's atmosphere. Lightning strikes the earth 100 times every second.

A rainbow can be seen only in the morning or late afternoon. It is a phenomenon that can occur only when the sun is 40 degrees or less above the horizon.

Salt Lake City, Utah, gets an average of 17 inches more snow annually than Fairbanks, Alaska. Santa Fe, New Mexico, gets an average of 9 inches more snow each year than New Haven, Connecticut.

## Weights & Measures

It takes 120 drops of water to fill a teaspoon.

A ten-gallon hat holds less than a gallon.

Tom Mix in a "ten-gallon" hat

There are two kinds of tons, a regular ton (2,000 pounds) and a long ton (2,240 pounds). There are also two kinds of pounds, an apothecary pound (12 ounces) and a troy pound (16 ounces).

## Worms & Sea Creatures

The earthworm *(Lumbricus terrestris):*

can clear and aerate half a pound of soil in a day. (There are, on the average, 3 million worms per acre of fertile soil.)

is hermaphroditic, or bisexual: it can self-fertilize or mate with another of its species.

has several sets of vital organs throughout its body, which is why it can be cut in half and still survive. If it is cut in the middle its two ends will usually regenerate; if it is not cut in the middle one segment will live. However, if it is cut in too many places the whole worm will die.

A hundred tons of barnacles collect on the bottom of a steamship every year.

The snail mates only once in its entire life. When it does mate, however, it may take as long as twelve hours to consummate the act.

Snails under water

When leeches mate, the leech playing the male role (leeches are hermaphrodites and can assume either sex) clings to the body of the female and deposits a sac of sperm on her skin. This sac produces a strong, flesh-deteriorating enzyme that eats a hole through the female's skin and fertilizes the eggs within her body.

Lobsters *do* feel pain when boiled alive. By soaking them in salt water before cooking, however, you can anesthetize them.

At birth barnacles look like waterfleas. In the next stage of their development they have three eyes and twelve legs. In their third stage they have twenty-four legs and no eyes. Barnacles stay fastened to the same object for their entire lives.

When young abalones feed on red seaweed their shells turn red.

Abalone shell

A 4-inch-long abalone can grip a rock with a force of 400 pounds. Two grown men are incapable of prying it up.

---

The starfish is the only animal capable of turning its somach inside-out. As it approaches its prey (usually a member of the mollusk family), the starfish reverses its viscera, protrudes them through its mouth, and projects them under the shell of its victim. Then it slowly devours the fleshy underparts of the helpless mollusk by a process of absorption.

Sea worms mate in the following way: at mating time, males and females swarm together. Suddenly the females turn on the males and bite their tails off. The tails contain the males' testes and sperm. When they are swallowed and acted upon by the females' digestive juices, they fertilize her eggs.

---

Snails have teeth. They are arranged in rows along the snail's tongue and are used like a file to saw or slice through the snail's food.

---

# Miscellaneous

The average lead pencil will draw a line 35 miles long or write approximately 50,000 English words. More than 2 billion pencils are manufactured each year in the United States. If these were laid end to end they would circle the world nine times.

The three balls traditionally displayed above pawnshops were inspired by Santa Claus. St. Nicholas, on whom the legend of Santa Claus is based, is said to have turned three brass balls into three bags of gold in order to save the daughters of a poor but honest man from earning their living in dubious ways. Since that time St. Nicholas has been patron saint of pawnbrokers as well as of helpless virgins.

People waiting for pawnshop to open, New York City, 19th century. Three balls on sign were inspired by a miracle attributed to St. Nicholas.

Galileo was the first man to suggest using a pendulum to run a clock.

Turning a clock's hands counterclockwise while setting it is not necessarily harmful. It is only damaging when the timepiece contains a chiming mechanism.

Rubber is one of the ingredients of bubble gum. It is the substance that allows the chewer to blow a bubble.

Of all the world's peoples, the only ones known not to use fire are the Andaman islanders and the Pygmies.

Pygmy hunters in the Congo, one of the two groups of people in the world who do not use fire

---

*Question:* When does the twenty-first century officially begin, on January 1, 2000, or on January 1, 2001? *Answer:* Since there never was a year 0 on our calendar, our calendar presumably started in the year 1. Adding two thousand years to the year 1 gives us an official starting date of 2001. However, in the nineteenth century the changeover was celebrated both on January 1, 1900, and January 1, 1901. There is no reason to believe the coming century will not be greeted in a similar way.

---

Christendom did not begin to date its history from the birth of Christ until 500 years after His death. The system was introduced in 550 by Dionysius Exigus, a monk in Rome.

---

The average housewife walks 10 miles a day around the house doing her chores. She walks 4 miles and spends 25 hours a year making beds.

---

# Volume Two

## Agriculture

Iowa has more land under cultivation than any other state—more than 24 million acres. Following in order are Texas, Illinois, Kansas, and Minnesota.

Almost all our breakfast cereals are made of grass. Oats, barley, corn, and wheat are all different varieties of grass and are all descended from the same botanical species. Moreover, most of the sugar we eat also comes from grass (sugar cane), as do most of our alcoholic beverages.

The United States produces more tobacco than it does wheat. By weight, the largest agricultural crop is corn, then peanuts, tobacco, wheat, and soybeans.

It takes 100 pounds of rain water to produce a single pound of food from the earth. Between 10 and 20 tons of water must pass through the roots of an acre of corn before one bushel of corn will be produced.

## Animals

The chow is the only dog that has a black tongue. The tongues of all other dogs are pink.

Kangaroo rats never drink water. Like their relatives the pocket mice, they carry their own water source within them, producing fluids from the food they eat and the air they breathe.

A crocodile weighing 120 pounds exerts a force of about 1,540 pounds between its jaws. A human being's jaws exert a force of only 40 to 80 pounds.

A python can swallow a rabbit whole and may eat as many as 150 mice in a six-month period.

*Python about to consume a rabbit.*

From 1890 to 1900, 20 tons of ivory were shipped every year from Siberia to London. All of this ivory was taken from the remains of woolly mammoths, which have been extinct since the Ice Age.

*Woolly mammoths, detail of a mural by Charles R. Knight.*

Most varieties of snake can go an entire year without eating a single morsel of food.

More than 99.9 percent of all the animal species that have ever lived on earth were extinct before the coming of man.

Almost half the pigs in the world are kept by farmers in China.

A skunk will not bite and throw its scent at the same time.

The woolly mammoth, extinct since the Ice Age, had tusks almost 16 feet long.

A rat can fall from a five-story building without injury. Two rats can become the progenitors of 15,000 rats in less than a year.

No one has ever been able to domesticate the African elephant. Only the Indian elephant can be trained by man.

According to tests made at the Institute for the Study of Animal Problems in Washington, D.C., dogs and cats, like people, are either right-handed or left-handed—that is, these animals favor either their right or left paws.

How to classify the platypus, a native of Australia and Tasmania, is a problem that has puzzled biologists and zoologists since the animal was discovered in the eighteenth century. This strange animal has characteristics of both mammals and birds. For instance, the platypus lays eggs, as birds do. Yet platypus mothers nurse their young, a typical mammalian characteristic. (However, the platypus has no nipples. The mother secretes milk from stomach glands and the baby laps it up.) The platypus has a leathery, ducklike bill (from which it gets the name "duckbilled platypus"), and its feet are webbed like those of aquatic birds. But at the end of the webs are claws just like a cat's or a raccoon's. After much argument, scientists finally decided that the platypus merited classification as a mammal—but only marginally.

*The duckbilled platypus, a zoological enigma.*

At birth, baby kangaroos are only about an inch long—no bigger than a large waterbug or a queen bee.

A full-grown moose may be 8 feet high at the shoulder and weigh almost a ton. The male moose sheds its antlers every winter and grows a new set the following summer.

A herd of sixty cows is capable of producing a ton of milk in less than a day.

A giraffe can go without water longer than a camel can.

Though the giraffe's neck is about 7 feet long, it contains the same number of vertebrae as a mouse's—seven. The giraffe's tongue is 18 inches long. It can open and close its nostrils at will, can run faster than a horse, and makes almost no sound whatsoever. The first giraffe ever seen in the West was brought to Rome about 46 B.C. by no less a personage than Julius Caesar.

The blue whale weighs as much as thirty elephants and is as long as three Greyhound buses.

An anteater is nearly 6 feet long, yet its mouth is only an inch wide.

*Giant anteater.*

A lion in the wild usually makes no more than twenty kills a year.

Turtles, water snakes, crocodiles, alligators, frogs, porpoises, dolphins, whales, and several other watergoing creatures will drown if kept underwater too long. Unlike fish, these animals require a certain amount of air in order to survive.

---

Lanolin, an essential ingredient of many expensive cosmetics, is, in its native form, a foul-smelling, waxy, tarlike substance extracted from the fleece of sheep.

---

Most dinosaurs lived to be more than a hundred years old.

---

The stegosaurus, a giant dinosaur that grew to more than 18 feet long and was armed with enormous bony plates on its neck, back, and tail, had a brain that weighed only 2 ounces and was no bigger than a walnut.

*Stegosaurus.*

---

The polar bear is one of the only large land mammals that has absolutely no fear of man. It will stalk people at every chance and has been known to charge large groups of hunters, sometimes into heavy gunfire, not slowing down even after its vital organs have been hit repeatedly.

---

The smell of a skunk can be detected by a human a mile away.

There is a rare variety of ivory that comes from the male narwhal (*Monodon monoceros*), a whale that inhabits Arctic waters. In infancy, this formidable creature loses all its teeth but two upper incisors. One of these continues to grow forward through the narwhal's upper lip, twisting corkscrew-fashion, until it develops into a spiral tusk that may reach 9 feet, almost two-thirds the length of the whale's body. Eighteenth- and nineteenth-century whale hunters stalked the creature for its precious ivory, and there are many tales of men being impaled on narwhal tusks and carried into the sea.

---

Nose prints are used to identify dogs in the same way fingerprints are used to identify human beings. Breeders and trainers keep a dog's nose prints on file as part of its permanent record, and insurance companies require them whenever a dog is to be bonded. At one time paw prints were used as a means of canine identification, but these proved less accurate than noses.

---

The weasel and the ermine are the same animal. This mammal's coat changes with the seasons—in its white winter coat it is known as an ermine, in its brown coat it is a weasel.

*Weasel in its brown summer coat.*

A newborn polar bear cub weighs only twice as much as a newborn human—about 15 pounds. Yet when fully grown, polar bears reach weights of up to 1,600 pounds.

Garter snakes, though reptiles, do not lay eggs. They bear live young, just as mammals do.

## Architecture and Construction

A bridge built in Lima, Peru, in 1610 was made of mortar that was mixed not with water but with the whites of 10,000 eggs. The bridge, appropriately called the Bridge of Eggs, is still standing.

It takes a person fifteen to twenty minutes to walk once around the Pentagon.

*Aerial view of the Pentagon, Washington, D.C.*

There are 10 million bricks in the Empire State Building.

The sixty-story John Hancock Tower in Boston is haunted by one of the more mysterious problems in skyscraper history: its windows, huge 4-by-11-foot panes of glass, pop out unexpectedly and shatter on the street below. The building, completed in 1972, was less than a month old when suddenly dozens of its windows began popping for no discernible reason. Determined to remedy the situation, the John Hancock Mutual Life Insurance Company replaced all 10,334 windows with 400-pound sections of half-inch tempered glass. The windows kept popping out. Today the mystery remains unsolved, and windows occasionally still pop. To protect passers-by, John Hancock has hired two permanent guards who do nothing but peer up and spot the cracked panes before they tumble to the sidewalk.

---

The base of the Great Pyramid in Egypt is large enough to cover ten football fields. According to the Greek historian Herodotus, it took 400,000 men twenty years to construct this great monument.

*The Great Pyramid of Cheops, with the Sphinx at left.*

---

Many houses in the rural districts of Nepal are constructed of cow dung mixed with mud, sand, and clay.

---

Japanese farmers, after removing the hulls from their rice crop and sorting out the white kernels, take the hulls from the leftover rice, mix them into a kind of paste, mold the substance into brick-shaped blocks, and build houses with them. Such buildings are known in Japan as "houses of rice skin."

---

The only manmade structure visible from space is the Great Wall of China.

*The Great Wall of China at Nankow.*

The Column of Trajan, built in 113 A.D. to commemorate the Roman emperor Trajan's victories against the Dacian tribes of the lower Danube, contains a continuous frieze a yard wide and 218 feet long in which more than 2,500 human figures as well as hundreds of boats, horses, vehicles, and pieces of military equipment are depicted. This great column, still standing today, rises 128 feet from the ground, is 12 feet thick at the base, and is made entirely of gilded bronze. Inside is a circular staircase where the ashes of Trajan were sprinkled.

In the mid-sixteenth century Hideyoshi, the so-called peasant ruler of Japan, ordered that all the swords in the nation be collected and melted down. The metal was then used, in 1586, to construct an enormous statue of Buddha. It took 50,000 artisans more than six years to build the statue, and exactly ten years after it was completed an earthquake razed it. Not a trace of this giant figure remains today.

The Incas considered bridges to be so sacred that anyone who tampered with one was put to death. Among the most impressive Inca bridges were the *chacas*, or rope bridges, that spanned great distances over gorges and rivers. They were made of plaited grasses woven together into a single cable as thick as a man's body, and they sometimes extended for 175 feet. It took as many as a thousand people to build such a bridge, and many of these remarkable structures lasted more than five hundred years.

---

The Escorial, the famous palace located outside Madrid, was built in the shape of a gridiron because Saint Lawrence, to whom the palace was dedicated, was roasted on one.

*The Escorial Palace, Madrid.*

## Art and Artists

The Venetian painter Tintoretto (1518–1594) once painted a picture of Paradise that was 72 feet long. It was made for the Doge's palace in Venice.

---

The painting *Saint Jerome* by Leonardo da Vinci, one of the great art treasures of the world, was discovered in a junk shop in the nineteenth century. Though highly valued for several centuries after its creation and kept in a special cabinet by its owner, Angelica Kauffman (a painter herself), the painting disappeared when Kauffman died in 1804. Ten years later Cardinal Joseph Fesch, an uncle of Napoleon, was exploring an antique shop in Rome one day and came upon an old box, the lid of which displayed this very Saint Jerome—minus its head. An astute collector, the cardinal recognized the work at once and bought it. Then came the *real* miracle. Several months later, while browsing in another back alley in Rome, Cardinal Fesch found a head of Saint Jerome that so resembled his work by Leonardo that he purchased it immediately. He brought it home and placed the head with the body. Remarkably, it fit. Thus one of the great paintings of the world was saved for posterity.

---

The *Discus Thrower* by Myron, one of the most famous of all Greek statues, is not Greek at all. The statue as we know it today is a restoration assembled in the nineteenth century from pieces of a Roman copy of the Greek original.

*Artist's rendering of the* Discus Thrower *by Myron*.

---

The French painter Rosa Bonheur (1822–1899) kept lions, monkeys, gazelles, chamois, goats, and deer in her back yard. She maintained this menagerie so that she might study animal anatomy firsthand.

---

The Impressionist painter Claude Monet (1840–1926) painted more than three hundred pictures of the same lily pads. The now-famous plants grew in a pond behind his house.

---

Before 1800, only two women achieved fame as artists. Both were painters. One was an Italian named Rosalba Carriera (1675–1757), who popularized the use of pastels in Paris; the other, Marie Anne Elisabeth Vigée-Lebrun (1755–1842), was a French portraitist who gained fame for her paintings of European royalty.

---

At an art auction held in June, 1978, at Sotheby's in London, an undisclosed London dealer bid $2 million for *objets d'art* twice in ten minutes—and lost the bidding both times. At the same auction, two small enamel figures sold for $2 million—in *two* minutes. A total of $11,812,918 was spent on art objects, by far the greatest sum ever paid at one auction.

---

*Drawing of Adolf Hitler at sixteen by a fellow art student.*

In his youth Adolf Hitler was a landscape and portrait painter and, according to some who have seen his work, not a bad one. It was Hitler's inability to get into the Vienna Art Academy, it has been said, that caused him to hate that city forever. Of Hitler's three hundred paintings, only about twelve still exist. Four or five of these are in the United States.

---

In the late Middle Ages, when a church member or patron of the arts commissioned a portrait of a saint, he generally had himself and his family painted into the picture. These pictures, known today as "donor portraits," depict the holy personalities many times larger than the donors, a symbolic statement concerning the relative importance of ordinary man compared with the divine. Today such pictures provide a wealth of information about how people looked and dressed in the fifteenth and sixteenth centuries.

---

An American artist named John Banvard (1815–1891) once painted a picture a mile long. As a youth, Banvard longed to become famous, and at the age of twenty-five he concocted the scheme of painting a colossal mural depicting 1,200 miles of landscape along the Mississippi River. Camping out along the Mississippi for more than a year, Banvard lived on hunted game and worked his way slowly upriver, making thousands of sketches as he traveled. He then returned to Louisville, built himself a studio, and furnished it with a mile of canvas. In order to keep the canvas manageable, he wrapped it around a large upright roller and pulled it out as needed, much the way one pulls paper towels off a dispenser. The part of the canvas that was painted was then rolled up on another large drum. According to people who saw the work in progress, the quality of craftsmanship was quite good, depicting, as one witness reported, "the remarkable truthfulness of the minutest objects upon the shores of the river.'' On its completion in 1846, the painting was displayed in Louisville, where it was an immediate success. Banvard then took it on tour across the United States and to Great Britain. The picture received international acclaim, and he soon became quite wealthy. When Banvard died, however, the painting disappeared. It was last seen in Watertown, South Dakota, where strips of it were being used as a stage set. Just how good this painting actually was we will never know, for no contemporary photographs of it exist.

---

Auguste Rodin (1840–1917), one of the great French sculptors, was allowed to freeze to death by the French government even though it knew of his plight and could have saved him. Rodin, forgotten in the last years of his life, was refused financial aid several times by the French state, even while the statues he had donated to the country were kept warmly housed in museums. In the winter of 1917 Rodin's application for a room in one of these museums was rejected, and a month later he died in a garret from frostbite.

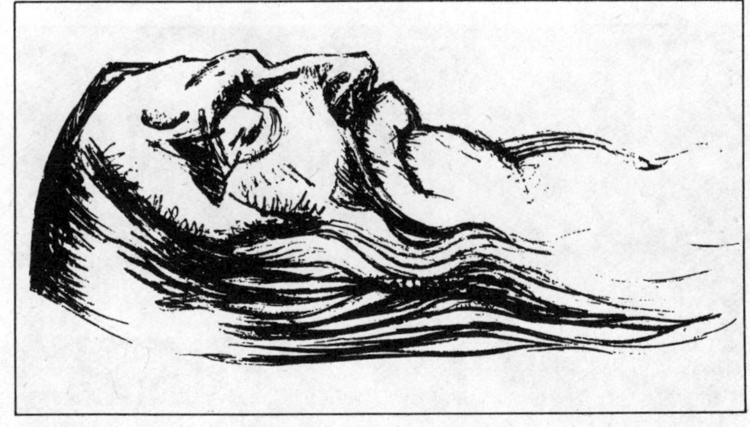

*Rodin on his deathbed, from a lithograph by John Storrs.*

---

Leonardo da Vinci's painting *The Last Supper* is perhaps the finest known example of the High Renaissance style, and is considered one of the great art treasures of the world. Yet the painting as we know it today can in no way be considered an original. Leonardo painted his masterpiece on the refectory wall of the monastery of Santa Maria delle Grazie in Milan between 1495 and 1497. He worked at it in fits and starts, finally leaving it unfinished (the picture was largely unappreciated in its time). By 1517, the work had already been seriously damaged by dampness, and a few years later the famous art historian Vasari referred to it as ''merely a mass of blots.'' By the following century monks inhabiting the monastery had lost all respect for the work and had broken a doorway through Christ's legs. The painting continued to decay, and in 1796 a garrison of French soldiers occupied the monastery and quartered their horses in the same room as the painting. The soldiers whiled away the time taking target practice at Christ's head. During World War II sandbags were piled against the painting to protect it from bombing. Nonetheless, a bomb landed squarely on the monastery and demolished the building, though miraculously most of the wall on which *The Last Supper* was painted was spared. All this abuse, however, more or less destroyed the painting, and *The Last Supper* that people see today is a heavily restored work in which only the outlines and a few brush strokes are by Leonardo.

The Last Supper,
*painting by Leonardo da Vinci.*

---

The Italian Renaissance painter Fra Filippo Lippi (ca. 1406–1469), while chaplain of the Convent of Santa Margherita in Prato, ran off with Lucrezia Buti, one of the young nuns. Lucrezia later bore Fra Filippo's son, Filippino Lippi (1457–1504), who himself became a famous painter. Fra Filippo is said to have used his abducted nun as the model for all the Madonnas he painted.

Madonna and Child, *painting by Fra Filippo Lippi.*

---

Though the Italian Renaissance flourished in Rome, not a single Renaissance artist, sculptor, or musician of any stature was born in that city. During the fifteenth and sixteenth centuries, practically all architects, painters, sculptors, and musicians were imported to Rome. When they had completed their projects, they almost always departed.

---

Anna Mary Robertson "Grandma" Moses (1860–1961), the famous American artist, did not start painting full-time until she was in her seventies. Once she began, however, she was nothing if not prolific. She painted steadily until the year she died, and her total output was about 1,600 paintings and 85 ceramic tiles.

Joy Ride, *painting by Grandma Moses.*

---

In his lifetime, Samuel Morse (1791–1872), inventor of the telegraph, was better known as a painter than as a scientist.

The Dying Hercules, *painting by Samuel F. B. Morse.*

Morse studied art at Yale University, where his specialty was ivory carving. In 1812 he won the gold medal from the Adelphi Society of Arts in England for his still lifes, and the following year his painting *The Dying Hercules* was shown at the Royal Academy, where it was rated among the nine best pictures in the exhibition. Within ten years Morse was internationally known as a portrait painter, and his rendering of the Marquis de Lafayette still hangs in New York's City Hall. It was only when Morse was in his forties that he became interested in telegraphic communication.

---

## Automobiles

---

As of 1972, there were fewer than 2,000 automobiles in the entire country of Albania.

---

For every 50 miles driven in an automobile, a person has a one-in-a-million chance of being killed in a motoring accident.

---

Most American automobile horns beep in the key of F.

---

In 1924 a Ford automobile cost $265.

*1924 advertisement for the Ford Runabout.*

The high roofs of London taxicabs were originally designed to keep gentlemen from knocking off their top hats as they entered and left the vehicles.

*Taxicab near Leicester Square, London.*

The price of the average American automobile doubled during the ten-year period between 1968 and 1978.

In 1950 the United States had 70 percent of all the automobiles, buses, and trucks in the entire world.

In 1905 the Bosco Company of Akron, Ohio, marketed a "collapsible Rubber Automobile Driver." The figure, deflated and kept under the seat when not in use, was a kind of dummy intended to scare thieves away when the car was parked.

The first automobile race ever seen in the United States was held in Chicago in 1895. The track ran from Chicago to Evanston. The winner was J. Frank Duryea, whose average speed was 7½ miles per hour.

In 1906 a car known as the Autocar was manufactured in the United States with a new invention—headlights (they burned kerosene). The Autocar, however, lacked another important accessory—the steering wheel. The driver directed the vehicle by means of a sticklike shaft situated to the right of the driver's seat.

---

The Buick, the first automobile manufactured by the General Motors Corporation, was actually built by a man named David Buick. Buick, a plumber by trade, also invented a process whereby porcelain could be annealed onto iron, hence making possible the production of the white porcelain bathtub.

*1906 Model F Buick.*

## Babies and Birth

As of 1977, 52 percent of children under eighteen years of age in Venezuela were born out of wedlock.

---

There are recorded cases of babies that have been delivered through the rectum. In rare instances, blockage of the mother's vaginal orifice may force an unborn child into the rectal area and the baby must be expelled through the anus. A nineteenth-century British doctor named Payne cited the case of a thirty-three-year-old woman who gave birth in this manner. Dr. Payne, seeing that the child was located near the rectum, anesthetized the mother and delivered the child by forceps with little hemorrhage and an easy removal of the placenta.

---

It is believed that 30 to 50 percent more male fetuses than female fetuses are conceived, yet only 5 to 6 percent more males are born. Prenatal (as well as infant) deaths are much higher among males than females.

---

In medieval China it was not unusual for a mother to breastfeed a child until the child was seven years old.

---

A newborn baby's head accounts for about one-quarter of its entire weight.

---

As of 1978, one out of every six fetuses conceived in the United States died through a surgical abortion.

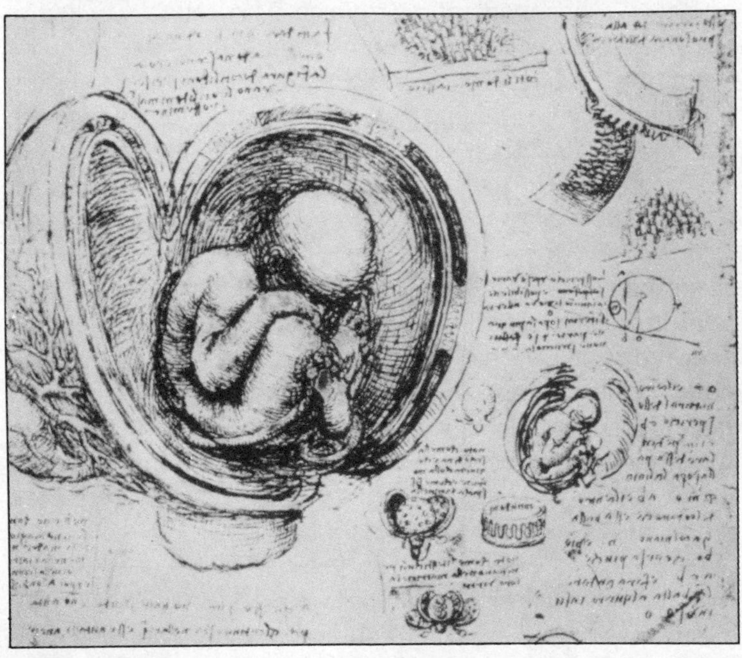

*Fetus, drawing by Leonardo da Vinci.*

---

It is possible for a fetus in the womb to get hiccups.

---

## Biology

During experiments conducted in 1962 at the University of Michigan, scientists successfully extracted memory from one animal and transferred it to another. The experiment was conducted in the following manner. Over a period of time planarian worms were trained to behave in a particular way when exposed to light. These worms were then cut into pieces and fed to untrained planarians, and the untrained worms were put through the same learning paces as their predecessors. The second batch of worms, those that had dined on the first, learned many times faster than the originals, indicating that knowledge had somehow been transferred through body tissue. Similar experiments were later conducted at Baylor University: mice were trained to run through a maze, and an extract was then made of their brains. This extract was fed to untrained mice, which then learned the same maze twice as fast as their predecessors. If placed in a different maze, the untrained mice showed no particular aptitude for learning the layout. The implication of these experiments is that memory can be transferred from one being to another somatically as well as experientially.

---

Scientists at the Institute for Cancer Research in Philadelphia have bred mice that have more than one set of parents. Known as "multimice," these creatures are spawned by taking two embryos created by two sets of parent mice, placing them together in such a way that the embryos grow together, then transplanting the entire organism into the womb of a third female mouse. The result is a baby mouse born with genetic characteristics of both sets of parents.

---

In a single human cell there are between 10,000 and 100,000 coded messages known as genes. If all the directions contained in all these genes were written down, the words would fill the equivalent of 10,000 volumes of the *Encyclopaedia Britannica.*

---

## Birds

The bateleur eagle of Africa hunts over a territory of 250 square miles a day.

*Bateleur eagle.*

A bird sees everything at once in total focus. Whereas the human eye is globular and must adjust to varying distances, the bird's eye is flat and can take in everything at once in a single glance.

Utility workers in the desert of southern California have developed a unique system for finding gas leaks. The desert areas of southern California are heavily populated by a bird known as the turkey buzzard, which has an exceptionally keen sense of smell. The utility companies add a substance to the natural gas (which is odorless in its pure state) that gives it a smell that arouses the turkey buzzard's mating instincts. Whenever there is a break in a line, vast numbers of excited birds are drawn to the spot. By looking for clusters of these anxious birds, linemen are able to determine the precise location of the leak.

---

*The ceram lory, an Australasian parrot.*

Parrots, most famous of all talking birds, rarely acquire a vocabulary of more than twenty words.

---

The bird with the largest population in the world is the red-billed quela (*Quelea quelea*), an inhabitant of Africa. To farmers red-billed quelas are known as "feathered locusts," for they travel in flocks that number in the millions and leave devastation behind them whenever they land on crops. At last count there were approximately 10 billion of these birds in existence. The only other bird with nearly so great a population was the passenger pigeon, which in 1840 had a population of about 9 billion. As a result of excessive hunting by man, the passenger pigeon was extinct less than eighty years later.

---

A robin has almost 3,000 feathers.

---

The female condor lays a single egg once every two years.

*Female Andean condor.*

---

An ostrich may weigh as much as 300 pounds. Its intestinal tract is 45 feet long.

Ostriches fleeing pursuers.

A bird ''chews'' with its stomach. Since most birds do not have teeth, a bird routinely swallows small pebbles and gravel. These grits become vigorously agitated in the bird's stomach and serve to grind food as it passes through the digestive system.

The ruby-throated hummingbird (*Archulochus colubris*) moves its wings at a rate of 200 wingbeats per second.

Hens do not have to be impregnated to lay eggs. The rooster is necessary only to fertilize the egg.

It may take more than two days for a chick to break out of its shell.

There is approximately one chicken for every human being in the world.

Ninety percent of all species that have become extinct have been birds.

The dodo, probably the best-known extinct bird.

More turkeys are raised in California than in any other state in the United States.

In 1956 a white leghorn chicken belonging to a farmer in Vineland, New Jersey, laid an egg that weighed more than a pound. This is the largest chicken egg recorded to date.

There are no penguins at the North Pole. In fact, there are no penguins anywhere in the Northern Hemisphere. All seventeen varieties of the bird are found below the equator, primarily in Antarctica.

Colony of king penguins.

## The Black Plague

In 1347, when the Black Plague was raging through Europe, the citizens of Lübeck, Germany, to appease the wrath of

God, descended on the churches and monasteries with enormous amounts of money and riches. The monks and priests inside one of these monasteries, fearful of contamination, barred their gates and would not allow the citizens to enter. The persistent crowd threw valuables, coins, gold, and jewels over the walls; the frightened monks threw all of it back. The back-and-forth tossing continued for hours, until the clerics finally gave up and allowed the riches to remain. Within hours piles 3 and 4 feet high arose, and for months following the incident—some say for years—the money remained untouched, a testament to the power of self-preservation over greed.

---

The following famous painters all died of the Black Plague: Ghirlandaio, Perugino, Hans Holbein the Younger, Titian, the brothers Pietro and Ambrogio Lorenzetti, and Giorgione.

*Self-portrait of Titian, one of many artists who fell victim to the plague.*

---

The following antiplague remedies were prescribed throughout Europe in the fourteenth century:

—Sitting between two great fires. This was a favorite method of Pope Clement VI.

Removal of plague patients in London. Note the "antiplague pipes."

—Killing all swallows. (These birds were believed to carry the disease.)

—Rubbing perfumes and scented oils over all the walls and furniture of a household.

—Smoking tobacco. (In Holland "antiplague pipes" were manufactured by the thousands.) This notion may not have been entirely erroneous, since the smoke kept away the plague-bearing flies.

—Breaking up the air with loud noises to dissolve the "static plague vapors." Bells were rung continually, and during later outbreaks of plague, in the seventeenth century, cannons and muskets were shot off.

—Letting birds fly about the sickroom so that they would absorb the poisons in the air and keep the vapors in motion.

—Bringing spiders into the household. Spider webs were believed to absorb all noxious miasmas.

—Standing in front of a latrine and inhaling the stench.

—Washing the body with goat urine. "A wash with urine does more than any other preventive," wrote a contemporary expert, "more particularly when in addition the urine is drunk."

—Drinking red wine in which new steel had been cooled.

—Placing pigs near a person dying of the plague so that their smell would heal him or her.

—Placing a piece of warm bread on dying person's mouth in order to absorb the lethal vapors.

—Placing a dried toad over a plague boil. Paracelsus, the great medieval physician, wrote: "Toads should be taken which have been dried thoroughly in the air of the sun and they should be laid on the boil, then the toad will swell and draw the poison out of the plague through the skin itself, and when it is full it should be thrown away and a new one applied."

—Applying the entrails of a young pigeon or a newborn puppy to the forehead.

—Wearing packets of arsenic in a locket, or writing the word "arsenicum" on a piece of parchment and hanging that around the neck. Arsenic supposedly had plague-repelling powers.

Visit to a plague patient in Venice.

—Opening the boils and burning them with a hot iron.
—Blistering the thighs with burning herbs and surgical instruments. The wounds that resulted from this treatment were kept open by artificial means, and fresh butter was rubbed into them in the hope that all toxins would be drained.

---

The Black Plague killed so many people in the French city of Avignon in the fourteenth century that Pope Clement was obliged to consecrate the entire Rhone River so that bodies could be thrown into it en masse for group burials.

*Hospital wagon taking the sick and dying out of Rome during a plague epidemic.*

---

## The Body

---

When astronauts remain weightless in space for prolonged periods, scientists have discovered, their bones lose a measurable amount of weight and thickness. This means that weightlessness actually causes human beings to shrink.

---

A person cannot taste food unless it is mixed with saliva. For example, if a strong-tasting substance like salt is placed on a dry tongue, the taste buds will register nothing. As soon as a drop of saliva is added and the salt is dissolved, however, a definite taste sensation results. This is true for all foods. Try it.

---

The human sense of smell is so keen that it can detect the odors of certain substances even when they are diluted to 1 part to 30 billion.

---

Human lips have a reddish color because of the great concentration of tiny capillaries just below the skin. The blood in these capillaries is normally highly oxygenated and therefore quite red. This explains why the lips appear pale when a person is anemic or has lost a great deal of blood. It also explains why the lips turn blue in very cold weather—cold causes the capillaries to constrict, and the blood loses oxygen and changes to a darker color.

The Ketchua Indians of the Andes Mountains in South America have 2 to 3 more quarts of blood in their bodies than people who live at lower elevations.

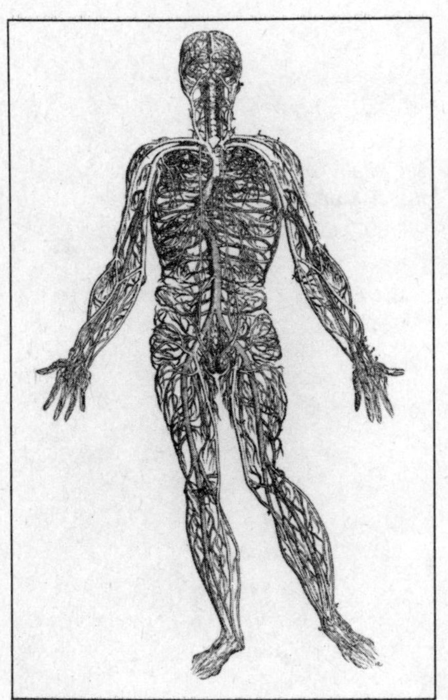

*The "vein man" drawn by Vesalius gives some idea of the size and complexity of the human circulatory system.*

If all the blood vessels in a single human body were stretched end to end, they would form a rope capable of going around the world.

Even if the stomach, the spleen, 75 percent of the liver, 80 percent of the intestines, one kidney, one lung, and virtually every organ from the pelvic and groin area are removed, the human body can still survive.

A loss of 20 percent of the body's water would result in certain and painful death. Ordinarily the body cannot go more than a week and a half without water; the longest recorded time anyone has gone without water is eleven days.

In one year the average human heart circulates from 770,000 to 1.6 million gallons of blood through the body, enough fluid to fill 200 tank cars, each with a capacity of 8,000 gallons.

In the seventh month of fetal life the adrenal glands, located just above the kidneys, are about the same size as the kidneys. At birth they are slightly smaller, and they continue to shrink throughout life. By the time a person reaches old age, the adrenals are so small they can hardly be seen.

The brain of Neanderthal man was larger than that of modern man.

*Sculptor's rendering of what the head of Neanderthal man is thought to have looked like.*

The lens of the eye continues to grow throughout a person's life.

Experiments conducted in West Germany and at the University of Southampton in England show that even mild and incidental noises cause the pupils of the eyes to dilate. It is believed that this is why surgeons, watchmakers, and others who perform delicate manual operations are so bothered by uninvited noise: the sounds cause their pupils to change focus and blur their vision.

An adult sitting in a relaxed position inhales approximately one pint of air with every breath.

If one were to unravel the entire human alimentary canal—esophagus, stomach, large and small intestines—it would reach the height of a three-story building.

As of 1975, 20 million Americans had lost all their teeth.

The indentation in the middle of the area between the nose and the upper lip has a name. It is called the philtrum. Scientists are somewhat baffled as to what purpose this concavity serves, and their theories by no means agree. Among the ancient Greeks this innocent little dent was considered one of the body's most erogenous zones.

A simple, moderately severe sunburn damages the blood vessels to such an extent that it takes four to fifteen months for them to return to their normal condition.

*Sunbathers,*
*drawing by Philip Pearlstein.*

The amount of energy expended during sexual intercourse is roughly equivalent to the amount required to climb two flights of stairs.

An average of 400 million sperms are contained in a single human ejaculation.

One out of every ten men in the United States is impotent.

One square inch of skin on the human hand contains some 72 feet of nerve fiber.

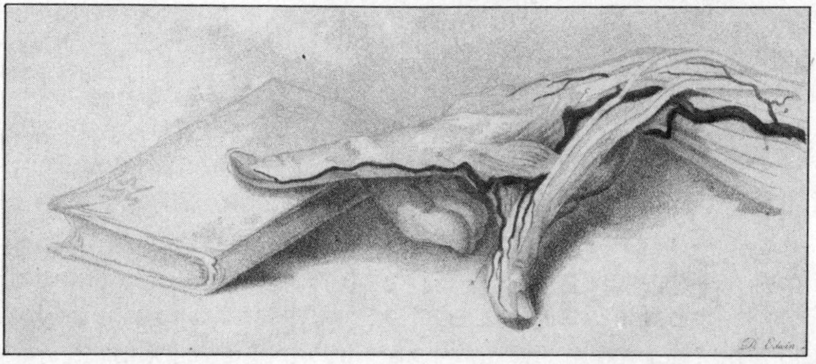

*The human hand, shown here with some of its muscles and blood vessels delineated, is rich in nerve endings.*

There are 35 million digestive glands in the stomach.

Apart from its vulnerability to fire, human hair is almost impossible to destroy. It decays at such a slow rate that it is practically nondisintegrative. It cannot be destroyed by cold, change of climate, water, or other natural forces, and it is resistant to many kinds of acids and corrosive chemicals. This is why it clogs sinks and drainpipes.

Men reach the peak of their sexual powers in their late teens or early twenties, and then begin a slow decline. Usually they are past their sexual prime by their late forties. Women, on the other hand, do not reach their sexual peak until their late twenties or early thirties, and they remain at this level through their late fifties or early sixties.

The hair of an adult man or woman can stretch 25 percent of its length without breaking. If it is less elastic, it is not healthy.

## Books

There are 10 million books in the Russian Public Library in Leningrad—enough to supply every man, woman, and child in the city with two free books. Remarkable as this may sound, however, the statistic is dwarfed by the book-count at the Library of Congress in Washington, D.C., which, as of 1973, had 72,466,926 books on its shelves, or more than seventy-two free volumes for every person in Washington.

---

Johannes Gutenberg was not the first man to produce a book printed with movable type. Printed books were made in China five hundred years before their appearance in Europe. These books were set in movable type made with metal or porcelain characters, were printed on paper (which also was invented in China centuries before it reached the West), and were bound in a manner much like contemporary volumes, complete with title page and cover.

---

The oldest known books in the world were made of clay. Actually earthen tablets on which written symbols were imprinted and baked, these "books" were used for recording land deeds and business transactions by the Babylonians five thousand years before movable type was invented in the West.

*Augustus Caesar.*

## The Classical and Ancient World

The famous quotation that appears on the front of the General Post Office in New York City—"Neither snow nor rain nor heat nor gloom of night stays these couriers from the swift completion of their appointed rounds"—is more than two thousand years old. It is taken from the writings of Herodotus, who lived in the fourth century B.C.

---

According to the Roman historian Suetonius, Augustus Caesar, the great Roman emperor, adorned his living quarters and private palaces with the bones of giants. What these bones really were remains a mystery. It has been guessed that the bones were either those of exceedingly tall men or were taken from the remains of mastodons and other prehistoric beasts.

---

Flamingo tongues were a common delicacy at Roman feasts.

*Flamingo tongues were among the culinary delights enjoyed by these Roman banqueters.*

The Roman emperor Commodos collected all the dwarfs, cripples, and freaks he could find in the city of Rome and had them brought to the Colosseum, where they were ordered to fight each other to the death with meat cleavers.

High-wire acts have been enjoyed since the time of the ancient Greeks and Romans. Antique medals have been excavated from Greek islands depicting men ascending inclined cords and walking across ropes stretched between cliffs. The Greeks called these high-wire performers *neurobates* or *oribates.* In the Roman city of Herculaneum there is a fresco representing an aerialist high on a rope, dancing and playing a flute. Sometimes Roman tightrope walkers stretched cables between the tops of two neighboring hills and performed comic dances and pantomimes while crossing.

According to the Greek historian Herodotus, Egyptian men never became bald. The reason for this, Herodotus claimed, was that as children Egyptian males had their heads shaved, and their scalps were continually exposed to the health-giving rays of the sun.

At the height of its power, in 400 B.C., the Greek city of Sparta had 25,000 citizens and 500,000 slaves.

There was a "pony express" in Persia many centuries before Christ. Riders on this ancient circuit, wearing special colored headbands, delivered the mails across the vast stretch of Asia Minor, sometimes riding for hundreds of miles without a break. The Greek historian Herodotus has left us this description of them: "Nothing mortal travels as fast as these Persian messengers. The entire plan is a Persian invention . . . along the whole line of road there are men stationed with horses in number equal to the number of days which the journey takes. . . . The first rider delivers his dispatch to the second, and the sec-

Socrates.

ond passes it to the third, and so it is borne from hand to hand along the whole line, like the light in a torch race."

Socrates, one of the most famous Greek philosophers, never wrote down a single word of his teachings. The only knowledge we have of his thinking today comes from notes taken by his great student, Plato.

## Communications and Media

There are more telephones than people in Washington, D.C.

In 1977, according to the American Telephone and Telegraph Company, there were 14.5 telephone calls made for every 100 people in the entire world.

According to the General Telephone Company of Pennsylvania, the typical American spends an average of one year (8,760 hours) of his or her life speaking on the telephone.

Americans have always enjoyed talking on the telephone, as this postcard indicates.

There are two radios for every man, woman, and child in the United States.

The average person in the United States spends fifty-two minutes each day reading the newspaper. This means that in a seventy-year lifetime (subtracting the first fifteen years as non-newspaper-reading time), the typical American spends a little less than two years—about 687 days—of his or her life reading the paper.

*Illustration by Leyendecker shows a man engaged in a popular American pastime—reading the newspaper.*

---

In 1976 more people with an income below $3,000 a year owned television sets in the United States than those with an income above $10,000.

---

According to the New York Telephone Company, of the 398 million telephones in the world, more than one-third (155 million) are in the United States.

---

It is estimated that 4 million "junk" telephone calls—phone solicitations by persons or programmed machines—are made every day in the United States.

According to the Federal Trade Commission, there are 20,000 television commercials made each year that are aimed exclusively at children. Of these, 7,000 are for sugared breakfast cereals.

On June 1, 1946, there were only 10,000 television sets in the United States. Five years later, there were 12 million.

According to the Television Code of Decency, a beer advertisement can never show a person actually *drinking* beer. Next time you see such an advertisement on television, notice that while the beer itself is prominently displayed, the subject always stops short of imbibing it.

In 1948 Milton Berle's budget for the ''Texaco Star Theater,'' the most popular one-hour show on television, was $15,000 for the entire hour. In 1978, this was far less than the cost of a one-minute television commercial.

*Milton Berle at the height of his career, on the ''Texaco Star Theater.''*

In every hour that one listens to the radio in the United States, one hears approximately 11,000 spoken words.

Anyone writing a letter to the New York *Times* has one chance in twenty-one of having the letter published. Letter writers to the Washington *Post* do significantly better: one letter out of eight finds its way into print.

## Crime

As of 1975, handguns were used in 51 percent of all murders committed in the United States. Knives were used in 20 percent of all murders, shotguns in 8 percent, and personal weapons such as rocks and bottles in 9 percent. Six percent of murders were committed by miscellaneous methods, and another 6 percent by poisoning. This, however, may be a deceptive statistic, as it is estimated that 64 percent of all murders by poisoning go undetected.

Forensic scientists can determine a person's sex, age, and race by examining a single strand of hair.

In past centuries infants in China were sometimes kidnapped and turned into ''animal children.'' Every day, starting with the back, the captors would remove a bit of the unfortunate child's skin and transplant pieces of the hide of a bear or dog in its place. The process was tedious, for the hide adhered only in spots, and the children had a habit of dying in the midst of treatment. The captors also destroyed their victims' vocal cords, forced them by means of ingenious mechanical contraptions to walk on all fours, and tortured them to such an extent that the innocents were soon bereft of all reason. One result of such atrocities was the ''wild boy of Kiangse,'' exhibited in the nineteenth century before a group of westerners in China. The child walked on all fours, made a peculiar barking sound, and was covered with a fuzzy, leathery kind of hide. An American doctor named Macgowan who witnessed this spectacle recorded that another method of creating child-monsters in China was to deprive the children of light for several years so that their bones would become deformed. At the same time they were fed certain foods and drugs that utterly debilitated them. Macgowan mentioned an Oriental priest who subjected a kidnapped boy to this treatment and then displayed him to incredulous observers, claiming he was a religious deity. The child looked like wax, having been fed a diet consisting mostly of lard. He squatted with his palms together and was a driveling idiot. The monk, Macgowan added, was arrested but managed to escape. His temple was burned to the ground.

---

In ancient China the punishment for small criminal infractions such as shoplifting or breaking a curfew was to brand the offender's forehead with a hot iron. Petty thieves and people who molested travelers had their noses sliced off. For the crime of damaging city bridges or gates, the ears, hands, feet, and kneecaps were cut off. Abduction, armed robbery, treason, and adultery were punished by castration. Death by strangulation was the price one paid for murder and for an even more unspeakable crime—drunkenness.

*Criminal being punished in ancient China.*

---

Based on the victim-to-population ratio, an adult has a greater chance of being physically assaulted in the state of Arizona than anywhere else in the country. The state with the second highest rate of assault is North Carolina; third is New Mexico.

---

In seventeenth-century Europe there were wandering bands of smugglers called *comprachicos* whose stock-in-trade was buying children, deforming them, and selling them to the aristocracy, who thought it fashionable to have freaks in court. The *comprachicos'* "arts" included stunting children's growth, placing muzzles on their faces to deform them (it was from this practice that Dumas took his theme for *The Man in the Iron Mask*), slitting their eyes, dislocating their joints, and malforming their bones. James II of England hired *comprachicos* to kidnap the heirs of families whose lines he wished to extinguish. Victor Hugo's *The Man Who Laughs* had a grotesque permanent smile carved by the *comprachicos.*

*Illustration from*
The Man in the Iron Mask
*by Alexandre Dumas.*

In New York City, official government automobiles are not subject to traffic summonses. In 1975, 6,000 tickets a month were issued to cars belonging to federal agencies, and not one was paid. The unpaid fines that year added up to $2.7 million.

In New York City in 1977, diplomats attached to the United Nations received a total of 250,000 parking tickets. The representative from Guinea led the list with 526 tickets.

According to the Federal Aviation Authority, airline security-check stations at airports have, since 1973, detected more than 15,000 firearms that passengers have tried to smuggle onto airplanes. More than 5,000 arrests have resulted from these discoveries.

## Death

The body of Francisco Pizarro, the Spanish conquistador who conquered Peru in the sixteenth century, was embalmed with special herbs after his death and preserved in the cathedral in the main square of Lima. His body can still be viewed today, displayed in a glass casket.

The National Academy of Engineering estimates that 15,000 deaths each year are directly attributable to air pollution. The National Institute of Occupational Safety and Health estimates that many of the 100,000 people who die each year from occupational exposure die as a result of hazardous air quality at work.

*Pollution in Pittsburgh in the 1890s. Today many people still die as a result of industrial pollution.*

Every man, woman, and child who has died has died of the same cause—hypoxemia. Hypoxemia is a general term for inadequate oxygenation of the blood and cellular tissue. After the heart has stopped beating, for whatever reason, the body's tissues are no longer supplied with life-giving oxygen. Their essential metabolic processes then cease, and death ensues.

Under the proper conditions of moisture and heat, the flesh of a buried body will turn to soap. Known as adipocere, this strange substance is a chemical much like baking soda mixed with fat (and thus almost identical in composition to soap) and is called ''grave wax'' by undertakers. For years the corpse of William von Ellenbogen, a soldier whose body turned to adipocere after he was killed in the Revolutionary War, was on display at the Smithsonian Institution.

---

Since its completion in 1937, more than 600 people have committed suicide by jumping off San Francisco's Golden Gate Bridge.

---

It is impossible to commit suicide by holding one's breath. At worst, the person who tries this will eventually lose consciousness. The lungs will then start to breathe again automatically.

---

In medieval Japan, it was believed that there was a single hair somewhere on the tail of a cat that could restore life to a dead person. For this reason cats were brought into the room of a dying person and placed next to his or her bed. As a last resort, relatives sometimes had the dying person pluck a single hair from the cat's tail in the hope that this one would prove to be the magic strand.

---

After the great ballet dancer Vaslav Nijinsky died, doctors cut open and examined his feet. They wanted to find out whether his foot bones were different from those of ordinary men, thinking that his bone structure might account for his ability to perform the extraordinary leaps for which he had been famous. The autopsy, however, revealed nothing unusual.

---

In ancient Egypt, when a rich man was mummified his heart was removed from his body and a heart-shaped stone carving of a dung beetle was put in its place.

---

In a churchyard near Cardiff, Wales, one can read the following inscription: "Here lieth the body of William Edwards of Cacreg, who departed this life 24th February, Anno Domini 1668, age one hundred and sixty-eight."

---

Henry IV of France (1553–1610) was exhumed nearly two hundred years after his death so that a death mask of his face could be made.

---

*Death mask of Henry IV.*

When an Australian Bushman died, his body was lowered into a grave where a special kind of gravedigger awaited it. This person's job was to slice up the corpse and hand out bits of the flesh to the mourners. The order in which the relatives partook of the feast was strictly prescribed. A mother ate from her children, and children from their mother. A man could eat his sister's husband and his brother's wife. A father, however, could not eat his children, nor children their father.

Nearly 5,000 Americans under the age of twenty-four committed suicide in 1977. An additional 100,000 tried to. Ninety percent of all suicides are females.

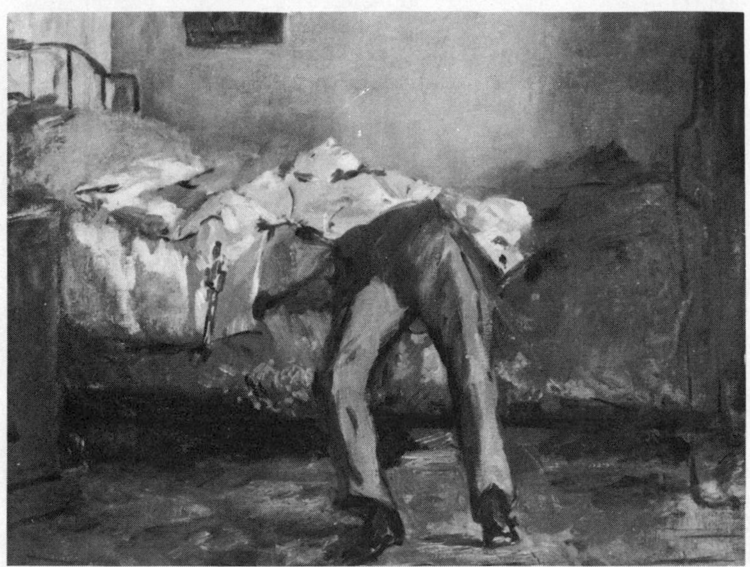

The Suicide,
*painting by Edouard Manet.*

The last will and testament of the great French writer François Rabelais (ca. 1490–1553) reads as follows: "I have nothing. I owe much. The rest I leave to the poor."

Dying words of the famous and the infamous:

Max Baer—"Oh, God, here I go. . . ."

Henry Ward Beecher (when asked on his deathbed if he could raise his arm)—"Well, high enough to hit you, Doctor."

Ludwig van Beethoven—"Applaud, friends, the comedy is finished."

Johann Wolfgang von Goethe—"Please close the window."

Georg Wilhelm Hegel—"Only one man understood me . . . and he didn't understand."

Samuel Johnson—"I am about to die."

John Keats—"I feel the flowers growing over me."

The Roman emperor Nero—"A great artist dies in me."

Carl Panzram (murderer of twenty-three people)—"I wish the whole human race had one neck and I had my hands on it."

Edgar Allan Poe—"Lord have mercy on my poor soul!"

François Rabelais—"I am going to a great perhaps."

Arnold Rothstein (famous gambler and gangster, when asked who shot him)—"My mudder did it."

Henry David Thoreau—"Moose . . . Indian . . ."

Oscar Wilde—"I am dying as I have lived, beyond my means."

*Oscar Wilde, who lived and died "beyond his means."*

---

## Demography

---

As of 1975, Florida had the highest percentage of married people in the United States (68.9 percent) and Alaska had the lowest (60.7 percent).

---

In 1800 only fifty cities on earth had a population of more than 100,000.

---

California has almost five times more fishermen than any other state. In 1977, 5.3 million fishing licenses were granted in California. The closest competitor, Michigan, sold only 1.6 million licenses.

---

There are more people in the borough of Queens in New York City (1,964,000) than in the entire country of Togo in West Africa (1,620,000).

---

Only 3.5 percent of the entire land area of Egypt is inhabited. The rest is desert. There are, furthermore, parts of Egypt where the population density is more than 250,000 people per square mile. In fact, while the country itself measures 387,000 square miles, more than twice the area of California, the entire population—about 39 million people—lives in an area less than four times that of Connecticut.

In 1700 there were more people living in Boston (population 7,000) than in New York City (population 5,000). The total population of the American colonies at that time was under 250,000.

*Street corner in 18th-century New York. At the time, Boston was more heavily populated.*

There are nine countries in the world where people have a higher life expectancy than in the United States. First is Sweden, then Norway, the Netherlands, Iceland, Denmark, Switzerland, and Italy. This statistic, however, pertains only to *white* Americans. The black population of the United States ranks thirty-third in life expectancy among nations, behind such countries as Chile, Jamaica, and Costa Rica.

The average life expectancy in Bangladesh is thirty-five years. Forty-five percent of those who die before thirty-five are mothers and infants. A child has only a fifty-fifty chance of living past five. Yet in this country only 11 percent of the population has ever visited a doctor.

---

In 1854 there were 700 people living in the area that is now California. One hundred twenty-five years later the same area had a population of 21,520,000. In other words, in little more than a century the population of this area increased approximately 30,000 times.

---

The life expectancy for women in the United States is nearly twice what it was a hundred years ago.

---

The life expectancy of American Indians is 10 percent shorter than that of white Americans.

---

In 1800 there was one slave for every six citizens in the United States (5,308,483 citizens; 896,849 slaves).

*19th-century slave sale in the U.S.*

---

If the world were a single town with a population of 100, one of those hundred people would have a college education, thirty would be able to read and write, fifteen would live in adequate housing (the rest would live in huts), and fifty would be hungry most of the time. Six of the hundred would control almost half the wealth of the town, and of these six, three would be Americans.

## Diamonds

Diamonds mined in Brazil are harder than those found in Africa.

A diamond will not dissolve in acid. The only thing that can destroy it is intense heat.

Of all the ore dug in diamond mines, only one carat in every 23 tons proves to be a diamond.

The largest diamond-in-the-rough ever found measured 3,106 carats and weighed more than a pound and a quarter. It was discovered in South Africa in 1905 by Sir Thomas Cullinan, who brought it back to England that same year. After the stone had changed hands several times it was finally given to King Edward VII on his sixty-sixth birthday. Edward promptly had the stone cut into ninety-six small gems and nine large ones, including the famous Star of Africa, which measured 530 carats. Other well-known large diamonds include the Excelsior stone (970 carats), the Jubilee (634 carats), the Jonker (736 carats), and the Imperial (457 carats).

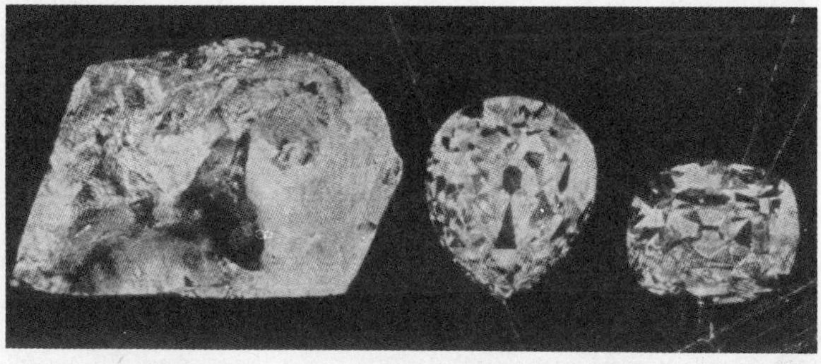

*The Cullinan diamond (left), with the two largest stones cut from it, including the famous Star of Africa (middle).*

The Victoria-Transvaal diamond, mined in Africa in 1950 and one of the world's hundred largest and most famous diamonds, appeared in a Lex Barker-Dorothy Hart movie called *Tarzan's Savage Fury*. It was used to represent the eye of a jungle god. Its appearance was sponsored by its owner, who was contemplating selling the gem and wanted the publicity.

In 1928 a farmer named William Hones, while planting horseradish in a field in Petersburg, West Virginia, found a greasy, shiny stone, which he brought home as a kind of curiosity. Fifteen years later it was discovered that his "curiosity" was a 32-carat diamond, one of the largest ever found in America. Diamonds in fact are not so rare in the United States as is often supposed. The Eagle diamond, weighing 16 carats, was found in Wisconsin some years ago, and other large stones have been discovered in Ohio, Illinois, and Indiana. The largest diamond found to date in the United States weighed 40 carats and was mined near Murfreesboro, Arkansas.

## Diseases

A 1971 study at the Harvard School of Public Health revealed that women who drink one or more cups of coffee a day are two and a half times more likely to get bladder cancer than women who drink no coffee.

As of 1977, diabetes was the third leading cause of death by disease in the United States. It has increased 50 percent since 1965, and today affects at least 10 million Americans.

Two out of three adults in the United States have hemorrhoids.

In 1971, at Memorial Hospital in New York City, a woman weighing less than 100 pounds ran a fever of 114 degrees—and survived without brain damage or physiological aftereffects.

---

The rate of hypertension is twice as high among blacks as whites in the United States; the rate of hypertension among men living in Vermont is also twice the national average. Women of all races are afflicted by this disorder far less than men.

---

Each year more than 300,000 American teen-agers become afflicted with some form of venereal disease.

---

A patient who receives blood from a paid donor is three to ten times more likely to contract hepatitis than one who receives blood from a voluntary donor. Paid donors are frequently derelicts or drug addicts and often carry the hepatitis virus in their blood streams.

---

Every year some 8,000 infants in the United States die from a mysterious ailment known as Sudden Infant Death Syndrome (SIDS), or crib death. Most of these children have been put to bed hours before their death, seemingly in perfect health. All die without a trace of struggle. As yet no one has been able to explain the cause of these deaths.

---

Of the 32 million Americans admitted to hospitals each year, some 1.5 million develop some disease that comes simply from being in the hospital. More than 15,000 people die of such a disease each year. So prevalent is this syndrome that doctors have given it a name—noscomial disease, from the Greek word *noscomium*, meaning "hospital."

---

A woman's arthritic pains will almost always disappear as soon as she becomes pregnant. No one knows why.

---

The death rate from cardiovascular diseases—heart attack, hardening of the arteries, and so on—has decreased in the United States since 1950.

---

Neuritis and neuralgia are not diseases. They are nerve pains *related* to disease. In fact, when a pain is identified as neuralgia, it is often because the exact cause is not known. Neuralgia differs from neuritis in that neuralgia pains come in paroxysms, while neuritis is more constant and even. Thus sciatica is a kind of neuralgia and a toothache a kind of neuritis.

---

In 1918 and 1919 a world epidemic of simple influenza killed 20 million people in the United States and Europe.

*Seattle policemen wear masks to protect them from contamination during the 1918–1919 flu epidemic.*

---

One cannot catch cold at the North Pole in winter. Neither can one contract the flu, nor most of the ailments transmitted by viruses and germs. The winter temperature is so low in this part of the world that none of the standard disease-causing microorganisms can survive.

---

The chances of an American woman getting breast cancer depend on a number of variables. For a woman whose sister, mother, or daughter has developed cancer in both breasts, the chances are five to three against. However, if one of these relatives developed cancer before reaching menopause, the odds are fifty-fifty. Women with the lowest chances of getting breast cancer are those whose ovaries have been removed before the age of thirty-five. Chances are almost as good for a woman who has had a child before the age of eighteen.

---

Men are twice as likely to contract leprosy as women.

*Leper house, illustration from a 13th-century French manuscript.*

---

Medical studies show that members of the Seventh-Day Adventist church, even those living in heavily polluted areas, have 1,000 percent less lung cancer than members of the general population in the United States. Moreover, Seventh-Day Adventists have appreciably lower rates of other cancers and of respiratory diseases, 40 percent less coronary trouble, and scarcely a quarter the amount of tooth decay found in the general population.

---

Ninety percent of all teen-agers suffer from some form of acne.

---

Teen-agers are 50 percent more susceptible to colds than people over fifty.

---

There is a strange and terrible disease known as bulimia in which the victim develops a ravenous, insatiable appetite. A woman observed in St. Bartholomew's Hospital in nineteenth-century London is recorded to have consumed three loaves of bread every day, along with three pounds of steak, large quantities of vegetables, a pound of cereal, and twenty glasses of water. An American doctor named Smith, reporting in the *Medical and Surgical Reporter* in Philadelphia, mentioned an even stranger case, that of a boy who ate continuously for fifteen hours every day and who had eight or nine bowel movements each evening. In one year this boy's weight increased from 105 to 284 pounds, and it was steadily increasing by about a half-pound a day. Despite his prodigious intake of food, the boy constantly complained of hunger. Another unpleasant ailment akin to this one is polydipsia, or constant thirst. Medical records mention a three-year-old child who drank two pailfuls of water every day. Sir M. MacKenzie, a British doctor, cited the case of a woman who drank four pailfuls of water a day and who once, appearing before a scientific commission, drank 14 quarts of water in ten hours, passed 10 quarts of urine, and continued to complain of thirst.

---

A condition known as hypertrophy (enlargement) of the tongue can sometimes reach such extremes that the tongue becomes too large for the mouth and protrudes over the chin, reaching down as far as the chest. This extraordinary enlargement may cause deformity of the teeth and jaw, and may even cause the sufferer to choke on his or her own tongue.

---

A collection of mysterious and unusual physical disorders:

***Amazia***—The complete absence of breasts.

***Athetosis***—Constant involuntary movements of the fingers and toes. In advanced stages of this disease sufferers continually wave their hands about in slow, languid motions and are totally unable to keep the fingers still. Often this disease is confined to one side of the body.

***Contagious follicular keratosis***—The whole body becomes covered with small spinelike growths of a dirty yellow color. The spines are very hard and, when cut off and placed in a container, rattle like scraps of metal.

***Diphallic terata***—The presence of more than one penis.

***Harlequin fetus***—A newborn child emerges covered with fatty epidermic plates about a sixteenth of an inch thick. These plates cover the entire body and face like a loosely built stone wall. The skin is so stiff and contracted that the eyes cannot be opened (or if they are open, they cannot be shut) and the lips are too stiff to suck. The child soon dies from starvation and loss of body heat.

***Mercyism***—The need to regurgitate after each meal and then immediately to eat another full meal. For some reason this disease was at one time observed to be common among physicians.

*This bearded lady, a member of P. T. Barnum's side show during the 19th century, was probably a victim of naevus pilosus.*

***Naevus pilosus***—Enormous moles or birthmarks with great amounts of hair growing out of them. The "bearded woman" and "orang-utan man" seen at circuses and carnivals are usually victims of this disorder.

***Plica polonica***—The skin and nails turn spongy and black, the hair follicles exude a gluey liquid, and the hair itself becomes painful to the touch. Oddly enough, this disease is found almost exclusively among Polish people.

***Polyorchidism***—The presence of more than two testicles. This is the opposite of the condition known as *anorchidism,* in which a male is born with no testicles at all.

***Saltatoric spasm***—Spasmodic muscular contractions of the calves, hips, knees, and back that cause the sufferer to spring up or jump about uncontrollably every time he or she attempts to stand.

***Xeroderma pigmentosum***—Small yellow warts cover the entire body. The skin is wrinkled and abounds in strange white scales. This disease, quite rare, usually attacks children.

## The Earth

If the moon were placed on the surface of the continental United States, it would extend from San Francisco to Cleveland (2,160 miles).

---

For the first 2 billion years of its existence, the earth had no life on it whatsoever.

---

Each year the United States loses 3.5 billion tons of soil through erosion. This amount of soil would fill a freight train

474,000 miles long, enough to circle the globe nineteen times at the equator. Experts estimate that since 1600, 25 percent of the available topsoil in America has been washed into the sea.

---

Approximately three-thousandths of all the water on the surface of the globe evaporates each year.

---

Approximately 70 percent of the earth is covered with water. Only 1 percent of this water is drinkable.

## Energy

Over any given twenty-four-hour period, the fifty major hotels and gambling casinos in the Las Vegas area use 1.5 million kilowatt hours of electricity, enough to provide power for a city of some 35,000 inhabitants. The power used by these entertainment establishments simply to light their marquees could supply the electricity for more than 1,000 homes.

---

According to the Federal Power Commission, as of 1976 the United States produced more than twice as much electricity as any other country in the world. Its closest competitor was the Soviet Union.

---

The average automobile traveling at 57 miles per hour gets only two-thirds the gas mileage of a car moving at 50 miles per hour.

---

One-quarter of all the energy in the United States is used to heat and cool homes and buildings, according to the U.S. Research and Development Administration.

---

In order to equal the amount of energy transmitted every day from the sun to the earth,it would be necessary to burn 550 billion tons of coal, more than could be mined (given present methods) in a thousand years.

---

According to the U.S. Bureau of Labor, the cost of fuel increased 182 percent between 1967 and 1977. Gas and electric costs have increased 110 percent.

The lighthouse in Creach d'Ouessant on the coast of Brittany in France gives out a light equal to that of 500 million candles. It would take 6,253,000 flashlights to make a light that bright.

## Executions

During the Inquisition in fifteenth-century Spain, prisoners condemned to burn were forced to walk to their doom wearing a special frock called a *sanbenito*. On it were painted pictures of the fiery mouth of hell. After the accused died, his name was written on the *sanbenito* and it was hung in his parish church, where it remained until it fell apart. Occasionally an old *sanbenito* would be replaced by a fresh one so that the infamy of the heretic who had worn it would be perpetuated through the ages.

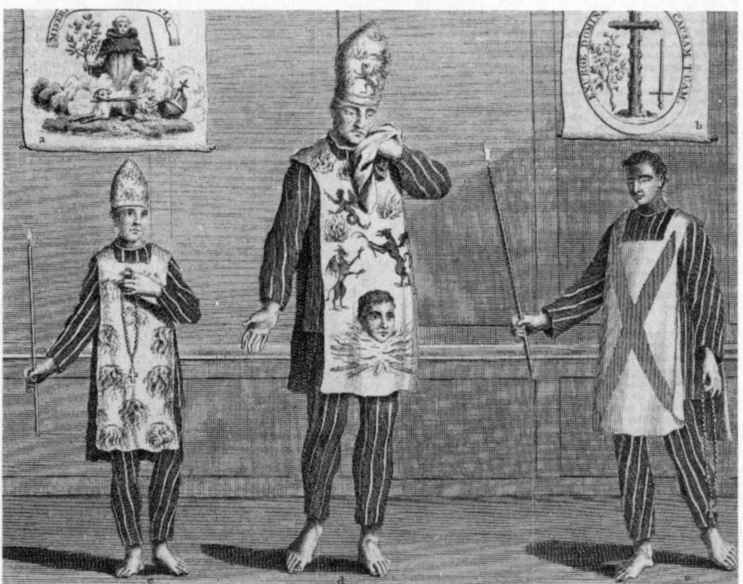

*Condemned prisoners in their sanbenitos during the Inquisition.*

Robert Damiens, an assassin and member of the Paris underworld in the eighteenth century, was hired by unknown conspirators to take the life of King Louis XV. The attempt failed, Damiens was apprehended, and the greatest torturers of the time were brought to Paris to try to get him to divulge the names of his associates. Damiens' skin was torn from his body, his hair, eyelids, and elbows were singed to shreds, his teeth and finger joints were wrenched out. He was dragged about at the end of a rope tied to a team of horses. He was sprinkled from head to foot with acid and seething oil. Throughout all this horror, Damiens, who finally died from his wounds, never revealed the names of his employers. Historians still argue both questions: Who was it that hired Damiens? And, more mysterious, why did he so steadfastly refuse to divulge their names?

*The torture and execution of Robert Damiens in Paris, 1757.*

---

At the moment of being hanged, many observers have noted, the victim, if male, often has an erection and may even ejaculate.

---

The Moravian Brothers, an evangelical Christian sect that originated in fifteenth-century Bohemia, believed in nonviolence and had a great abhorrence of bloodshed. Members of this community, however, were at times unavoidably called on to execute offenders. Their merciful way of doing so was to tickle their victims to death.

## Fallacies

The state of Pennsylvania was not named after William Penn. In a letter written to Robert Turner on January 5, 1681, Penn revealed the real source of the state's name: ''And they added Penn to it and though I much opposed it and went to the King to have it struck out and altered, he said it was past and he would take it upon him, for I feared lest it should be looked on as a vanity in me. But the King said, 'we will keep it, but not on your account, my dear fellow, don't flatter yourself. We will keep the name to commemorate the Admiral, your noble father [Sir William Penn].' ''

The Landing of William Penn, October 1862, *painting by J. L. Ferris.*

Cellophane is not made of plastic. It is made from a plant fiber, cellulose, which has been shredded and aged. Cellophane was invented in 1908 by a Swiss chemist named Jacques Brandenberger who was trying to make a stainproof tablecloth and ended up with cellophane instead.

Horace Greeley did not coin the phrase "Go west, young man." It was first said by John Soule, editor of the Terre Haute *Express*, in 1851. Greeley simply heard the statement and popularized it in his own paper, the New York *Tribune*. It caught on, and Greeley was given credit for it.

*Horace Greeley.*

Contrary to popular belief, the mongoose is not immune to the venom of the cobra. If bitten it will die as quickly as any other animal. The mongoose is able to defeat its archenemy in battle simply because it is faster and has better reflexes.

Big Ben is not a clock. It is a bell located in the clock tower of the Houses of Parliament in London. It weighs 13½ tons, is 9 feet in diameter, and stands higher than a man (7½ feet). Nor is the bell an ancient English landmark: it was installed a little more than a hundred years ago, in 1859.

*Though most people call this world-famous clock "Big Ben," the name actually belongs to the bell within the clock tower.*

Saint Joan of Arc was not French. She was born in 1412 in Domrémy, which at the time was an autonomous state outside the jurisdiction of the French monarchy. Neither was she a heroine in France until the nineteenth century. Having fallen

*15th-century statue of Joan of Arc.*

into oblivion shortly after her death, Joan was at best a minor figure in French legend. On coming to power at the beginning of the eighteenth century, Napoleon needed a hero symbol to help promote nationalism in France, and he hit upon Joan of Arc. She was not actually canonized until the twentieth century.

---

The story of the little Dutch boy who placed his finger in a dike to save a town from a flood is an American invention. It was never heard of in Holland before the twentieth century.

---

Contrary to popular opinion, the Pyramids of Egypt were not among the Seven Wonders of the Ancient World, although the Sphinx was. The other six wonders were the Hanging Gardens of Babylon, the statue of Zeus at Olympia, the Mausoleum of Halicarnassus, the lighthouse at Pharos, the Colossus of Rhodes, and the Temple of Diana at Ephesus.

*The Mausoleum of Halicarnassus, one of the Seven Wonders of the Ancient World.*

---

The Tower of London is not one particular tower, but a group of buildings covering 13 acres along the north bank of the

Thames River. The central ''White Tower,'' built in 1078 and used as a fortress, a royal residence, and finally as a prison, is the ''tower'' of which the English so often spoke in horror.

*Aerial view of the Tower of London.*

The Pennsylvania Dutch are not Dutch, but German. Catgut strings are not made from catgut, but from sheep intestines. Bedstraw is not straw; it is an herb that grows wild in woods and marshes. Shooting stars are not stars; they are meteors and meteorites. *Old Ironsides* did not have iron sides—its sides were made of wood. Hay fever is not caused by hay; it is an allergy caused by various kinds of pollen.

## Fashion

To preserve their elaborate coiffures, geishas in ancient Japan slept with their heads on bags filled with buckwheat chaff.

During the Renaissance, fashionable aristocratic Italian women shaved their hair several inches back from their natural hairlines.

A fashionable 18th-century headdress.

In eighteenth-century England, women's wigs were sometimes 4 feet high. These remarkable headdresses were dusted with flour and decorated with stuffed birds, replicas of gardens, plates of fruit, or even model ships. Sometimes the wigs were so elaborate they were worn continuously for several months. They were matted with lard to keep them from coming apart, which made mice and insects a constant hazard. Special pillows had to be constructed to hold these giant creations, and rat-resistant caps made of gilt wire were common items. Mercifully, the wig craze died out quite suddenly in England in 1795, when a hair-powder tax made their upkeep too expensive.

---

In the eighteenth century the French Comte d'Artois owned a set of diamond buttons, each of which had a miniature clock encased inside it.

---

The Greeks in the time of Alexander the Great liked blond hair as much as we do today. Men and women alike bleached their locks with potash water and herbal infusions, creating a reddish-blond color considered to be the height of style and beauty.

---

According to the U.S. Food and Drug Administration, two out of five women in America dye their hair.

---

In 1400 B.C. it was the fashion among rich Egyptian women to place a large cone of scented grease on top of their heads and keep it there all day. As the day wore on, the grease melted and dripped down over their bodies, covering their skin with an oily, glistening sheen and bathing their clothes in fragrance.

---

The San Blas Indian women of Panama consider giant noses a mark of great beauty. They paint black lines down the center of their noses to make them appear longer. Among San Blas men, an enormous nose is the mark of a great leader.

In India it is perfectly proper for men to wear pajamas in public. Pajamas are accepted as standard daytime wearing apparel.

---

It was the style among eighteenth-century Englishmen to wear pantaloons so tight they had to be hung on special pegs that held them open, allowing the wearer to jump down into them. This was the only way fashionable gentlemen could get their trousers to fit properly.

---

In 1500 B.C. in Egypt a shaved head was considered the ultimate in feminine beauty. Egyptian women removed every hair from their heads with special gold tweezers and polished their scalps to a high sheen with buffing cloths.

---

The French philosopher Voltaire owned eighty canes. His contemporary, Jean Jacques Rousseau, owned forty. Canes in fact were in great vogue in eighteenth-century France, and women as well as men carried them. Women's canes often came equipped with perfume bottles, music boxes, or romantic pictures hidden inside.

*Voltaire, with one of his eighty canes.*

In nineteenth-century England it was considered vulgar to hold an umbrella under one's arm. Well-bred people gripped their umbrellas in the middle, with the handle turned toward the ground. Only silk umbrellas were considered fashionable by the British upper crust, and these only if they were blue or green. For the general public, moreover, umbrellas were an unaffordable luxury. When it rained the ordinary man or woman would hire an umbrella from a local stand, usually at the cost of one and a half pence per hour.

## Firsts

The first place the famous Dutch explorer Henry Hudson set foot on when he arrived in New York was Coney Island. In 1609, Hudson approached what is now New York Harbor and disembarked precisely on the spot where one of the world's largest and most famous amusement parks would someday stand.

*Henry Hudson landing at what is now Coney Island.*

Austria was the first country to use postcards.

Martin Luther was the first person to put lights on a Christmas tree. Luther reportedly placed candles on his *tannenbaum* to represent the stars above Bethlehem on the night of Christ's birth. Many of his followers adopted the practice and soon the custom spread throughout Europe.

*Martin Luther and his family gathered around their candlelit Christmas tree.*

The first belch ever broadcast on national radio was heard in 1935. Melvin H. Purvis, head of the Chicago office of the FBI, was making a guest appearance on a program sponsored by Fleischmann's yeast. In the middle of delivering a commercial for Fleischmann's, Mr. Purvis inadvertently emitted the dreaded sound, and for years afterward this brand of yeast was known as "Purvis's folly."

The first steam engine ever built was a miniature toy train. It was constructed in 1798 by a former boat salesman named John Fitch, who, unable to make a living selling the orthodox boats of the time, began experimenting with steam-driven vehicles. In 1798 he invented both the first free-moving railway engine and the first moving model train. He also invented a steamboat.

The first message ever sent over a telegraph wire was "What hath God wrought?" It was sent from the U.S. Supreme Court room in Washington, D.C., to Baltimore, Maryland, in 1844 by the inventor of the telegraph, Samuel Morse.

In 1978 a Scottish police sergeant invented the world's first electronic bagpipe. The instrument, created by Sgt. Angus MacLellan, looks like the traditional Scottish bagpipe but is run by a battery and requires no blowing.

The first monument constructed in India to commemorate an American was dedicated to a black man. Unveiled in Bombay in 1947, it was a statue of the famous black horticulturist, George Washington Carver.

## Fish

A species of starfish known as *Linckia columbiae* can reproduce its entire body—that is, grow back completely—from a single severed piece less than a half-inch long.

A tuna can swim 100 miles in a single day.

*The tuna, one of the swiftest fishes in the sea.*

Lemon sharks grow a new set of teeth every two weeks. They grow more than 24,000 new teeth every year.

Goldfish lose their color if they are kept in dim light or are placed in a body of running water, such as a stream. They remain gold only when kept in a pond or in a bowl with adequate illumination.

## Flowers, Plants, and Trees

The so-called bee and fly varieties of orchid form themselves into perfect replicas of female flies and bees and reproduce the scents of these insects with such accuracy that male bees and flies are irresistibly attracted to them. Once they have landed on the orchid's petals, the insects help pollinate the species.

*European bee orchid.*

A single orchid plant of the genus *Cymbidium* was sold in the United States in 1952 for $4,500.

Each seed of the palm tree *Lodoicea seychellarum* weighs 30 pounds.

Seeds of the leguminous plant known as the Arctic lupine, found frozen in holes in northern Canada and estimated to be ten thousand years old, have been planted by scientists and have grown! The seeds of the lotus plant, unfrozen and unpreserved, will sometimes germinate after lying fallow for two hundred years.

It is estimated that millions of trees in the world are accidentally planted by squirrels who bury nuts and then forget where they hid them.

Rattan palms found in the jungles of Southeast Asia have vinelike stems that trail along the jungle floor up to 250 feet in all directions.

There is an organization in Berkeley, California, whose members gather monthly to discuss and honor the garlic plant.

Called "The Lovers of the Stinky Rose," this unusual organization holds an annual garlic festival and publishes a newsletter known as *Garlic Time.*

---

The baobab tree of Australia has a short, fat trunk that develops into a shape that is an almost perfect replica of a bottle. It is known throughout Australia as the "bottle tree."

---

There are 250,000 species of flowering plants on the earth today.

---

Redwood trees sometimes grow to heights of 350 feet and produce bark that is more than a foot thick. Yet they spring from a seed that is only a sixteenth of an inch long. These seeds are so small that 123,000 of them weigh scarcely a pound.

*Massive trunk of a California redwood tree.*

## Food and Diet

According to the American Popcorn Institute, Americans consumed almost 7.5 billion quarts of popcorn in 1977. Of this amount only 10 percent was eaten in movie theaters and other places of amusement; 90 percent was eaten at home.

---

On the average, each American consumes 117 pounds of potatoes, 116 pounds of beef, 100 pounds of fresh vegetables, 80 pounds of fresh fruit, and 286 eggs per year.

In the United States in 1976, a pound of potato chips cost two hundred times more than a pound of potatoes.

*Eight varieties of potatoes—all cheaper, pound for pound, than potato chips.*

Eighteen ounces of an average cola drink contain as much caffeine as a cup of coffee.

There are 15,000 different kinds of rice.

In ancient China and certain parts of India, mouse flesh was considered a great delicacy. In ancient Greece, where the mouse was sacred to Apollo, mice were sometimes devoured by temple priests.

In ancient Rome it was considered a sin to eat the flesh of a woodpecker.

In the Middle Ages, chicken soup was believed to be an aphrodisiac.

Half the foods eaten throughout the world today were developed by farmers in the Andes Mountains. Potatoes, maize, sweet potatoes, squash, all varieties of beans, peanuts, manioc, cashews, pineapples, chocolate, avocados, tomatoes, peppers, papayas, strawberries, mulberries, and many other foods were first grown in this region.

The staple food of the Kanembu, a tribe living on the shores of Lake Chad in Africa, is algae. The Kanembu harvest a common variety known as *Spirulina* from the lake, dry it on the sand, mix it up into a spicy cake, and eat it with tomatoes and chili peppers.

Among many native tribes in South Africa, termites are roasted to a nutlike consistency and eaten by the handful, like party snacks. It might also be noted that at certain specialty food shops in the United States and Europe, the connoisseur of exotic delicacies can purchase such treats as chocolate-covered ants, candied bees, and pickled bull's scrotum.

---

Rice is the chief food for half the people of the world.

---

*The tomato. Americans love it, au naturel and in ketchup and other sauces.*

According to the U.S. Department of Agriculture, Americans eat more than 22 pounds of tomatoes every year. More than half this amount is eaten in the form of ketchup and tomato sauce.

---

According to the U.S. Department of Agriculture, consumption of green and yellow vegetables has decreased 6.3 pounds a year per person since the late 1940s. The use of cereal and flour products has dropped about 30 pounds a year per person, and consumption of noncitrus fruits has declined at about the same rate. The only fruits whose rate of consumption has increased since World War I are citrus fruits.

---

Everyone knows about vitamins A, B, C, D, and E. Few are aware that there are also vitamin K (promotes proper liver function and vitality), vitamin T (helpful in treating anemia), vitamin H (also called biotin), and vitamin U (promotes healing of ulcers).

---

Refined sugar is the only food known that provides calories but no nutrition. About 100 pounds of sugar are eaten per person each year in the United States, and only 36 percent of it is taken directly. The rest is "hidden" in commercially sweetened and prepared foods like ketchup, baby food, canned fruits, and cereals. Children, it is estimated, consume 3 to 4 pounds of refined sugar a week.

---

According to a report issued by the Senate Committee on Nutrition and Human Needs, improved nutrition in the United States would cut the national health bill by approximately one-third. The committee also claims that a diet composed of 10 percent protein, 10 percent fat, and 80 percent complex carbohydrates (plus exercise done in moderation) could save 98 percent of those who die of heart disease every year.

---

Rennet, a common substance used to curdle milk and make cheese, is taken from the inner lining of the fourth stomach of a calf.

---

Though most people think of salt as a seasoning, only 5 out of every 100 pounds produced each year go to the dinner table. The rest is used for such diverse purposes as packing meat, building roads, feeding livestock, tanning leather, and manufacturing glass, soap, ash, and washing compounds.

---

The nutritional value of squash and pumpkin seeds improves with age. These seeds are among the few foods that increase in nutritive value as they decompose. According to tests made at the Massachusetts Experimental Station, squash and pumpkin seeds stored for more than five months show a marked increase in protein content.

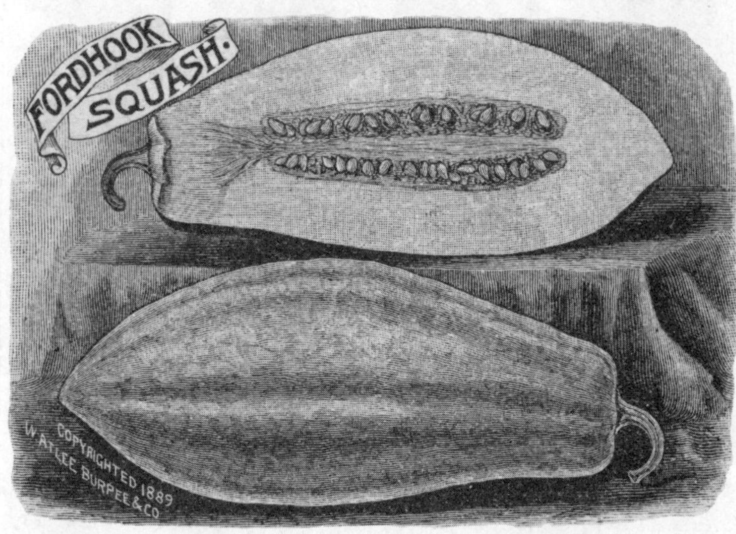


*The Fordhook squash. Its seeds, like those of pumpkins and all other squashes, improve with age.*

---

The Bible mentions salt more than thirty times.

---

## Games

Gin and canasta are both descended from an ancient Chinese game, mah-jongg, which is more than a thousand years old.

In the famous Parker Brothers game ''Monopoly,'' the space on which a player has the greatest statistical chance of landing is Illinois Avenue. This is followed by the B & O Railroad, Free Parking, Tennessee Avenue, New York Avenue, and the Reading Railroad.

Computers that are well advanced (i.e., highly programmed) at playing chess are capable of beating 95 percent of all chess players well versed in the game.

Playing cards in India are round.

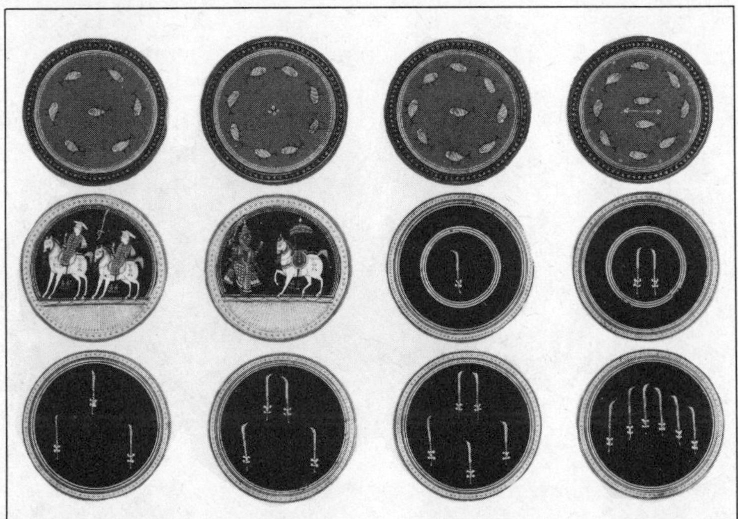

*19th-century round playing cards from India.*

George Washington, Thomas Jefferson, and John Adams were all avid collectors and players of marbles. In their day, marbles were called ''small bowls'' and were as popular with adults as with children.

## Geography

There is only one river in the world that has its source near the equator and from there flows into a temperate zone: the Nile. For some little-understood reason, the flow of most rivers is in the opposite direction.

*The Nile, one of the world's longest and most unusual rivers.*

---

Juneau, Alaska, has a greater land area than any other city in the Western Hemisphere. In 1977 the main city and outlying districts were consolidated, making Juneau officially 3,108 square miles in size. Of this area, 1,476 square miles are dry land, 928 are an icecap, and 704 comprise water. Compare this 3,108 square miles with other large cities: Jacksonville, Florida, traditionally considered the largest American city, has an area of 840 square miles. Houston, Texas, boasts 450, Los Angeles 455, and New York City 320.

---

Alaska has a sand desert with dunes over 100 feet high. It is located along the flatlands of the Kobuk River in the northwestern part of the state.

---

Alaska is the only state without a state motto.

---

In 1867, when Secretary of State William Seward purchased Alaska, one of the most resource-rich areas in the world, for the unbelievably low price of $7.2 million, he was showered with abuse by the American people and was almost forced to resign. Newspapers dubbed the acquisition "Seward's Icebox," "Walrussia," and "Icebergia." Seward, however, stood by his decision and named the country Alakshah, which means "great country" in the Aleut language.

---

The states of Arizona and Hawaii have never adopted Daylight Savings Time. Neither has Puerto Rico, the Virgin Islands, or American Samoa.

---

If the Nile River were stretched across the United States, it would run just about from New York to Los Angeles.

---

The needle of a compass does *not* point directly north. It points either a little to the east or a little to the west, not enough to make any difference to the average hiker. The difference is known to navigators as the "variation of the compass," and they take it into consideration when making critical geographical calculations. The phenomenon is due to the fact that the magnetic north and south poles do not coincide with the geographic north and south poles.

---

The highest mountain in all the British Isles, Ben Nevis in western Scotland, is only 4,406 feet high. In many other countries a "mountain" of this size would be considered something less than a large hill.

*Ben Nevis, Great Britain's highest mountain.*

---

Of the twenty-five highest mountains on earth, nineteen are in the Himalayas.

*Kanchenjunga, one of the titans of the Himalayas.*

Canada, the second largest country in the world (3,851,809 square miles), could fit into the largest country, the Soviet Union (8,647,250 square miles) more than twice.

Antarctica is the only continent that does not have land areas below sea level.

On a clear day one can see five states from atop the Empire State Building in New York City: New York, New Jersey, Connecticut, Massachusetts, and Pennsylvania.

The U.S. coastline—Atlantic, Pacific, and Gulf—involves twenty-five of the forty-eight mainland states.

The city of Los Angeles (455 square miles) is more than one-third the size of the entire state of Rhode Island (1,214 square miles).

The nation of Bangladesh covers approximately the same land area as the state of Wisconsin. Yet it ranks eighth in population among all the world's countries.

Before 1903 Panama was part of South America. After 1903 it was part of North America. This was due to an arbitrary decision of the Panamanian government, which in 1903, after staging the last of fifty revolutions (perhaps a record in itself) against its parent country, Colombia, gained its freedom, both to dissociate itself from Colombia and to decide which continent it wished to be part of. After less than a year's consideration, the government decided that the country should be North American, and so it has remained ever since.

Travelers to La Paz, Bolivia, often become ill the moment they arrive in the city. Why? La Paz is 11,900 feet above sea level, the highest metropolis in the world. People with ailing hearts or bronchial problems are warned to stay away, and even those in perfect health usually cannot avoid some illness resulting from the altitude.

## Government and Government Services

In 1976 there were fewer than half as many post offices in the United States as there were in 1900. The reason for this is that improved service and high-speed travel have reduced the need for post offices in many small communities.

There is an executive officer of the U.S. government whose job consists solely of investigating applications to the president of the United States for clemency and pardon.

According to the U.S. Department of Agriculture, 34 percent of all land in the United States is owned by the federal government.

If you've ever wondered what the numbers on your Social Security card signify, here is a breakdown of the mysterious code:

1. The first three numbers show what part of the country you applied from.

2. The next two numbers show, in coded form, the year you applied.

3. The last four numbers indicate your citizen's number kept on file by the government.

---

Before 1863 postal service in the United States was free.

*19th-century American village post office.*

## Holidays

The custom of using Christmas wreaths can be traced to the belief that the crown of thorns that Christ was forced to wear when he was crucified was made of holly.

---

Christmas was once illegal in England. In 1643 the Puritans outlawed all Christmas celebrations, banned the keeping of Christmas trees, and made the singing of Christmas carols a crime. These laws were maintained until the Restoration. Many Puritans in New England also adhered to these regulations, curtailing Christmas festivities to such a degree that even the making of mince pies was forbidden.

---

In Brazil, Christmas is celebrated with fireworks.

*Gift-giving at Christmas, a tradition that goes back to the ancient Romans.*

The practice of exchanging presents at Christmas originated with the Romans. Every December, the Romans celebrated a holiday called the Saturnalia. During this time the people gave each other good-luck presents of fruit, sweets, pastry, or gold. When the Christians began to celebrate their own holiday at this time of year, they simply took over the tradition.

Three billion Christmas cards are sent annually in the United States.

George Washington is the only man whose birthday is a legal holiday in every state of the United States.

Mother's Day was started by a woman named Anna Jarvis of Grafton, West Virginia. In 1907 Mrs. Jarvis began a campaign for the nationwide celebration of motherhood. At first no one paid much attention to her, but gradually churches and local town organizations began inviting her to speak at their meetings. Soon her notions caught on throughout the country, and on May 9, 1914, President Woodrow Wilson made the holiday official.

The following are all legal holidays in the United States:

Fast Day (fourth Monday in April, in New Hampshire).
Arbor Day (January 18, in Florida).
Kamehama Day (June 11, in Hawaii).
Nathan B. Forrest's Birthday (July 13, in Tennessee).
Cherokee Strip Day (September 16, in Oklahoma).
Will Rogers Day (November 4, in Oklahoma).
Repudiation Day (November 23, in Maryland).

## Human Oddities

In late-nineteenth-century France there was an individual known as *"l'homme proté,"* or the "protean man." He had exceptional control over all his muscles and could protrude or distort any part of himself at will. He could harden the muscles of his stomach so that if hit with a hammer they would not recoil. He could distend his abdomen to create the appearance of enormous obesity or draw it in until he looked like a living skeleton. According to Quatrefages, a celebrated French physician of the time, *l'homme proté* could shut off all the blood from the right side of his body and control the beating of his heart, feats he credited to his great muscular control.

---

At a meeting of the Physical Society of Vienna on December 4, 1894, a five-and-a-half-year-old girl was exhibited who weighed 250 pounds. She subsisted on a normal diet and was otherwise in good health. The only unusual feature of the girl's physiology was that she never perspired.

---

In 1657 Jakob van Meekren, a Dutch physician, recorded the case of a Spaniard named Georgius Albes, who could stretch the skin of his left breast up to his left ear and pull the skin at the base of his neck up over his chin. He was able to perform these feats because of a condition known as dermatolysis, a phenomenon that also explains the abilities of many so-called India-rubber men seen at carnival side shows.

---

In the late nineteenth century doctors discovered a Mexican porter named Paul Rodrigues who had a horn more than 4 inches long protruding from the upper part of his forehead. The horn was divided into three principal shafts and had a circumference of about 14 inches. Rodrigues wore a special pointed cap to hide it. This case was by no means unique. Sir W. J. Erasmus Wilson, a nineteenth-century English dermatologist, recorded ninety cases of human horns—forty-four females and forty-six males. Of these ninety cases, the majority of the horns were situated on the head. A few, however, grew from the face (several on the nose), some from the thighs, back, and foot, and one from the penis.

*Francis Trovillou, who, like Paul Rodrigues, had a horn growing from his forehead.*

---

Richeborg, a dwarf who was raised as a servant of the Orléans family in eighteenth-century France and who stood 23 inches high at maturity, was employed by the aristocracy as a secret agent during the French Revolution. Disguised as an infant and wrapped in swaddling clothes, Richeborg was taken in and out of Paris in the arms of his "nurse," all the while carrying crucial secret dispatches. Richeborg died in Paris at slightly less than a hundred years of age.

---

*At 8 feet 8 inches tall, Thomas Bell, "the Cambridge giant," was only 3 inches shorter than the tallest man in history.*

William Evans, a giant in the retinue of Charles I of England who was reputed to have been over 8 feet tall, carried a dwarf in his pocket whenever he came to court. The combination of giant and dwarf, it is recorded, amused the king.

---

The tallest man ever known was an American named Robert Wadlow. Born in Alton, Illinois, in 1918, Wadlow was 6 feet tall by the time he was eight years old, and at fifteen he was 7 feet 5 inches. He reached a final height of 8 feet 11 inches (and a weight of 491 pounds) on his twenty-first birthday. Alton died the following year of an inflamed leg (caused by improperly fitted leg braces) and was buried in a coffin that measured slightly under 11 feet. Gigantism, the disorder Wadlow suffered from, does not, interestingly enough, attack the entire body. Usually it involves only the lower extremities, so that in most cases the head and trunk are of more or less normal size while the lower torso and legs attain extreme proportions.

---

Josephine Clofullia, the most famous bearded lady of all time and a prominent attraction in P. T. Barnum's side show in the nineteenth century, had a beard 6 inches long when she was only sixteen. Josephine was an ardent admirer of the French monarch Napoleon III, and she styled her beard after his. So sincerely flattered was the ruler when he learned of this imitation that he sent Madame Clofullia a large diamond, which she wore, appropriately, in her beard.

## Injuries and Accidents

The American Speech and Hearing Association estimates that more than 40 million Americans are daily exposed to dangerously loud noises, not all of which are machine-made. For instance, the screaming of a baby has a higher decibel level (90 dB) and hence is more damaging to the delicate inner ear than an alarm clock (80 dB), a vacuum cleaner (70 dB), or heavy traffic (75 dB). Permanent hearing impairment, studies say, begins with sound levels of about 85 decibels. Thus prolonged exposure to the sound of a jackhammer (100 dB), a power mower (105 dB), an auto horn (120 dB), live rock music (130 dB), or a jet engine (140 dB) can cause irreparable damage to one's hearing.

---

Three million people in the United States have an impairment of the back or limbs that is the direct result of an accidental fall.

*Woman taking a spill at the dinner table. Millions of Americans are injured each year in accidental falls.*

---

According to the National Electronic Injury Surveillance System, 125,312 people were injured in 1977 while in or around a bed. These injuries resulted from such mishaps as tripping over the bed, hurting oneself on the headboard, or simply falling out of bed.

---

A survey conducted by the New York League for the Hard of Hearing determined that 50 percent of disco disc jockeys have suffered hearing damage. Of these, 33 percent have become partially deaf.

---

In 1975, 27,522 people were injured in skateboard accidents in the United States. Between 1974 and 1975, skateboarding moved from eighth to third on the list of the most dangerous sports in America.

*A skateboarder displays his proficiency at what is now the third most dangerous sport in America.*

---

According to the British Royal Society for the Prevention of Accidents, women are two and a half times more likely to have an automobile accident when they are menstruating. According to researchers, reflex and sensory alertness are impaired during the monthly period, and spatial judgment may be altered.

---

In the nineteenth century, flypaper, hat linings, playing cards, paper collars, Christmas-tree candles, wallpaper dyes, and wreaths of artificial flowers all contained lethal amounts of arsenic and all caused countless cases of accidental poisoning.

---

In November, 1972, a student skydiver named Bob Hail jumped from his plane and quickly discovered that neither his regular parachute nor his backup chute had opened. He dropped 3,300 feet at a rate of 80 miles per hour and landed on his face. "I screamed," Hail recalled later. "I knew I was dead and that my life was ended right then. There was nothing I could do.'' A few moments after landing, however, he got up and walked away with nothing worse than a broken nose and some missing teeth. No one has been able to explain how he escaped unhurt.

---

Unquestionably the most notable head injury of all time was sustained by a man named Phineas P. Gage, known in medical history as the ''American Crowbar Case.'' Gage, a twenty-five-year-old foreman on the Rutland and Burlington Railroad, was preparing a blast of dynamite on September 13, 1847, when the blast went off prematurely, driving a 3-foot-long, 13-pound tamping iron completely through the left side of his face. Passing along the left anterior lobe of Gage's cerebrum and out the back of his head, the bar smashed most of his brain. Though knocked backward by the blast and obviously shaken up, Gage remained conscious after the accident and stayed wide awake while his wound was dressed and doctors examined him. For a short time delirium set in and he lost the sight in his left eye. But shortly after that Gage became rational again and was back at work within several months. He lived for some years after the incident and was studied by innumerable doctors, who could make nothing of the case. After Gage died, the iron bar, along with a cast of the patient's head, was placed in the museum of the Massachusetts Medical College.

---

In 1972 physicians at the Walter Reed Army Medical Center estimated that of the more than 500,000 men who were receiving military combat training, more than half would sustain permanent hearing loss due to the noise of the weaponry.

## Insects, Spiders, and Other Invertebrates

Many insects hear with their hair. A number of insects, such as the male mosquito, have thousands of tiny hairs growing along their antennae. When a sound is sent out, these hairs vibrate, and the vibration is sent to the insect's central nervous system, where it is translated into sound perceptions. Thus, in a sense, the cockroach, whose sound-receiving hairs are located on its abdomen, ''hears'' with its belly. The caterpillar, covered with hairs, has ''ears'' over its entire body.

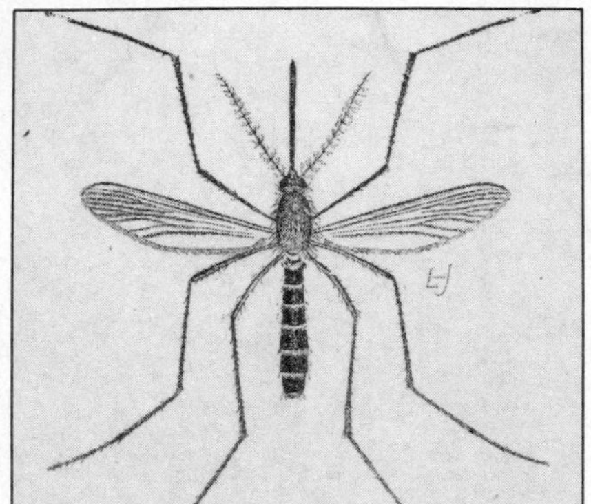

The mosquito, the world's hardiest insect.

The hardiest of all the world's insects is the mosquito. It has been found in the coldest regions of northern Canada and Siberia and can live quite comfortably at the North Pole. It is equally at home in equatorial jungles.

The buzzing of flies and bees is not produced by any sound-producing apparatus within the insects' bodies. It is simply the sound of their wings moving up and down and back and forth at a rapid rate.

There are more insects in one square mile of rural land than there are human beings on the entire earth.

A flea is capable of jumping 13 inches in a single leap. In human terms, this would be equivalent to a person leaping 700 feet in one bound.

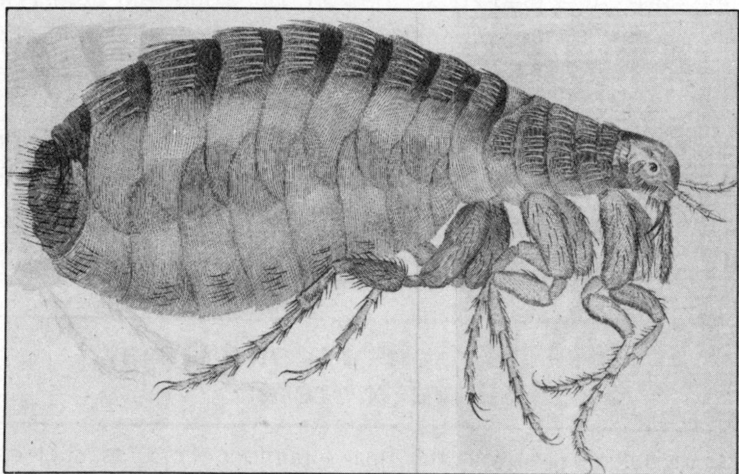

The tiny flea, a prodigious jumper.

Moths and butterflies pollinate flowers in the same manner as bees—they move from plant to plant carrying pollen on their hairy feet and promote cross-fertilization just as effectively as bees.

*Two meadow brown butterflies pollinating heath flowers.*

A mature, well-established termite colony with as many as 60,000 members will eat only about one-fifth of an ounce of wood a day.

There are endangered insect species, just as there are endangered mammals, birds, and fishes. According to the U.S. Office of Endangered Species, there are twenty-six species of insects that have already become extinct, and six species of California butterflies (the San Bruno elfin, lotus blue, mission blue, Smith's blue, El Segundo blue, and Lange's metalmark) are on the endangered list.

Scientists discover approximately 7,000 to 10,000 new insect species every year—and they believe that there are between 1 million and 10 million species as yet unfound.

There are approximately 1 million species of animals on the earth. Of these, approximately 800,000 are insects. If the name of every species of insect were printed in an average-size book, it would take about 6,000 pages to list them all.

Insects can perceive a range of light far greater than that discernible by man. Most insects, for instance, can see ultraviolet

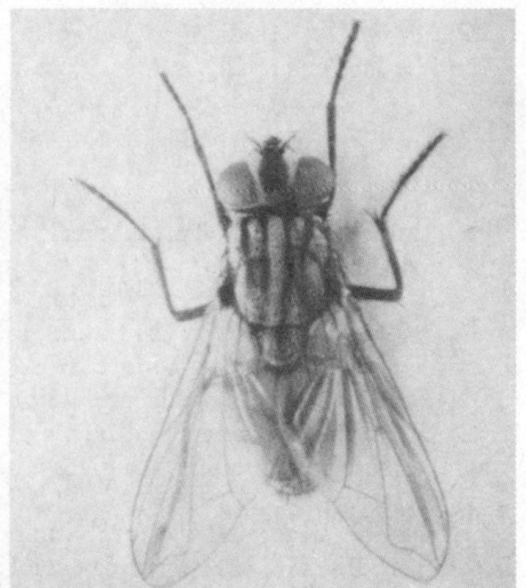

The house fly,
a notorious germ carrier.

light, and many varieties of beetles can see infrared. Insects are unable to focus their eyes, however, and can discern objects clearly only from several inches away. Most insects' eyes are made up of tiny six-sided lenses, and sometimes (in the dragonfly, for instance) as many as 30,000 of these lenses cover the retina. This means that insects do not perceive a single image, as humans do, but see a staggering number of separate images that, when combined, would appear to us as a colossal mosaic. Insects, furthermore, have no eyelids. Their eyes are always open.

---

A housefly can transport germs as far as 15 miles away from the original source of contamination.

---

A mosquito's wings move at the rate of 1,000 times a second.

---

Assuming that all the offspring survived, 190,000,000,000,000,000,000 flies could be produced in four months by the offspring of a single pair of flies.

---

A spider is not an insect. It is an arachnid—which means that it has eight legs instead of the insect's six, and has no wings or antennae. The same is true of the daddy longlegs, scorpion's mite, and tick—none is technically part of the insect class.

These thorn spiders, like all spiders, are arachnids, not insects.

---

There is no sure way to tell a moth from a butterfly. Though there are differences of physiology and habit between them, it is almost impossible to isolate a single differentiating characteristic that applies uniformly to both species.

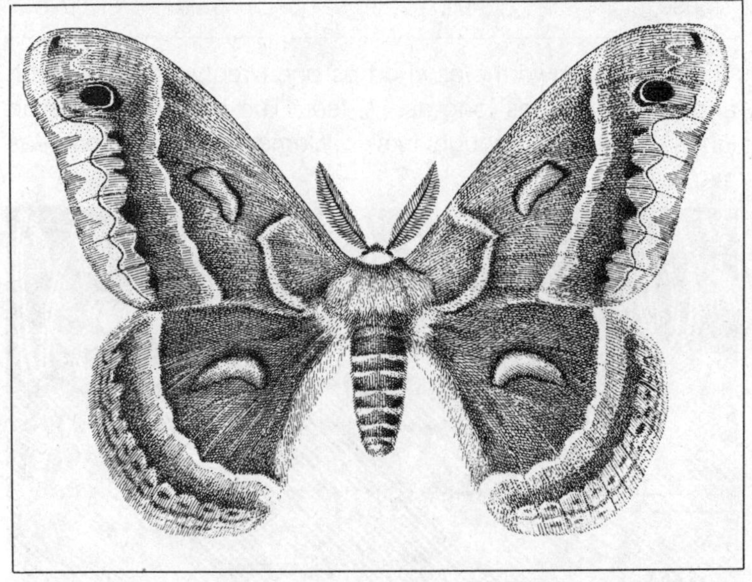

*The cecropia moth, like most moths, is nearly indistinguishable in many ways from a butterfly.*

The skeleton of an insect grows *outside* its body. This so-called exoskeleton is made of a fiberlike material called chitin, which is lighter and far more flexible than bone. The exoskeleton, however, does not grow as the insect grows, and as a result many insects shed their outer covering and grow an entirely new skeleton several times before they reach full maturity.

Bees create their own air conditioning. When the weather becomes especially hot and the temperature inside the hive threatens to melt the wax, one group of bees stations itself at the entrance to the colony while another remains inside. Both groups then flap their wings simultaneously, sometimes at a rate of 400 flaps per second. Thus they create a cross-draft that pulls the hot air out of the hive and draws cooler air in.

There really *are* such things as "cooties." Though most people believe that "cooties" is just a nonsense word used by children to describe unpleasant insects, cooties are in fact a kind of body lice. The word is from the Malay *kutu*, meaning "louse."

There are earthworms as short as one-twenty-fifth of an inch and earthworms as long as 11 feet. The earthworm has no lungs; it breathes through its skin. Some earthworms have as many as ten hearts.

*As this fanciful woodcut suggests, earthworms can be quite short or very long.*

A queen bee uses her stinger *only* to sting another queen bee. She never uses it on workers, drones, or people. The queen's stinger, moreover, is smooth and saber-shaped, not barbed, as other bees' stingers are. Thus she, unlike all other bees, can sting repeatedly without hurting herself.

Mosquitos do not bite. They stab. A mosquito has no jaws; when attacking a victim it pierces it with its long proboscis and sucks the blood up through a nasal tube. At one "sitting" a mosquito can absorb one and a half times its own weight in blood.

Many species of butterflies, like birds, fly south for the winter.

Migrating butterflies at Long Beach, N.Y.

Moths—at least in the form we know them—are not responsible for damaging woollen clothing. Our wearables are attacked only by moths in the larval stage, and then only by one family of moths, the Tineidae.

The tiny houseflies so often encountered are not, contrary to popular belief, "baby flies." Baby flies are maggots. The small houseflies are adults of a different species from the ordinary housefly.

The monarch butterfly can discern tastes 12,000 times more subtle than those perceivable by human taste buds.

The Nephila spider of India spins its webs with strands that are more than 20 feet long.

Spiders have transparent blood.

Spiders do not eat their victims, they *drink* them. Able to take food only by sipping it in liquid form through their tubelike mouths, spiders first cover their victims with a special fluid that causes them to dissolve. They then suck up the dissolved tissue. It is by this means that a tarantula is able to ingest an entire small mouse, bones and all, in about a day and a half.

*Giant spider feeding on a hummingbird.*

Most varieties of spiders have eight eyes. These are arranged on top and near the front of the head, usually in two rows of four each.

The American lobster can move through the water at a rate of 25 feet a second.

*The American lobster*, Homarus americanus.

The giant African snail *Achatina achatina* grows to a foot long and reaches weights greater than a pound.

Mother-of-pearl is not always white. It can be pink, blue, purple, gray, or even green. Nor is it produced only by the pearl oyster. The abalone and the pearl mussel both have shells that are lined with fine-quality mother-of-pearl.

## Inventions

In July, 1950, a patent was issued for an automatic spaghetti-spinning fork.

According to U.S. Patent Office records, Thomas Jefferson was the inventor of the first hideaway bed ever patented in the United States. Though the original plans for the bed have disappeared, we know from contemporary descriptions that when the bed was not in use it was hoisted to the ceiling and secured by a complicated system of pulleys and ropes.

---

Thomas Alva Edison invented the following:

1. Wax paper.
2. The mimeograph machine.
3. The carbon telephone transmitter.
4. The phonograph.
5. The electric light.
6. The magnetic ore separator.
7. The radio vacuum tube.
8. The motion-picture camera.
9. The dictating machine.
10. A variety of Portland cement.
11. An electric vote recorder.
12. The duplex and automatic telegraph machine.
13. A new kind of storage battery.
14. An ore-crushing machine.
15. The phonograph record.
16. The chemical phenol.
17. An electric pen.
18. The three-wire electrical wiring system.
19. Underground electric mains.
20. An electric railway car.
21. A version of the stock ticker.
22. An electric railroad signal.
23. The light socket and light switch.
24. A method for making synthetic rubber from goldenrod plants.
25. A machine that, in his words, was "so sensitive that if there is life after death, it will pick up the evidence."

*Thomas Edison in his laboratory.*

---

On June 22, 1882, the U.S. Patent Office granted a patent for a propeller-driven rocking chair. The chair had a large propeller-shaped fan mounted at its head, and as it rocked, the propeller turned, eventually moving the chair on its own power. It was a perpetual-motion machine and an air conditioner in one.

---

Charles Goodyear.

The bowie knife, the knife with a guard between the long, heavy blade and the handle to protect the user, though associated with and credited to the famous defender of the Alamo, James Bowie, was actually invented by his lesser-known brother, Rezin Pleasant Bowie. James was more adept at using the knife, carried it everywhere, and soon became identified with it.

Charles Goodyear (1800–1860), the man who developed vulcanized rubber and the first to produce it commercially, began his experiments in prison. In jail for debt, Goodyear started tests in his prison cell in 1834. After his release several years later, he hit upon vulcanization quite by accident when he dropped some rubber mixed with sulfur on a stove and noted that it did not dissolve.

## Language

A surprising number of English words pertaining to the nose—its function, its appearance, and its social connotations—begin with the letters *sn*. Some of these words are: snarl, sneer, sneeze, snicker, sniff, snipe (a long-billed bird), snivel, snob (one who turns up his nose), snoop (to stick one's nose into another's affairs), snoot, snore, snooty, snort, snot, snout, snub, snuff, and snuffle.

The word ''horse'' in horseradish has no relationship to the animal of the same name. It is used to mean ''coarse'' or ''rough,'' as in the terms ''horse mackerel'' and ''horse bean.''

In the early nineteenth century the words ''trousers'' and ''pants'' were considered obscene in England. Women referred to trousers as ''inexpressibles'' or ''a pair of dittoes.'' Later in the century the taboo was carried to such lengths that piano legs were covered lest they remind one of their human counterparts. In 1836 Charles Dickens wrote the following lines in *Oliver Twist:*

" 'I tossed off the clothes, got safely in bed, drew on a pair of ———' "

" 'Ladies present, Mr. Giles,' murmured the tinker.

" '——— of shoes, Sir,' said Mr. Giles, laying great emphasis on the word."

---

The term "doubleheader," meaning two baseball games played back to back, comes from railroad terminology. When two engines in the switching yard were hooked up back to back on a single train, the train was called a "two-header," or, more commonly, a "doubleheader."

---

The following words were all invented by Americans in the past 125 years: *apartment house, appendicitis, barroom, blizzard, bloomers, cocktail, coeducation, electrocute, filibuster, gangster, hydrant, moron, mortician, nickelodeon, realtor, saloon*, and *telegram*. The following words are all twentieth-century creations: *beautician, bromide, buildup, dust bowl, highbrow, sundae, superhighway*, and the verbs *to audition, to package*, and *to vacation*. The following terms have become part of American usage since 1945: *balding, baby sit, cutback, free-wheeling, genocide, giveaway, name calling, rat race, soap opera, spot check, stateside, tape recording*, and *top secret*.

---

The following terms were coined during the administration of Franklin Delano Roosevelt: *bottleneck, brain trust, coordinator, court-packing, directive, economic royalist, good-neighbor policy*, and *to process*.

---

*Glamorize, sanitize, motorize, vitalize, finalize, personalize, tenderize, customize*, and *comfortize* are all words invented by advertising agencies in the twentieth century.

---

According to many language experts, the most difficult kind of phrase to create is a palindrome, a sentence or group of sentences that reads the same backward and forward. A few examples:

Red rum, sir, is murder.
Ma is as selfless as I am.
Nurse, I spy gypsies. Run!
A man, a plan, a canal—Panama.
Mirth, sir, a gay asset? No, don't essay a garish trim.
He lived as a devil, eh?

---

The word ''sabotage'' is derived from a French word for ''shoe.'' In France, a *sabot* is a kind of heavy boot or shoe worn by workmen. During the Industrial Revolution, when machine-driven mills were first introduced in France, workers displaced from their jobs by these automata would throw their shoes into the gear mechanisms, wrecking the engines and thus *sabot*aging the business.

---

The term ''disc jockey'' was coined by *Variety* in 1937 to describe radio announcers who stayed up all night ''riding'' discs, or records.

---

The word ''fiasco,'' meaning a failure, is derived from the ancient Italian art of glass blowing. If a Venetian glass blower made a mistake while creating a fine, delicate bottle, the ruined vessel was turned into an ordinary drinking flask, which is known in Italian as a *fiasco.*

---

''Xmas,'' used instead of the word ''Christmas,'' is not a modern abbreviation. It originated with early Greek Christians in the second and third centuries A.D. In Greek, the letter *chi,* which is printed as an X, is the first letter of Christ's name. The X itself was often used as a sacred symbol because it resembled the Holy Cross, and many large X's can still be seen on the walls of Roman catacombs, where they were drawn as symbols of Christ and the Crucifixion.

---

The mathematical term ''googol,'' which stands for the number 1 followed by 100 zeros ($10^{100}$), was invented by a nine-year-old boy, the nephew of the mathematician Edward Kasner. One day Kasner heard his nephew use the term humorously and told his colleagues about it. Soon afterward the phrase was adopted throughout mathematical circles.

---

Salt, the most widely used seasoning in the world, was given as monthly wages to Roman legionnaires. It was called ''salt money,'' or *salarium,* and it is from this word that our word ''salary'' comes.

---

Punctuation did not come into use until the advent of printing in the fifteenth century. Before that, words written by scribes were runtogetherlikethis.

*Portion of a 6th-century manuscript of Vergil's* Aeneid. *Note the absence of spaces between words.*

---

The word ''fan,'' meaning an admirer or a devotee, is short for the word ''fanatic.''

---

The letters R.S.V.P. are an abbreviation for the French *répondez s'il vous plait* (''please respond''). They do not stand for ''respond very promptly,'' as is often supposed.

---

The term ''O.K.'' is believed by some etymologists to be derived from a Choctaw Indian word, *okeh,* which means ''it is so.'' President Woodrow Wilson was so convinced that this term was of Indian origin that he always wrote the word in its original form. The more common etymology of this word explains it as having originated in 1840, when the Democratic party's political club was known as the O.K. Club. (The word *okeh*, incidentally, was at one time used as a trade name by a manufacturer of phonograph records.)

---

The word "bury," used as part of the name of a town—as in Danbury or Middlebury—is taken from Old English and means "a place that is heavily fortified and protected; a fortress."

---

Do the Americans and the British speak the same language? Perhaps. But one might not know it from the hundreds of differences in the words we use for the same common things. Here are a few examples:

| ***American*** | ***British*** |
|---|---|
| Apartment | Flat |
| Automobile | Motorcar |
| Checkers | Draughts |
| Elevator | Lift |
| French-fried potatoes | Chips |
| Garbage man | Dustman |
| Garters | Suspenders |
| Gasoline | Petrol |
| Gearshift | Gear lever |
| Hood (of a car) | Bonnet |
| Kerosene | Paraffin |
| Lawyer | Solicitor |
| Molasses | Treacle |
| Newsstand | Kiosk |
| Phone booth | Call box |
| Potato chips | Crisps |
| Suspenders | Braces |
| Thumbtack | Drawing pin |
| Trunk (of a car) | Boot |
| Windshield | Windscreen |

---

Of the 1,500 languages in use in the world, only 30 are spoken by more than 10 million people.

---

Some unusual words and their meanings:

- ***acersecomic***—one whose hair has been cut.
- ***colporteur***—one who sells Bibles and religious tracts.
- ***genethliac***—pertaining to birthdays.
- ***hecatomb***—a great slaughter.
- ***hoful***—cautious.
- ***kill-priest***—a strong drink.
- ***lip-clap***—kissing.
- ***macaronic***—jumbled, mixed up.
- ***periapt***—a charm or amulet.
- ***quacksalver***—a charlatan, especially a fraudulent doctor.
- ***quean***—a loose, disreputable woman.
- ***sternutation***—the act of sneezing.
- ***stoopgalant***—that which humbles the mighty.
- ***vaticide***—the murder or murderer of a prophet.

The word "mandarin," used both to describe a major dialect of the Chinese language and the former ruling class of China, is not a Chinese word. "Mandarin" was originally a corruption of a Hindi word, *mantri*, which means "counselor" or "minister of state."

*Three 19th-century mandarins. Though the people were Chinese, the name they were known by was not.*

It is estimated that of the 450,000 words now in general use in the English language, only about 250,000 would be understood by William Shakespeare. It is also estimated that of the 200,000 words that have been added to our language since Shakespeare's time, about half have come into use during the past fifty years.

One out of every eight letters used in written English is an *e*.

## Laws

Private automobiles were forbidden on the island of Bermuda until 1948. This is one reason that there are still so many bicycles there.

Impotence is grounds for divorce in twenty-four states in the United States.

It is illegal to own a dog in Reykjavik, Iceland.

Legally, two automobiles do not have to come into direct contact for their drivers to be involved in a traffic accident. According to the National Committee on Uniform Traffic Laws and Ordinances, if a driver contributes *in any way* to a crash, he or she is legally involved.

A wedding ring is exempt by law from inclusion among the assets in a bankruptcy estate. This means that a wedding ring cannot be seized by creditors, no matter how much the bankrupt person owes.

In Idaho a citizen is forbidden by law to give another citizen a box of candy that weighs more than 50 pounds.

In New York State it is illegal to shoot at a rabbit from a moving trolley car.

According to law in the state of Arkansas, "No person shall be permitted, under any pretext whatever, to come nearer than fifty feet of any door or window of any polling room, from the opening of the polls until the completion of the count and the certification of the counted returns."

Until 1834, it was forbidden for any soldier or military unit of the U.S. Army to carry the American flag into battle. In 1834 the privilege was awarded to American artillery units only. The Marine Corps could not carry the flag until late in 1876, the cavalry in 1887. Before these dates only regimental colors were taken to war.

*Union soldiers carrying the flag into battle at Fredericksburg, 1862, lithograph by Currier & Ives.*

According to the Recruitment Code of the U.S. Navy, anyone "bearing an obscene and indecent" tattoo will be rejected.

In Alaska it is illegal to look at a moose from the window of an airplane or any other flying vehicle.

Every citizen of Kentucky is required by law to take a bath once a year.

In 1970 an Arizona lawyer named Russel H. Tansie filed a $100,000 damage suit against God. The suit was filed on behalf of Mr. Tansie's secretary, Betty Penrose, who accused God of negligence in His power over the weather when He allowed a lightning bolt to strike her home. Ms. Penrose won the case when the defendant failed to appear in court. Whether or not she collected has not been recorded.

A Venetian law decrees that all gondolas must be painted black. The only exceptions are gondolas belonging to high public officials.

*Gondolas on the Grand Canal, Venice.*

The following means of making a living are, according to New York City statutes, illegal: the skinning of horses or cows, the burning of offal, the growing of ragweed, and the burning of bones.

In San Salvador drunk drivers are punished by death before a firing squad.

It was illegal for women to wear buttons in fifteenth-century Florence.

Women were not allowed to vote in France until 1944.

In 1976 Cecilia M. Pizzo filed a lawsuit against the U.S. government to nullify the Louisiana Purchase. This monumental land acquisition, which was made in 1803 by Thomas Jefferson and which included a good portion of the southern and central United States, was, according to Ms. Pizzo, both unconstitutional and an illegal seizure of her family's original landholdings. A New Orleans federal judge ruled that Ms. Pizzo had filed her case 167 years too late. The six-year statute of limitations on such suits, the judge ruled, had run out.

Before enactment of the 1978 law that made it mandatory for dog owners in New York City to clean up after their pets, approximately 40 million pounds of dog excrement were deposited on the streets every year.

## Literature

Arthur Jean Nicolas Rimbaud (1854–1891), the great French Symbolist poet, wrote almost all his notable poetry between the ages of fifteen and twenty. In 1879, after having spent his adolescence and young adulthood in wandering, scandal, and debauchery, Rimbaud suddenly repudiated his art, traveled to the Middle East, set up a business in Ethiopia, and spent the rest of his life as a merchant. He never wrote another poem.

*Arthur Rimbaud, painting by Emlen Etting.*

Emily Dickinson (1830–1886), America's most famous woman poet, published only seven poems during her lifetime. All of these, moreover, were published anonymously and often against her will. Dickinson, a recluse most of her life after an unfortunate early love affair with a married minister, wrote her poetry in absolute secrecy and rarely shared her work even with her family. It was only after her death that volumes of her writings were discovered, and it was not until 1890, four years after she died, that the first collection of her work was published.

---

In the seventeenth century it was the vogue among some English poets to write poems in the shape of ships, hourglasses, crosses, flowers, human beings, stars, and other objects. When a couple was married their respective families often hired a poet to write a wedding poem in the shape of an altar; to commemorate a death a funeral poem might be written in the shape of a skull. The following poem, "The Pillar of Fame," by the English poet Robert Herrick, is a representative example:

**Fame's pillar here at last we set,**
**Out-during marble, brass, or jet;**
**Charmed and enchanted so**
**As to withstand the blow**
**Of overthrow**
**Nor shall the seas**
**Or outrages**
**Of storms, o'erbear**
**What we uprear**
**Tho' kingdoms fall**
**This pillar never shall**
**Decline or waste at all**
**But stand for ever by his own**
**Firm and well-fixed foundation.**

---

The nursery rhyme "Old King Cole" is based on a real king and a real historical event. King Cole is supposed to have been an actual monarch of Britain who ruled around 200 A.D. (According to legend, he was one of the most popular kings of his time.) The king was especially famous for his love of music—hence the line "he called for his fiddlers three." Another actual personage from nursery rhymes is Jack Horner. According to history, a man named Jack Horner was sent by the bishop of Glastonbury to King Henry VIII of England with the title deeds to three large private estates. The deeds were extremely valuable, so Horner transported them hidden in a large Christmas pie. Supposedly he opened the pie along the way and helped himself to one of the deeds, thus pulling out a ''plum.'' Still another bit of nursery-rhyme history comes from the court of Queen Elizabeth I. The queen is said to have teased her courtiers, much the way a cat teases a mouse. She herself was very fond of dancing to the tune of a fiddle. One of her courtiers was nicknamed ''Moon'' and another ''Dog.'' Moreover, Elizabeth had a lady-in-waiting known as ''Spoon.'' One day, we are told, a gentleman of the court known as ''Dish'' eloped with Mistress Spoon, inspiring the following:

Hey diddle, diddle,
The cat and the fiddle,
The cow jumped over the moon.
The little dog laughed to see such sport,
And the dish ran away with the spoon.

*Old King Cole,*
*thought to be a beloved early*
*English monarch.*

The brothers Grimm (Jacob and Wilhelm), collectors of the famous *Grimm's Fairy Tales*, were not storytellers, nor were they simple lovers of fairy tales. The Grimms were language scholars, the greatest of their time by most accounts, and the stories were collected and codified in the early nineteenth century as an exercise in comparative German philology and grammar.

*Illustration by Gustave Doré from "Little Red Ridinghood," one of the fairy tales collected by Jacob and Wilhelm Grimm.*

---

In downtown Lima, Peru, there is a large brass statue dedicated to Winnie-the-Pooh.

---

Though it is not widely known, the Italian painter Michelangelo (1475–1564) was considered by his contemporaries to be one of the greatest poets of all time. About 250 of his poems and sonnets have come down to us today and are still read by scholars, historians, and poets.

---

Part of Lewis Carroll's classic *Through the Looking Glass* was omitted from the original publication and was only made known to the general public after 107 years of obscurity. The section, which featured a giant wasp wearing a wig, was left out because Carroll's illustrator, John Tenniel, refused to illustrate it. "A wasp in a wig," said Tenniel, "is altogether beyond the appliances of art."

---

For several decades the well-known Belgian mystery writer Georges Simenon wrote, on the average, one novel every eleven days. Besides the more than 230 novels he penned under his own name, Simenon wrote 300 other books under a pseudonym.

---

## Magic and the Occult

---

The magician's word "abracadabra" is actually an ancient sorcerers' spell that historians have traced to early medieval times. The English writer Daniel Defoe related that in London during the Black Plague, amulets with the following inscription were worn to keep away the disease:

A B R A C A D A B R A
A B R A C A D A B R
A B R A C A D A B
A B R A C A D A
A B R A C A D
A B R A C A
A B R A C
A B R A
A B R
A B
A

---

Nearly two-thirds of the college and university teachers questioned on the subject of the occult said they believed that the existence of extrasensory perception was an established fact or a likely possibility.

---

In parts of Japan, if a black cat crosses one's path, it is considered a sign of *good* luck.

---

The magician's stock word "hocus-pocus" is taken from the name of a mythological sorcerer, Ochus Bochus, who appears in Norse folktales and legends.

## Manners and Customs

Tibetans, Mongolians, and people in parts of western China put salt in their tea instead of sugar.

In most parts of the Middle East, men and women clean themselves after toilet by splashing water onto their privates with their left hand. This is why it is considered the basest act conceivable in the Middle East to take food or drink with the left hand.

Among the Chippewa Indians, when a woman was menstruating she was banished to a hut of branches outside the camp and made to wear a long hood during the time she was "unclean." Furthermore, it was believed that any object touched by a menstruating woman was defiled and would bring misfortune or even death to anyone who used it. Therefore she was not allowed to touch any of her household furniture or to come in contact with any objects used by men. She was forbidden to use the common trails or walk on the ice of rivers or lakes, to come near any area where men were hunting or fishing, or even to converse with her own children. She was permitted to drink only out of a swan's bone. Any woman who broke these taboos was severely punished.

During the Middle Ages in England and France there was a custom among nobles, kings, and peasants known as the *droit du seigneur*. When any of the subjects of a great lord married (be he the noble of a king or the peasant of a noble), the lord himself had the privilege of deflowering the bride. Although in the later Middle Ages this right was rarely exploited, it was a common part of the marriage ritual in earlier days. The practice, however, was not as prurient as it sounds to us today. During the Middle Ages, loyalty and complete obedience to one's lord was the single most important element of the feudal system—and there was no greater sign of this loyalty than the offering of one's bride.

---

During the French Revolution, snuffboxes made of lead stripped from the roof of the Bastille were sold throughout Paris, and ownership of such a box was a sign of great prestige. These boxes usually displayed pictures of the guillotine, and often depicted scenes of bloody decapitations.

---

Tablecloths were originally meant to serve as towels with which guests could wipe their hands and faces after dinner.

*Man with a tablecloth draped over his lap does not have bad manners. Tablecloths originally served the same function as napkins do today.*

---

In the mountainous districts of northeastern Burma, a peculiar form of hospitality known as *perah* was practiced until the mid-twentieth century. Whenever an enemy was killed in battle, the blood was drained from his body, poured into a special bamboo reed, and set out in the open air to dry. When the victorious warrior wanted to treat friends and visitors to a great delicacy, he cracked open these reeds and allowed them to dine on the congealed blood.

---

In the eighteenth century, patients in the insane asylum of the Hospital of St. Mary of Bethlehem in London were placed in cages and exhibited to curious onlookers like animals at a zoo. A popular afternoon's entertainment consisted of visiting the inmates of this institution and taunting them with sticks, rocks, and burning missiles. It is from the name of this asylum, commonly called "Bethlehem," that the word "bedlam" is derived.

*Inmates of the asylum at London's Hospital of St. Mary of Bethlehem, whose name gave us the word "bedlam."*

---

In the early nineteenth century, many members of Congress came to sessions wearing knives in their belts. A popular poem about Henry Clay's reaction to the knife-wielding habits of one such congressman, a Mr. Slick, appeared in several newspapers of the time:

> "Young man," quoth Clay, "avoid the way of Slick of
> Tennessee,

Of gougers fierce, the eyes that pierce, the fiercest gouger he:
He chews and spits as there he sits, and whittles at the chairs,
And in his hand, for deadly strife, a bowie-knife he bears."

---

From ancient times until the nineteenth century in China, long fingernails were considered a mark of great beauty and, for members of the scholar-ruling class, a symbol of distinction indicating that they never worked with their hands. To protect their nails—which were sometimes more than 2 inches long—from cracking, both men and women attached special silver or gold covers to them. They wore these protective shields even when they slept.

*A Chinese aristocrat with well-cultivated long fingernails, 1889.*

---

During the Civil War undertakers were addressed as "Doctor."

---

During an annual ceremony in Morocco known as the Great Feast, it was the custom for a man to wrap himself in the bloody skins of a sacrificed sheep and run through the crowd of celebrators, whipping everyone within reach with a flap of the skin or a foot of the sheep. To be struck by this hide was considered enormously auspicious: a person struck on the head, it was believed, would have no headaches in the coming year; if one was struck on the stomach, indigestion and all forms of abdominal disorders would be prevented.

## Manufacturing and Technology

The character known as the Mad Hatter in Lewis Carroll's *Alice in Wonderland* and the phrase "mad as a hatter" are both based on a tragic episode in manufacturing history. In the eighteenth and nineteenth centuries, hatmakers used various chemicals in their work, among them mercury for curing felt. Mercury is a deadly poison, and the thousands of workers who handled this noxious substance developed pathological symptoms—including kidney damage, anemia, inflammation of the gums, as well as insanity—known today as "hatter's syndrome." It is estimated that at one time more than 10 percent of all the workers in hat factories ended their lives insane.

*The Mad Hatter, illustration by John Tenniel from Lewis Carroll's* Alice in Wonderland.

---

The United States uses 70 million tons of cement every year—approximately one-fifth of the cement used throughout the world annually.

---

The variety of aluminum used to manufacture airplane wings is capable of withstanding loads of more than 90,000 pounds per square inch. Aluminum can be spun into a filament so fine that 1½ pounds of it could encircle the earth.

---

More steel in the United States is used to make bottle caps than to manufacture automobile bodies.

---

The human race as we know it has existed for approximately 50,000 years. This makes it approximately 800 lifetimes old, assuming a lifetime to be from sixty-five to seventy years. Of these 800 lifetimes, about 650 were passed by cave dwellers. Nearly all the manufactured products, luxury items, and technological conveniences we enjoy today were invented or perfected within only the last five to seven lifetimes.

---

When sulfur matches were first manufactured, in the late nineteenth century, the workers who made them, usually young girls, licked the point of each match to make it stiff after dipping it in the requisite chemical solution. The solution contained radioactive zinc sulfide, which attacked the workers' teeth, jaws, and finally their entire bodies. No one knows how many thousands of young girls died of radioactive poisoning before they turned thirty.

*Young women working in a match factory in 19th-century London.*

---

It took Henry Ford's Motor Company seven years to manufacture 1 million automobiles. One hundred thirty-two working days after this figure was reached (in 1924), the company had made 9 million more cars.

---

The first manufactured item ever exported from the United States was tar. It was sent from Jamestown, Virginia, to the colony's sponsors in England in 1608. There is some evidence that a cargo of sassafras had been sent previously from Cape Cod, but this was a natural substance and not commercially produced.

---

It is estimated that a plastic container can resist decomposition for as long as 50,000 years.

---

It has been estimated that if one cubic kilometer of a mineral-rich asteroid were brought to earth it would be worth about $5 trillion. Such an asteroid would provide the world with about two hundred years' supply of nickel and enough steel to run industries in every country for the next fifteen years, given the current rate of use.

## Marriage

In 1976 a Los Angeles secretary named Jannene Swift officially married a 50-pound rock. The ceremony was witnessed by more than twenty people.

---

In the marriage ceremony of the ancient Incas, the couple was considered officially wed when they took off their sandals and handed them to each other.

---

Each year approximately 250,000 American husbands are physically attacked and beaten by their wives.

---

The Roman emperor Nero married his male slave Scorus in a public ceremony.

*The emperor Nero.*

---

It is recorded in the genealogical tables of the book *Kentucky Marriages, 1797–1865* that one Moses Alexander, aged ninety-three, married a Mrs. Frances Tompkins, aged one hundred five, in the town of Bath, New York, on June 11, 1831. It is also recorded that the newlyweds were both found dead in their bed the following morning.

---

The Mormon leader Brigham Young had twenty-seven wives.

Brigham Young.

## Mathematics and Numbers

The Incas and certain other pre-Columbian tribes in Peru developed the decimal system hundreds of years before it was used in Europe.

At 12:34 on May 6, 1978, there was a peculiar lining up of dates and hours that will not happen again until the year 2078. On that day the numbers in the hour 12:34 were followed by the number sequence of the month, day, and year for May 6, 1978, which reads 5/6/78. The resulting sequence was 12345678.

The highest number recognized by orthodox mathematics is the centillion. This is a 1 followed by 600 zeros. Any number higher than a centillion is considered an unimaginable abstraction belonging to the realm of infinity. However, attempts have been made to define such abstractions. For example, a megiston is the number 10 raised to the six-billionth power. The googolplex is even higher—it is 10 raised to the googol power (a googol is a 1 followed by 100 zeros).

If you flip a coin ten times, the odds against its coming up with the same side showing each time are 1,023 to 1.

When the Spanish conquistadors entered Peru in the sixteenth century, they found historians of the Inca tribe who kept records of practically every aspect of life in the Incas' 3,000-mile kingdom—marriages, population, livestock accounts, deaths, births, amounts of grain harvested, and hundreds of other social and political data—on nothing more complex than a set of strings. These strings, known to the Indians as *quipu*, consisted of a main cord on which a number of smaller colored strings were arranged. Knots were tied at various in-

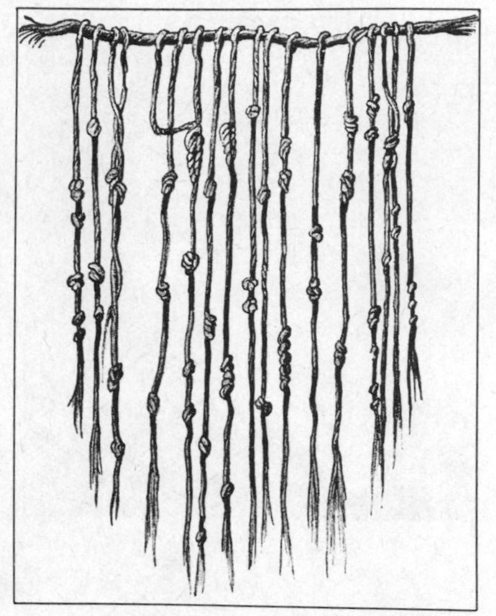

*An Inca* quipu.

tervals along the colored strings. The cords were strung, tied, and worked by specially trained men known as *quipu-camayoc,* who spent their entire lives doing nothing but studying new uses for these strings and recording every event that occurred in Inca society. When the Spanish historian Pedro de Cieza de Leon asked Inca priests about these strings in 1549, he was told that "knots counted from one to ten and ten to a hundred, and from a hundred to a thousand. Each ruler of a province was provided with accountants, and by these knots they kept account of what tribute was to be paid . . . and with such accuracy that not so much as a pair of sandals would be missing." With the coming of the Spanish to Peru the use of the *quipu* declined, and today there is not a person alive who remembers how they were really used.

## Medicine

According to acupuncturists, there is a point on the head that you can press to control your appetite. It is located in the hollow just in front of the flap of the ear.

The world's first artificial heart was made of Dacron. It was implanted into a patient by Dr. Denton Cooley in Houston, Texas, on April 4, 1969. Four days later it was rejected by the patient's body and the patient died.

The insulin used to treat diabetes in human beings is taken from pigs and sheep. The substance produced in these animals is exactly the same as that found in the human body and has precisely the same sugar-stabilizing effect.

Taliacotius, a sixteenth-century Italian surgeon, devised an operation for rebuilding damaged tissue in the human nose. The patient's arm was raised to the face and held there, the inner part of the arm against the open flesh of the nose, by means of a special apparatus or system of bandages. The arm was kept adhered to the nose for several weeks, at the end of which time the two were supposed to have grown together. The surgeon then cut the joint between arm and nose, leaving enough flesh for a new nose, and the apparatus was removed.

---

The ℞ sign used today on pharmaceutical prescriptions was originally an astrological sign for the planet Jupiter. The use of this sign originated in the Middle Ages, when doctors believed that the planets influenced health. Jupiter was thought to be the most powerful of all the heavenly bodies in curing disease.

---

In Nepal, cow dung is used for medicinal purposes. The Nepalese, believing that dung has antiseptic properties, often pack a woman's vagina with it after she has given birth. This practice is thought to be responsible for the high incidence of tetanus among new mothers in Nepal.

---

Forty percent of the American population has never visited a dentist.

*Much to his chagrin, this little boy will not be among the 40 percent of Americans who never see the dentist.*

---

The theory of immunization, and of smallpox immunization in

particular, was known to Chinese doctors more than seven hundred years before its discovery in 1796 by the English physician Edward Jenner. To immunize a child against smallpox, known euphemistically as "the budding of blossoms," a doctor took a pustule from a smallpox patient, pulverized it, and blew the powder into the child's nose through a specially molded tube. It was believed that since only the scabs were used, the mild case of smallpox caused by this "injection" would bestow natural immunity on the child without causing him to become too sick. Another method of immunization was to wrap a child in a robe smeared with pus taken from someone with a mild case of smallpox so that the child's skin would be permeated by the secretions. This technique was also practiced by doctors in medieval India.

---

A typical surgical skin graft is done with a slice of skin eight-thousandths of an inch thick.

---

In ancient China, doctors were forbidden in the name of propriety to see their female patients naked. To circumvent this prohibition, doctors on house calls brought with them a small ivory carving of a woman's naked body. This carving was passed into the curtained bedchamber of the ailing woman along with instructions on how to mark the troubled organs. The statue was then handed out through the curtains and the doctor made his diagnosis on the basis of the markings.

---

Dentists in medieval Japan extracted teeth by pulling them out with their fingers.

---

According to the Center for Health Administration, one out of every ten Americans spends one day a year in the hospital.

---

Runners in ancient Greece believed that the spleen was a hindrance to endurance and long-distance running. Consequently they had a vast pharmacopoeia of herbal concoctions especially designed to shrink this vital organ. One popular spleen-shrinker was a beverage made from a plant of the genus *Equisetum*. The drink was mixed with a variety of herbs and taken for three days before a race. According to contemporary witnesses, it proved enormously helpful in promoting endurance (whether it shrank the spleen we do not know). Hippocrates, the famous Greek physician, mentioned a certain mushroom that, when burned over the area of the spleen, melted the organ completely.

*Ancient Greek runners depicted on an Attic vase, 6th century B.C.*

---

In 1977, more abortions than tonsillectomies were performed in the United States.

## Money

As of 1978, the nation with the world's highest income per person was not the United States. Nor was it Switzerland, Germany, or even Saudi Arabia. It was Kuwait. Here the average income for every man, woman, and child is $15,480 per year. The per capita income of Switzerland, second on the list, is slightly more than half of Kuwait's. Sweden follows Switzerland, and the United States is fourth, with a per capita income of $7,890.

---

The cedi, syli, won, kip, kwa, ouguiya, tughrik, leu, lek, and lev are the basic currency units of Ghana, Guinea, North and South Korea, Laos, Papua-New Guinea, Mauritania, Mongolia, Romania, Albania, and Bulgaria.

---

Paper money developed in Europe in the following manner. During the Middle Ages it was customary for wealthy families to store their gold, jewels, and coins in vaults kept in the cellars of goldsmiths' shops. The goldsmiths gave written receipts for all valuables received, and these articles could be redeemed with the receipts at any time. Eventually the receipts themselves were being used as currency by those who didn't want to take the trouble to go to the vault every time they needed money, and businesses throughout Europe began accepting them as readily as gold. The practice gradually spread: paper money became a common form of legal tender, and its use contributed to the establishment of the banking system, which was in full swing by the sixteenth century.

---

It is not known whether the first printed items of all time were used as money or in games. These ancient bits of printing, paper slips produced by the Chinese sometime during the Tang dynasty (618–906), seem to have been used interchangeably as currency and as a variety of playing cards. To this day no one has been able to determine what their primary purpose really was.

---

The first paper money to appear in North America was printed on playing cards. In 1685 the French colonial government in Canada, suffering from a lack of francs, began issuing money printed on pasteboards from the standard playing deck of the time. These cards were signed by the colonial governor and were circulated throughout French Canada. Though this odd form of currency was intended to be used only until the money arrived from France, it was so popular among the colonists that it was kept in circulation for the next hundred years.

---

Until 1857, any foreign coins made of precious metal were legal tender in the United States.

---

Before 1933, the dime was legal as payment only in transactions of $10 or less. In that year Congress made the dime legal tender for all transactions.

---

The U.S. Treasury used to print a $100,000 bill. This bill displays a portrait of Woodrow Wilson and has the denomination boldly engraved in the corners, as all U.S. bills do. None of this exclusive currency, however, is in circulation. It is used only in transactions between the Federal Reserve System and the Treasury Department.

---

Approximately 90 billion pennies have been placed into circulation in the United States since the beginning of this century.

---

As of 1977, a pair of dungarees cost $50 in the Soviet Union.

---

Here is how to tell in which city a U.S. coin was minted. If the coin bears the letter D it was minted in Denver; if it is stamped with an S it was minted in San Francisco. A coin with no mint mark at all comes from Philadelphia.

---

Before the sixth century B.C. Chinese coins were cast in the shapes of miniature shells, spades, and knives. These objects had been the principal items of barter in China prior to the minting of coins.

*Ancient Chinese money in knife and spade shapes.*

---

If the current rate of inflation continues, a worker making $5.00 an hour in 1978 would, in the year 2077, make $4,799 an hour.

---

Based on typical earnings for each period, in 1900 a factory employee would have had to work 101½ hours to earn enough money to purchase an electric sewing machine; today he must labor only 22 hours to own the same product. The same worker would have had to put in a week of labor to earn the rail fare from Washington, D.C., to Atlanta; today he need toil only one and a half days. It took 53 minutes to earn the money needed to purchase a dozen eggs in 1900; now only 13 minutes are required.

---

According to the Bureau of Labor Statistics, the average American family in 1978 had to earn at least $17,106 a year to live moderately well. This amount allowed the woman of the house three new dresses every two years, the man two suits, and the couple nine movies a year.

---

In 1914, the first year income tax was collected, Americans paid an average per capita tax of forty-one cents, and only 1 percent of the population was obliged to pay taxes at all.

---

In 1977 Americans paid more than $227.5 billion in taxes, according to the U.S. Department of Commerce.

---

According to the U.S. Chamber of Commerce, if the total amount of yearly income tax one owed were withheld from weekly paychecks before a person could earn any take-home pay, the average taxpayer would not earn a cent of personal income until the middle of May. In other words, the average American taxpayer works almost three out of every eight hours for Uncle Sam.

---

As of 1977, a U.S. citizen with an annual income of $25,000 or less had one chance in fifty-six of having his annual tax return audited by the Internal Revenue Service.

---

Since 1971, any money lost through bribery has been tax deductible. According to the Internal Revenue Service's official taxpayers' guide, ''bribes and kickbacks to governmental officials are deductible unless the individual has been convicted of making the bribe or has entered a plea of guilty or *nolo contendere.''*

---

The oil used by jewelers to lubricate clocks and watches costs about $3,000 a gallon.

A 1977 study at Purdue University revealed that by the time a restaurant has purchased its quota of glasses and paid for breakage, washing, ice, serving machinery, and service, it costs the restaurant an average of twelve cents each time a customer is served a glass of water.

In 1973 New Yorkers spent $100 million buying flowers.

In 1978, according to the Office of Management and Budget, the U.S. federal budget reached the half-trillion-dollar mark. This means that the American government now spends almost $1 million a minute, every minute of the day, every day of the year. Each day the government spends $1.37 billion.

There are more female than male millionaires in the United States. According to *U.S. News and World Report*, 50.4 percent of all American millionaires are women, a phenomenon due both to women's increased earning capacity in recent years and to the fact that women tend to live longer than men and hence inherit their husbands' fortunes.

## Movies and Movie Stars

The Hollywood director D. W. Griffith made 450 motion pictures between 1908 and 1913.

*D. W. Griffith.*

The city of Hollywood was founded by a temperance society, which intended to establish it as a model community. Its founder was a man named Horace Wilcox, who acquired the land on which Hollywood now stands in 1888. He laid out an orchard at the foot of the Hollywood hills, built homes and churches, set aside areas for parks and libraries, and then decreed that only nondrinkers could settle in his Arcadian village.

For twenty years the town was in fact an utterly blissful community with no crime, no firearms, no jail, and no locked doors. The mayor performed his duties free of charge as a public service. Until 1900 there were no more than 500 people in this sleepy hamlet, and at the trustees' annual meeting in 1903, the biggest problem was what to do about farmers driving their sheep through the town square. A decade later the film companies arrived.

---

Since the first Dracula film in 1923 (*Nosferatu*), eighteen movies have been made on the subject.

*Bela Lugosi as Dracula.*

---

The first famous western star, Bronco Billy Anderson, who had a bit part in the first western movie ever made (*The Great Train Robbery*, 1903), was so inept at horseback riding that it took three men to lift him into the saddle.

---

In 1914, movie theaters became so popular in America, and movie attendance increased so greatly, that ushers at several of New York's theaters were drilled by West Point graduates in the logistics of moving masses of people through small spaces.

---

Mary Pickford, the famous early film star and symbol of innocent American girlhood, was Canadian. She was born in Ontario in 1893. Her real name was Gladys Mary Smith.

*Mary Pickford, "America's sweetheart," was born in Canada.*

---

When Humphrey Bogart was a baby, a portrait of him painted by his mother was used as a trademark for Mellin's baby food. The baby Bogart was known to millions as "the Mellin's Baby" and was familiar to Americans long before he became a screen star.

---

As of 1977, Walt Disney Productions had won fifty-one Oscar awards.

---

Cyprus has one motion-picture theater for every eight members of its population. Saudi Arabia, as of 1976, had no movie theaters at all.

---

A wealthy teen-ager named Thomas Rhodes once offered Douglas Fairbanks $1 million if he would teach him gymnastics. (The actor was an expert gymnast.) Fairbanks, a multimillionaire himself, rejected the offer and reportedly told Rhodes he was too liberal with his money. If he would invest the million in Liberty Bonds, Fairbanks said, he would teach Rhodes the stunts for free.

*Douglas Fairbanks working out.*

## Music and Musicians

Franz Schubert composed music so swiftly, easily, and prolifically that he often couldn't recognize his own work when it was later set before him.

---

Mozart wrote his last and, many think, his greatest symphony, No. 41 (the "Jupiter") in less than sixteen days. His last three symphonies were written in a period of three months in 1788.

Though these three works are today considered some of the finest music ever composed, Mozart was not able to get even one of them performed during his lifetime.

---

Mozart's opera *Zaide* was not performed until seventy-five years after the composer's death. Found among his manuscripts after he died, the opera was considered too short for a full evening and too long to be part of a double bill. Hence it is still rarely presented.

---

*Kaddara*, an opera written by Hakon Borrensen and produced in Copenhagen in 1921, is the only opera ever written about Eskimos.

---

Egyptian musicians played a harp that looked almost exactly like the one played today. The major difference is that most Egyptian players strummed the strings with a stick rather than with their fingers. For reasons that are unknown today, in Old Kingdom Egypt only men were allowed to play this instrument.

*Ancient Egyptian harpist.*

---

A snake charmer does not charm snakes with a flute. The instrument he uses is a large gourd to which several bamboo stems are attached by means of a piece of beeswax. The sound of this ancient instrument is closer to that of the bagpipe than to the flute.

*A Hindu snake charmer. The instrument he is playing sounds more like a bagpipe than like a flute.*

The Roman emperor Nero was an expert bagpiper. According to the Roman historian Suetonius, Nero "knew how to play the pipe with his mouth and the bag thrust under his arm." Toward the end of his life the emperor played the instrument in public at the Roman athletic games. The bagpipe, it might be added, is not a Scottish invention but an ancient instrument that musicologists have traced to pre-Christian Asia.

William Shakespeare published two well-known textbooks on voice training for opera singers, *The Art of Singing* and *Plain Words on Singing.* This William Shakespeare, however, was not the famous playwright, though he was English. He lived from 1849 to 1931 and was a distinguished concert and oratorio singer.

The composer Richard Wagner (1813–1883) was haunted all his life by the number 13. There were thirteen letters in Wagner's name, and the sum of the figures in the year of his birth was thirteen. He made his first public appearance in 1831, the numbers of which again added up to thirteen. He completed *Tannhäuser* on April 13, and it was performed in Paris on March 13, 1861. On August 13, 1876, he began the first presentation of the *Ring of the Nibelungen.* The year he was made director of the state theater at Riga, the theater opened on September 13. Wagner wrote thirteen operas, was exiled from Saxony for thirteen years, and died on the thirteenth day of the month in the thirteenth year of the new German confederation.

Most flutes used by professional musicians are made of sterling silver, 14-carat gold, or platinum.

The famous Russian composer Nicolai Rimsky-Korsakov (1844–1908), creator of the popular *Scheherezade*, did not know how to read music until he was in his late teens. He did not start studying music at all until he was a student in St. Petersburg, and then only in a very superficial way. His real musical education began when he joined the Russian navy, at which time he educated himself in the fine points of music and wrote his first symphony while on a three-year cruise.

*Nicolai Rimsky-Korsakov.*

Between 1927 and 1935, more than 250 songs were written to honor Charles Lindbergh. One of them, "Lucky Lindy," is still occasionally played today.

The famous Christmas carol "Silent Night" was written in three hours on Christmas Eve, 1818, by a parish priest in Austria named Josef Mohr. Earlier that day, Mohr had baptized a baby (the first stanza of "Silent Night" may have been inspired by the event), and on leaving the christening learned that the church organ had broken down. Fearing that his parishioners would be saddened by the lack of music on

Christmas Eve, he rushed to the house of a friend, Franz Gruber, the church organist. There the two men composed the famous hymn, and at midnight mass Mohr and Gruber, accompanied by a guitar, sang the carol for the first time.

---

"The Star-spangled Banner" did not become the official anthem of the United States until 1931.

---

If the coils of a French horn were straightened out, the instrument would be 22 feet long.

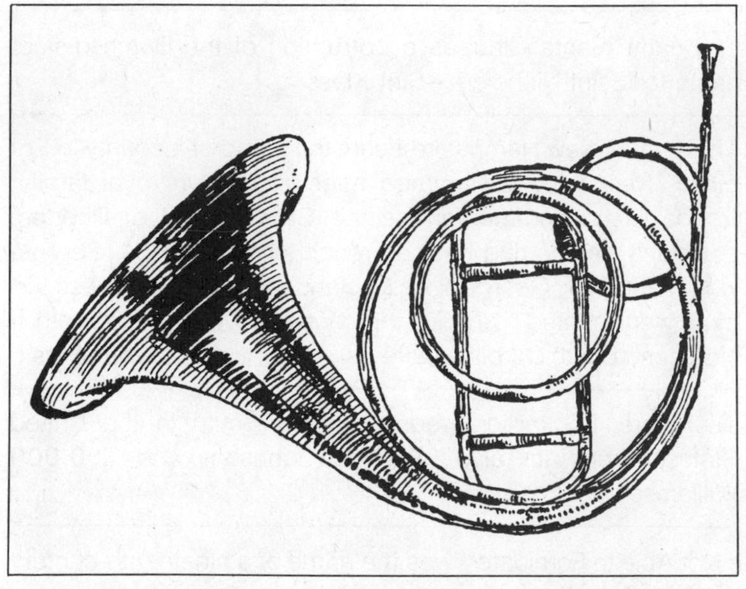

*French horn.*

---

Neither the saxophone, the tuba, the cornet, nor the valve trumpet existed before 1800.

## Names: People, Places, and Things

There is a club in the United States whose only membership requirement is that one be named Jim Smith. The club was founded by James H. Smith, Jr., of Camp Hill, Pennsylvania. Smith felt that the kidding he and others had taken for the ordinariness of their name should be combated by a show of international solidarity. At present there are 781 members of this club, some living as far away as Scotland and New Zealand. Members meet once a year for their annual "Jim Smith Fun Festival," and at these meetings, reports their president, "If you say 'Hey, Jim,' twenty heads will turn."

---

Montezuma, ruler of the Aztecs and adversary of the Spanish explorer Cortez, had a nephew named Cuitlahac. Translated, Cuitlahac's name means "plenty of excrement."

---

The name Santa Claus is a corruption of the Dutch dialect name for Saint Nicholas—Sint Klass.

---

The state of New Hampshire bears the name of a county in England. New York was named after an English royal family. Rhode Island commemorates the Greek Island of Rhodes. Louisiana was named for the French king Louis XIV. Georgia was named for George II of England. Virginia and West Virginia were named to honor the "Virgin Queen," Elizabeth I. North and South Carolina were named for England's Charles I.

---

There are 1.3 million people named Smith in the United States. There are also 900,000 Johnsons and 750,000 Williamses.

---

"Not Able to Fornicate" was the name of a nineteenth-century northwestern American Indian chief.

---

The real names of some famous personalities:

Julie Andrews—Julia Wells
Ann-Margret—Ann-Margret Olsson
Fred Astaire—Frederick Austerlitz
David Ben-Gurion—David Green
Richard Burton—Richard Jenkins
Joan Crawford—Lucille La Sueur
Tony Curtis—Bernard Schwartz
Kim Darby—Derby Zerby

Doris Day—Doris von Kappelhoff
Marlene Dietrich—Maria Magdalena von Losch
Phyllis Diller—Phyllis Driver
Kirk Douglas—Issur Danielovitch
Greta Garbo—Greta Gustaffson
Judy Garland—Frances Gumm
Cary Grant—Archibald Leach
Dean Martin—Dino Crocetti
Roy Rogers—Leonard Slye
Mickey Rooney—Joe Yule, Jr.
Dinah Shore—Frances Shore
Natalie Wood—Natasha Gurdin

*Judy Garland—née Frances Gumm—as Dorothy in* The Wizard of Oz.

---

It is possible for any American citizen to give whatever name he or she chooses to any unnamed mountain or hill in the United States. The only stipulation is that the person does not name it after himself. To name a hill or mountain, all you have to do is obtain a U.S. Geological Survey topographical map and find a peak that has no official title. After writing to the Chamber of Commerce or the county clerk to make certain that the hill is still unnamed, send your suggested name to Donald Orth, Executive Secretary of Domestic Geographical Names, U.S.G.S. National Center, Mail Stop 523, 12201 Sunrise Valley Drive, Reston, Virginia 22092. Approximately a thousand new names are accepted in this way by the secretary each year.

---

The original name of the island of Réunion in the Indian Ocean was Bourbon.

---

There is more than one Kremlin in Russia. In fact there are many. *Kremlin* is simply a word used to designate the seat of any town or city government in Russia. It is derived from an ancient word meaning ''fortress.''

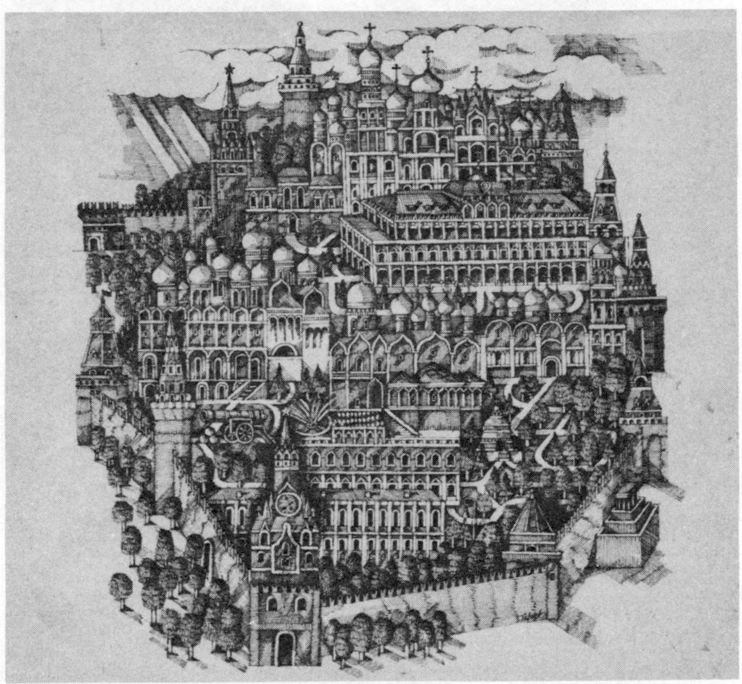

*The Kremlin, Moscow.*

---

The crescent of Gianuzzi, isles of Langerhans, crypts of Lieberkühn, canal of Gugier, circle of Willis, area of Cohnheim, pyramids of Malpighi, antrum of Highmore, spaces of Fontana, cistern of Pecquet, and angle of Ludwig are *not* tourist sites or places to spend the summer, but parts or areas of the human body. Most are named after the anatomists who first described them, and they are listed in *Gray's Anatomy*—along with Scarpa's triangle, Gower's tract, Goll's column, the pouch of Douglas, the convolutions of Broca, and the jelly of Wharton.

---

Llanfairpwllgwyngyllgogerychwyrndrobwllllantsiliogogogoch is the Welsh name of the town of Llanfair in Wales. At the Llanfair railroad station a 20-foot-long sign makes this fact clear to all arrivals. Translated, the name means "Saint Mary's Church in a hollow of white hazel, close to a whirlpool and Saint Tysilo's Church and near a red cave."

---

The following are all names of towns in the United States: Chicken, Alaska; Climax, Colorado; Combined Locks, Wisconsin; Embarrass, Wisconsin; Enigma, Georgia; Experiment, Georgia; Mars, Pennsylvania; Mexican Hat, Utah; Old Joe, Arkansas; Smackover, Arkansas; Social Circle, Georgia; Waterproof, Louisiana; Why, Arizona; and Zigzag, Oregon.

---

The Baby Ruth candy bar was named after the first baby girl ever born in the White House, Ruth Cleveland, daughter of President Grover Cleveland.

---

Pooler Jones, Lazy Plate, Jayne Hill, Untorn Ribbon, Buckthorn, Barber Perfect, and Underwood Tack are all names for various types of barbed wire.

---

The following is the name of an Indian chief who died in 1866 in Wisconsin: Chief Lepodotemachoselachogaleokranioleipsanodrimupotrimmatosiphioparaomelitokatakeclummenokichleipkossuphophattoperisteralektruonoptegkephalokigklopelsiolagoosiraioealetraganopterugon.

---

The term "rib-eye steak" was invented by a restaurateur from Clarksville, Virginia, named Howard N. Roberts. In 1951 Roberts acquired a large number of specially boned prime ribs, which, after much deliberation, he decided to call "rib-eye steaks." The name caught on immediately but did not bring Roberts the fame he rightly deserved. When he hired a lawyer to have the name trademarked he learned that he had started proceedings a month too late. At last report, Mr. Roberts's restaurant was still serving its famous steaks.

---

There is a town in New Mexico called Truth or Consequences. It was named in the following way. In 1950, Ralph Edwards, moderator of the radio show "Truth or Consequences," offered free national publicity to any town in the United States that would rename itself after his program. The town of Hot Springs, New Mexico, volunteered, and within a year it was as good as its word, altering its title to Truth or Consequences. It even went so far as to dub the park in the center of town "Ralph Edwards Park." Edwards devoted hours of radio time to the town and traveled there to pose for publicity pictures.

---

Alabama, Arkansas, Colorado, Florida, Georgia, Illinois, Indiana, Iowa, Kansas, Kentucky, Louisiana, Michigan, Minnesota, Missouri, New Hampshire, North Carolina, Ohio, Oklahoma, Oregon, South Dakota, Tennessee, Texas, West Virginia, and Wisconsin all have towns named after Andrew Jackson.

---

"There's only one Hollywood," the saying goes. This is not entirely true. Actually there are eleven Hollywoods. In addition to the movie capital in California, there are Hollywoods in Alabama, Arkansas, Florida, Georgia, Louisiana, Maryland, Mississippi, Missouri, South Carolina, and West Virginia.

---

A list of names for things you probably never knew had names:

***aglet***—the plastic or metal tip of a shoelace.

***bolster***—the part of a knife (usually located toward the middle) that separates the blade from the handle.

***bow***—the top part of a key.

***chuck***—the hole in a pencil sharpener into which the pencil is placed.

***counter***—the piece of leather used to stiffen the rear part of a shoe.

***flan***—the flat side of a coin that has not yet been stamped.

***kerf***—the slit or cut line made by a knife or saw.

***kickspace***—the inset area for the feet beneath a kitchen or bathroom counter.

***moon***—the crescent-shaped white area on the lower part of a fingernail.

***platen***—the tubular roller around which paper is inserted in a typewriter.

***plunger***—the disconnect button on a telephone.

***rictus***—the space or gap inside the open beak of a bird.

***serifs***—the tiny cross strokes at the tops and bottoms of printed letters.

***tang***—the prong of a fork.

***worm***—the spiral-shaped part of a corkscrew.

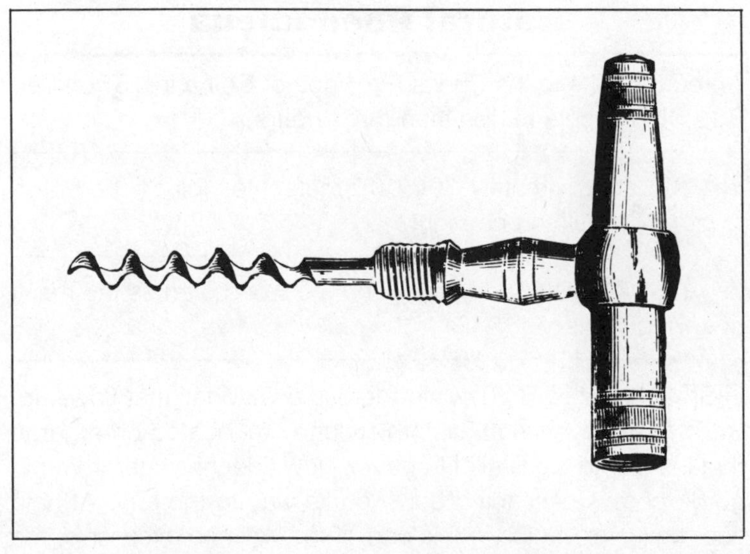

*Corkscrew (with worm).*

---

The state of Wyoming is named after a valley in Pennsylvania. The name came into use in 1865, when an Ohio congressman named J. M. Ashley suggested that part of the Western Territory be given a specific name. He proposed naming it after the Wyoming Valley in northeastern Pennsylvania, site of a famous massacre during the American Revolution. The name itself is derived from a Delaware Indian word, *m'cheuwomink*, which means "upon the great plain."

---

There is only one state in the United States named after a president—Washington.

---

What do the following names have in common? Tirana, Manama, Thimphu, Gaborone, Bandar Seri Begawan, Praia, Moroni, Paramaribo, Godthaab, Vaduz, Malé, and Dili. They are all capitals of nations (respectively: Albania, Bahrain, Bhutan, Botswana, Brunei, Cape Verde, Comoro Islands, Surinam, Greenland, Liechtenstein, Maldives, and Portuguese Timor).

## Natural Phenomena

An earthquake in the Shensi Province of China in 1556 killed 830,000 people in less than three hours.

---

In 1868 approximately 100,000 meteorites fell on the Polish town of Pultusk in one night.

---

In 1976, 700,000 people around the world died as the result of earthquakes.

---

In St. John, New Brunswick, there is a waterfall that flows upward. The Reversing Falls of St. John are located on a gorge that leads into the Bay of Fundy. At low tide the water from the gorge comes cascading down on its way to the bay. At high tide, however, which in this part of the world is excessive, the bay's water level rises 5 feet higher than that of the river itself. This causes a "bore," or rushing tide, to flow back into the river, and thus it pushes the water back up the falls.

---

There are parts of Europe, especially in southern France, where it has rained red rain. Known as "blood rains," such showers were for years thought to herald the apocalypse. Some scientists believe that they are caused by a reddish dust that is blown all the way from the Sahara Desert. Others believe that the red color comes from microorganisms in the water.

---

Here is a method for determining how far away a thunderstorm is located. Wait for a lightning flash. Then count the seconds that pass until the sound of thunder is heard. Sound travels about 1 mile in five seconds. Thus if there are five seconds between the lightning flash and the thunderclap, the storm is approximately a mile away. If ten seconds pass, it is 2 miles away, and so forth.

---

The energy released by a large earthquake may be equal to that released by 200 million tons of dynamite—10,000 times more power than was given out at the detonation of the first atomic bomb.

---

In the Bay of Fundy, located between New Brunswick and Nova Scotia in Canada, the tide sometimes rises 10 feet in one hour and attains heights as great as 60 feet from the beginning of the tide to the end.

---

In the city of Reykjavik, Iceland, one can see the stars eighteen out of twenty-four hours during the heart of winter. During the summer, sunlight is visible for twenty-four hours a day.

## Occupations

According to the U.S. Labor Department, the occupations that will be most in demand between 1978 and 1988 are airplane mechanic, computer programmer, cashier, cook, chef, dental assistant, draftsman, emergency medical technician, geologist, industrial-machinery repairman, lithographer, machine-tool operator, nurse's aide, physician, plumber, and police officer. Jobs that will offer the least chance of financial success and will be the most difficult to obtain are aerospace engineer, bookkeeper, college teacher, compositor and/or typesetter, historian, mathematician, newspaper reporter, physicist, school counselor, and stenographer.

---

The United States produces about 7,000 fewer doctors each year than the 22,000 it requires to meet medical needs. Law schools, on the other hand, are turning out about 5,000 more lawyers each year than are needed in our present legal system.

*Doctor and patient, 1930 painting by Norman Rockwell. The U.S. does not have enough physicians to meet current needs.*

---

As of 1977, says the U.S. Department of Labor, 4.5 million Americans held two jobs.

---

Streetcar conductors, taxi drivers, and business executives have the highest statistical chance of getting peptic ulcers.

---

The most dangerous job in the United States, statistically

speaking, is that of sanitation worker. Next on the list is fireman, followed by police officer, leather tanner (because of industrial poisons), coal miner, dock worker, meat packer, and logger.

---

No one over 6 feet tall can qualify to become an astronaut in the U.S. space program.

---

In the nineteenth century, European and American glass blowers, because of constant dryness of the throat and mouth, worked up such extreme thirsts that they had to drink enormous quantities. A doctor named McElroy, making observations in an American glass factory in 1877, noted that in nine working hours a glass blower might imbibe 50 to 60 pints of water, and this without the excreta or urine being measurably increased. When not working, McElroy added, the glass blowers drank no more than 3 or 4 pints of water a day. Occasionally a workman on the job would become so bloated that he would stop perspiring and, unable to move, would have to be carried out to the factory office, where rest and friction rubs finally restored his ability to sweat.

*Glass blowers in 19th-century New York.*

---

In India, letter carriers in the nineteenth century carried a long stick with several iron plates fixed to the end. If they were set upon by wild beasts or snakes, they rattled the stick at their attackers. In the nineteenth century, the typical load carried by an Indian mailman might exceed 80 pounds. In certain areas of the country, these mailmen would travel their route at a trot, covering as much as 100 miles in less than two days.

*Letter carriers running their route in 19th-century India.*

## Paradoxes

Three enigmatic paradoxes:

***Zeno's Paradox.*** Imagine a point at any location along the arc of an arrow fired from point A to point B, and let us call this point C. In its flight from point A to point B, the arrow must at one moment pass through point C. If it passes through point C, common sense tells us, at the very moment of its occupancy it inhabits no other point. That is to say, the arrow is at point C and at no other point along the arc. If this is true, then for that moment the arrow is standing still, as it is at this one point and at no other. Thus logic tells us that each time an arrow occupies one point along an arc it is standing still, not being at any other place but at that one point. And so the movement of an arrow is, paradoxically, made up of nothing but a chain of stationary positions.

***The Endless Race.*** A racer decides to run in a straight line from point A to point B. The paradox says he will never reach point B. Why? For this reason: if he wishes to go from point A to point B, the runner must first go half that distance. And in order to go half that distance he must first go half the distance of half the distance. And in order to go half the distance of half the distance he must go half *that* distance—and so on. Thus the runner can never go the whole distance, since he must continually cross this infinite number of half distances.

***The Hangman.*** There is a hangman who stands on a hill along a road to town. Every person who passes is asked the same question: "Where are you going?" If the passer-by answers honestly, he or she is allowed to continue. If he tells a lie, he is hanged. There is, however, one reply for which the hangman can neither hang the person nor let him go. What is that reply? The answer: suppose a man comes along the road and the hangman asks him, "Where are you going?" The man replies that he is coming here so that the hangman can hang him. This answer creates an irreconcilable paradox. It is unfair for the hangman to hang the traveler, for the traveler has told the truth. If he lets the traveler go, however, it is also unfair, for then the traveler would have been lying.

## People

John Paul Jones (1747–1792), famous naval hero of the American Revolution, was a bastard by birth, an actor by trade, lived under an assumed name most of his life, practiced piracy, was wanted for two murders, was tried for the rape of a young girl, and died penniless. Born out of wedlock in Scotland and originally named John Paul, he became an actor with a stock company in Jamaica at the age of eleven, playing a role in Steele's *Conscious Lovers*.. He later shipped out as a sailor on a West Indies slave ship, where he flogged one shipmate to death and killed another (many say in self-defense) on

*John Paul Jones, painting by Charles Willson Peale.*

the island of Tobago. Fleeing to America, he assumed the name Jones to avoid detection and eventually distinguished himself during the American Revolution. After the war, Jones became a mercenary sailor, at various times consorting with pirates and selling slaves. Later, when sailing under the Russian flag, he was accused in St. Petersburg of assaulting a young girl and only after a lengthy trial was he acquitted. The latter part of Jones's life was lived more or less in embittered anonymity, and he died forgotten in France, buried in an unmarked grave in St. Louis Cemetery. It was not until a century later, through the efforts of an American ambassador named Horace Porter, that his remains were exhumed, brought back to the United States, and buried in a tomb at Annapolis—which today is a national shrine.

---

Charles Joseph Bonaparte (1851–1921), chairman of the National Civil Service Reform League, secretary of the navy under Theodore Roosevelt, and finally attorney general of the United States, was a grandnephew of Napoleon Bonaparte.

---

*Paul Revere, painting by John Singleton Copley.*

Paul Revere, famous American patriot, was once court-martialed for cowardice. Revere was in command of a garrison of soldiers at Castle William, near Boston, from the beginning of the Revolutionary War until 1779. In the last year of his command he participated in the so-called Penobscot Expedition, an attempted invasion of a British stronghold in Maine. The invasion failed miserably, Massachusetts lost a considerable number of ships in the effort, and Revere was accused of cowardice and insubordination. Though his court-martial was short and he was cleared on all counts, the famous silversmith left the military in some disrepute and was never able to clear his name completely of the scandal.

---

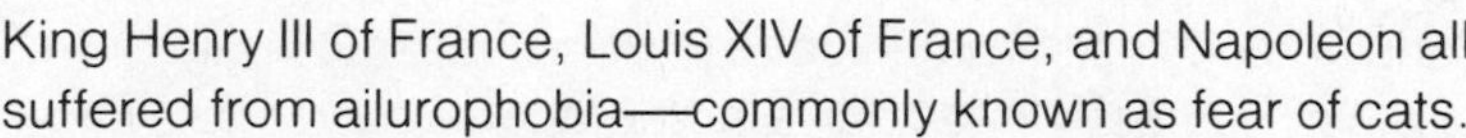

King Henry III of France, Louis XIV of France, and Napoleon all suffered from ailurophobia—commonly known as fear of cats.

---

Uncle Sam, long-time symbol of the United States, was originally a butcher. During the War of 1812, Samuel Wilson, a well-to-do meat packer from Troy, New York, supplied the American army with barrels of pork, which he stamped "EA–US." That same year a group of visitors toured Wilson's plant and asked what the letters signified. A workman jokingly replied that the US stood for "Uncle Sam" (an eyewitness account of this dialogue was reported in the New York *Gazette and General Advertiser* on May 12, 1820), and the name caught on. By the next decade the character of Uncle Sam was appearing in numerous political cartoons.

---

In 1966 a former British major named Roy Bates moved, with his wife and son, to a 10-by-25-foot cement caisson built 7 miles off the British coast during World War II. Bates named the platform "Sealand," declared it to be an independent country, crowned himself king and his wife queen, issued postage stamps, designed passports, and even created a Sealand dollar. Today Sealand is the world's smallest country, and King Roy still reigns. Since they are beyond the 3-mile limit, Bates and his kingdom are outside the jurisdiction of any other country.

---

When William Congreve, the great English playwright, died in 1792, he left his worldly goods to his eccentric and devoted mistress, Henrietta, Duchess of Marlborough. Henrietta became so deranged with grief at the death of her paramour that she ordered a death mask made of Congreve's face, attached it to a life-size dummy, and spent the rest of her life treating the mannequin as if it were alive. Visitors were obliged to bow to the dummy, exchange pleasantries with it, and pretend that it was really Congreve himself. Every morning Henrietta dressed the dummy, and every night she undressed it and laid it next to her in bed. She held long conversations with it, had her servants treat it like a living lord, called doctors to examine it when it became "ill," and ordered that it be buried in her coffin with her when she died.

---

In 1972 a Japanese soldier named Yokoi Shoichi was discovered hiding deep in the jungles of Guam, living on a diet of rats, snails, frogs, insects, and wild nuts. He had been there for twenty-seven years, since the end of World War II, and was unwilling to give himself up because of ''shame and dishonor.'' Finally persuaded to ''surrender,'' Shoichi was returned to civilization in Japan, where doctors declared him to be in normal health, though slightly anemic. An exhibition of his jungle clothes and artifacts at a Tokyo department store drew more than 350,000 curious visitors. After some time in civilization Shoichi met a forty-four-year-old widow. The two fell in love, married, and set out on a honeymoon—back to Guam!

---

The famous British playwright Noel Coward, the American inventor Thomas Alva Edison, the Irish playwright Sean O'Casey, the British novelist Charles Dickens, and the American humorist Mark Twain never graduated from grade school.

*Noel Coward, a grade-school dropout.*

---

Miguel Cervantes, author of the Spanish classic *Don Quixote*, applied to live in America in 1590. He desired a post in the Spanish colonies, he told the authorities, but they turned him down. *"Busque por aca en que se haga merced"*—"Let him look for something closer to home"—they replied.

*Illustration by Jose Moreno Carbonero from* Don Quixote, *Miguel Cervantes' masterwork.*

After Jimmy Walker, mayor of New York from 1926 to 1932, was asked to leave office because of "accounting problems," he went on to become an active member of the show-business world. Walker wrote several hit tunes, one of which he performed with George Jessel in Madison Square Garden in 1938. He was elected president of the National Association of Performing Arts and eventually became head of Majestic Records.

Orville Wright, who with his brother Wilbur invented the airplane, was himself badly injured in an airplane crash. The same accident also took the life of the first person ever to die in an airplane. On September 17, 1908, Wright and Lt. Thomas Selfridge of the U.S. Signal Corps took off on a flight from Fort Meyer, Virginia. Midway through the trip the propeller snapped, and the plane plummeted 150 feet to the ground. Wright was hospitalized and Selfridge was killed.

Before Manuel Benitez, the famous Spanish bullfighter, retired from the ring in 1972, he was earning more than $3 million a year.

Czar Alexander III of Russia, the Duke of Aquitaine, Godfrey of Bouillon the Crusader, and Leonardo da Vinci were all famous in their time for having uncommon physical strength. Leonardo was said to be able to lift great weights and to throw a metal ball farther than any of his contemporaries.

Sir Henry Wyat, a noble at the court of Richard III (1452–1485), was sent to the Tower of London by the monarch for political crimes, and was condemned to die of starvation. Sir Henry's pet cat, however, followed him to the Tower and every day crept down through the chimney and brought him a freshly killed pigeon. In this way Wyat was kept alive for months. The king, hearing of the miracle, relented and ordered Wyat released.

---

Benjamin Franklin is credited with originating the following famous proverbs, which appeared in the 1758 edition of his *Poor Richard's Almanac:*

A penny saved is a penny earned.

Early to bed and early to rise make a man healthy, wealthy, and wise.

God helps those who help themselves.

---

*Jane Pierce, "the shadow in the White House" from 1853 to 1857.*

Jane Pierce, the wife of President Franklin Pierce, was a recluse for more than half her husband's term in office (1853–1857). She did not even attend her husband's inaugural ball. Her seclusion began scarcely two months before Pierce's swearing-in ceremony, when she saw her eleven-year-old son Benjamin die in a railroad accident. She withdrew to her White House bedroom for the next several years and almost never appeared in public. Newspapers referred to the melancholy first lady as "the shadow in the White House." Though she eventually began venturing out, Mrs. Pierce remained in mourning and wore black for the rest of her life.

---

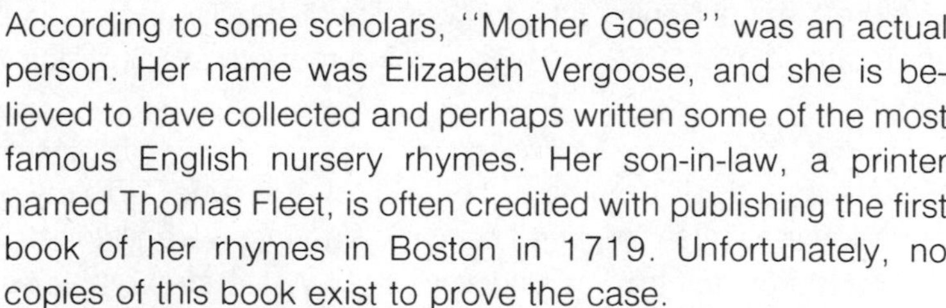

According to some scholars, "Mother Goose" was an actual person. Her name was Elizabeth Vergoose, and she is believed to have collected and perhaps written some of the most famous English nursery rhymes. Her son-in-law, a printer named Thomas Fleet, is often credited with publishing the first book of her rhymes in Boston in 1719. Unfortunately, no copies of this book exist to prove the case.

---

Arnold Rothstein, the famous American gambler, never went out without $100,000 in cash in his wallet. Because of this idiosyncrasy, and his willingness to take enormous risks (he once bet $250,000 on the turn of a card), he was known among gamblers as "The Big Bankroll."

---

Joseph M. W. Turner (1775–1851) one of the greatest and most successful of all English painters, spent the latter part of his life as a recluse, living in seclusion under the assumed name of Booth. Although Turner was loved and respected throughout Europe, he lived alone amid mounds of rubbish, filth, and discarded canvases, rarely changing his clothes (his landlady had to bathe and dress him), and hoarding the vast fortune he had amassed.

J. M. W. Turner at his easel.

The Christmas carol "Good King Wenceslas" is based on an actual historical personage. Wenceslas was not a king, however, but a tenth-century duke who later became the patron saint of Czechoslovakia. Duke Wenceslas was famous for his piety and compassion, and is reputed to have gone to the woods during the severe Bohemian winters and chopped wood for widows, poor people, and orphans.

Joseph Caspar Mezzofanti, an Italian priest born in 1774, could learn a foreign language in a single day. Once called on to hear the confessions of two foreign criminals condemned to die the following morning, Mezzofanti learned their language in one night and conversed with them at sunrise before their execution. At his death Mezzofanti was fluent in thirty-nine languages (including Chinese, Coptic, Chaldean, Gujarati, Persian, Turkish, Russian, all the Romance languages, Hindi, Hebrew, Old English, Suriac, Arabic, Greek, Geez, Algonquin, and Armenian), was able to speak eleven more languages moderately well (including Welsh, Serbian, Kurdish, Bulgarian, and Angolese), and could understand, though not speak, twenty others, including some of the most obscure tongues known to man: Tibetan, Old Icelandic, Lappish, and Chippewa.

James Marshall, the man famous for being the first to discover gold in the state of California (he found the original traces at Sutter's Mill on January 24, 1848), died an impoverished alcoholic. Although Marshall began the Gold Rush and did make a small amount of money from his discovery, the land where the gold was found belonged to someone else and he was quickly turned away. From that time on he was unable to make a major strike and, discouraged, he took to drink. He ended up in the gutter, where he passed his last days.

---

Daniel Webster, Abraham Lincoln, John Marshall, and Stephen A. Douglas, four of the most famous lawyers the United States has ever produced, never went to law school.

---

Wendell Lewis Willkie, Republican candidate for president in 1940, was originally named Lewis Wendell Willkie. According to Willkie, when he enlisted in the army during World War I, the army mistakenly reversed the sequence of his first and second names, and try as he might, he could not get them to change it back. Finally Willkie accepted the alteration and was known as Wendell Willkie from then on.

---

The French composer Charles Alkan (1813–1888) was one of the great pianists of his day. Yet he would perform only on rare occasions, stating that he wished to spend all his spare time reading the Jewish scriptures, especially the Torah. Alkan passed many years absorbed in the study of his beloved religious works until one day a massive volume of the Torah fell off a shelf, hit him on the head, fractured his skull, and killed him.

---

Thomas Parr, known as ''Old Parr,'' an English servant born in 1483, lived 152 years. He did not marry until he was eighty years old, and his first wife lived thirty-two years after the couple was wed. Eight years after his wife's death, Parr married again. At the age of 130 he still worked diligently on his master's farm, plowing the fields and pounding the grain. By the time he was 150 his age and his great intelligence attracted the attention of King Charles I, who sent for him. Perhaps because of the excitement of the journey to London and the attendant celebrations (he was mobbed by admirers), Parr took sick and died at the age of 152 years and 9 months, having lived under nine kings of England. The famous physician William Harvey examined his body and found all his internal organs to be in a perfect state. No apparent cause of death could be determined, and it was assumed that Old Parr had simply died of overexposure. A monument to him was erected at Westminster Abbey.

*Portrait of Thomas Parr made just before his death at the age of 152.*

The longest recorded life span in modern times was that of Javier Pereira, a Zenu Indian from Colombia. Pereira died in 1955 in his hometown of Monteria at the age of 166. His age was attested to by friends, municipal records, and Pereira himself, who could remember with great clarity the battle of Cartagena (fought in 1815), various Indian massacres, and a famous famine. Toward the end of his life a bemused Pereira was brought to New York, where he was examined by a coterie of medical experts. Though they found him remarkably well preserved, with the blood pressure of a young man, arteries intact, a good heart, and a clear mind, they conceded that he was indeed a very, very old man, "more than 150 years old." When quizzed on his formula for longevity, Pereira advised, "Don't worry, drink lots of coffee, and smoke a good cigar."

---

Vaslav Nijinsky (1890–1950), the famous Russian ballet dancer, was able to cross and uncross his legs ten times during a single leap, an elevation known in ballet as an *entrechat dix*. No other dancer has ever been able to duplicate this feat.

---

Arnold Bly was able to inscribe the Lord's Prayer on a grain of rice and to write legibly on a strand of human hair. Bly gave demonstrations of his remarkable lettering ability at the 1939 World's Fair in New York, and several of his inscribed grains of rice still survive.

---

A peasant named Kirilow was presented to the empress of Russia in 1853 for the following reason. He had been married twice. His first wife bore fifty-seven children, including four sets of quadruplets, seven sets of triplets, and two sets of twins. His second wife gave birth to fifteen children—six sets of twins and one set of triplets. At the time of his presentation to the empress, all seventy-two of Kirilow's children were still alive.

## Physics and Chemistry

If the chemical sodium is dropped in water and a match is taken to the mixture, it will immediately and violently ignite. If sodium is immersed in a pot of kerosene, however, it will not burn at all.

---

According to the Theory of Relativity, the mass of an object increases with its velocity. In nonscientific terms, this means that things get bigger as they move faster. The process has been demonstrated in laboratories. In several experiments, objects accelerated to 86 percent of the speed of light have doubled in weight. The theory also postulates the rather incomprehensible notion that given enough speed, an object will become as large as the universe itself.

---

Ten of the 105 known elements had been discovered and were in use in prehistoric times: gold, silver, lead, iron, copper, zinc, tin, sulfur, carbon, and mercury. The largest individual contribution to the table of elements was that of the nineteenth-century English chemist Sir Humphrey Davy, who identified boron, barium, calcium, potassium, sodium, and strontium in 1807 and 1808. He also demonstrated that diamonds are composed of pure carbon and discovered the hilarious properties of nitrous oxide—"laughing gas."

*Sir Humphrey Davy lecturing at the Surrey Institute, etching by Rowlandson.*

---

The air around us is not weightless. In fact, it can be weighed almost as accurately as iron or lead. A column of air 1 inch square and 600 miles high, for instance, weighs approximately 15 pounds, about twice as much as an average newborn baby. This weight is what creates the phenomenon known as "atmospheric pressure."

---

Sound travels fifteen times more swiftly through steel than through air.

---

A pipe 2 feet in diameter will allow four times more fluid to pass through it than a pipe 1 foot in diameter—the volume of a pipe varies as the square of its diameter.

If you punch a series of holes in a paper cup filled with water, the water will squirt out farthest and fastest from the lowest holes. The reason is that water pressure is greatest at the bottom of the cup. For the same reason, dams are made thicker at the bottom than at the top.

## Presidents

''You sock-dologizing old mantrap'' were the last words ever heard by Abraham Lincoln. They were spoken by an actor named Asa Trenchard in the play *Our American Cousin*. The roars of laughter that followed these lines drowned out the sound of the gunshots fired by John Wilkes Booth.

*The assassination of Abraham Lincoln at Ford's Theater on April 14, 1865.*

William Henry Harrison was president of the United States for only thirty-one days. He caught cold the day of his inauguration and died of pneumonia in the White House on April 4, 1841, a month after he had been sworn in.

So beloved was George Washington among the French that when he died in 1799 Napoleon Bonaparte ordered ten days of mourning throughout France.

*George Washington, painting by Charles Willson Peale.*

Harry S Truman was President Truman's full name; the S is not an abbreviation but a name in itself, and when properly written is not followed by a period. Using a single letter as a middle name was a common practice in the United States and England before World War II.

At one time all American presidents, their wives, and important political figures were exempt from having to pay postage. All they had to do was sign their name in the corner of the envelope, a practice that became known as "franking." Today many valuable autographs sold to collectors are taken from these franked envelopes.

Every student at Washington and Lee University in Lexington, Virginia, receives financial aid from George Washington. Washington left the university a land grant of 50,000 acres, which was, at that time, the largest legacy ever donated to an American university. Today that land is worth millions of dollars, and the interest on profits from its sale has so far amounted to $400,000, all of which is used to help students.

Thomas Jefferson invented the calendar clock.

Groton, the prestigious prep school in Connecticut, has been attended by sixteen Roosevelts.

John Adams, Thomas Jefferson, James Madison, Martin Van Buren, Zachary Taylor, Andrew Johnson, and Ulysses S. Grant all died in thc month of July.

## Psychology

The following is a standard test used by many psychiatrists to determine if a person is susceptible to hypnosis. The patient is told to stand in the center of a room with his eyes shut. The tester stands behind him and asks the patient to fall back into his arms without resistance. The tester assures the patient that he will not be hurt and tells him to trust the tester completely. If the patient falls back without hesitation, he will be easily hypnotized. If not, he won't.

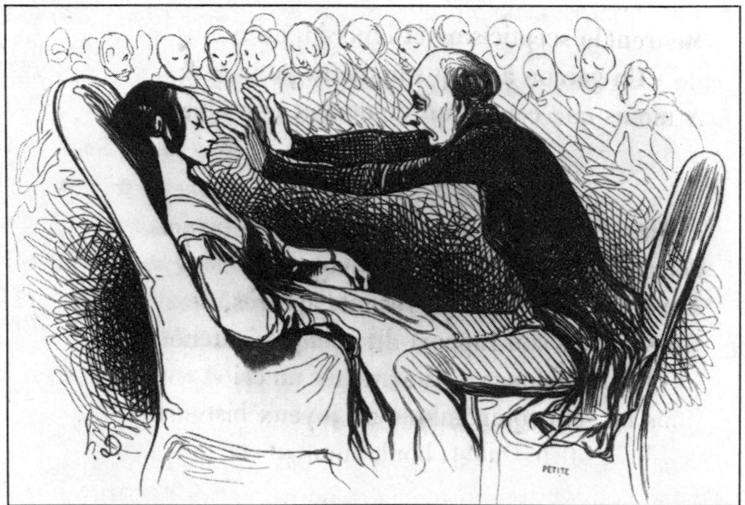

*A hypnotist at work, drawing by Honoré Daumier.*

---

Based on the total number of people tested since IQ tests were devised, women have a slightly higher average IQ than men.

---

Females learn to talk earlier, use sentences earlier, and learn to read more quickly than males. Males have a greater incidence of reading disabilities, stutter more, read with less speed and accuracy, and by the time they reach maturity have a smaller vocabulary than females.

---

According to studies made at Northwestern University, men change their minds two to three times more often than women. Most women, the experiments found, take longer to make a decision than men do, but once they make a decision they are more likely to stick to it.

---

Experiments conducted at several college laboratories demonstrate that hard rock music played to colonies of termites cause the insects to enter a kind of frenzy and to chew through wood at twice their normal rate.

---

## Religion

The Dome of the Rock in Jerusalem is one of the few shrines in the world simultaneously sacred to three religions: Christianity, Judaism, and Islam. According to the Jews, the rock beneath the dome marks the spot where Abraham prepared to sacrifice his son Isaac, and later was the site where Solomon built his temple. Christians believe that Christ once preached a sermon on the spot, and for Moslems this is the holy ground where the Prophet Muhammad made his famous Night Flight on the back of the winged *barak*.

*Dome of the Rock, Jerusalem.*

---

St. Lucia and St. Apollonia, *engraving by Toschi after Parmigiano.*

---

Saint Lucy is depicted in paintings as carrying her own eyes on a dish. When still a young and beautiful maiden, Lucy supposedly looked at and fell in love with an equally young and handsome man. Feeling this passionate glance to be a betrayal of her vows of chastity, Lucy plucked out the eyes that had offended her so that she might never again look with lust. Her prospective lover was so impressed with Lucy's piety, the story says, that he converted to Christianity.

---

A group of religious fanatics in Russia called the Skoptzies was famous in the eighteenth and nineteenth centuries for practicing self-castration. Advocating chastity, they took this notion to the extreme, citing Biblical references in Matthew 19:12 ("and there be eunuchs which have made themselves eunuchs for the kingdom of heaven's sake") and Luke 23:29 ("blessed are the barren"). The operations were performed by both men and women, who used razors, pieces of glass, sharpened bone, or hot irons to do the deed to themselves. The greater number of Skoptzies submitted to the "first purification," which required that they remove their own testicles and scrotum. These initiates were said to have given up the "keys of hell" but to retain the "keys to the abyss." Those who removed their penis as well were awarded the honor of "Bearers of the Imperial Seal," and these initiates of the "second purification" were considered "worthy of mounting white horses." Female members of this sect did not remove their ovaries, but mutilated their external genitalia, mammae, and nipples. The highest degree of feminine participation was the complete amputation of the breasts.

---

After Protestants, Catholics, and Jews, there are more Buddhists in the United States than members of any other religion. As of 1976, America had 60,000 active practitioners of Buddhism.

---

Forty-seven Bibles are sold or distributed throughout the world every minute of the day.

---

The American Bible Society, a group that boasts fewer than 750,000 members, has distributed a billion Bibles since it was founded in 1816.

The devil is never referred to by his common name Lucifer in the entire New Testament. Only once is the name used in the Old Testament (Isaiah 14:12), and then it refers to the king of Babylon and not to the Satan we generally associate it with. The name Lucifer, interestingly enough, means "light-bearer" (hence a match is known as a "lucifer"), and has none of the evil connotations of some of the devil's other names, like Beelzebub ("lord of the flies") and Satan ("to accuse"). The planet Venus, when seen in the morning sky, is known to astronomers as Lucifer—that is, the star that heralds the coming light of day.

*The devil struggling with an angel, carving from the cathedral of La Madeleine at Vézelay.*

Contrary to popular belief, there are almost no Buddhists in India, nor have there been for about a thousand years.

Though Buddhism was founded in India around 470 B.C. and developed there at an early date, it was uprooted from India between the seventh and twelfth centuries A.D. and today exists almost exclusively outside that country, primarily in Sri Lanka, Japan, and Indochina.

---

Saint Lawrence (d. 258 A.D.), deacon to Pope Sixtus II, turned to his executioners while being burned to death and remarked, "I am cooked on that side; turn me over, and eat."

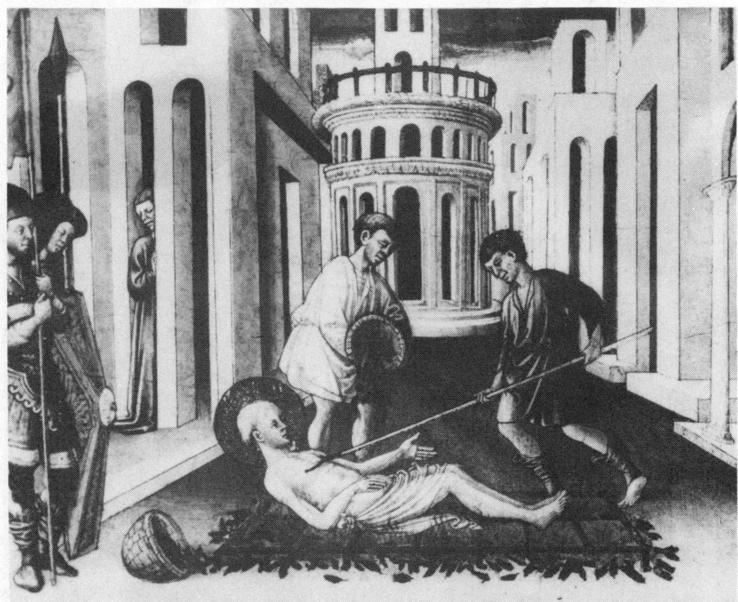

The Martyrdom of St. Lawrence, *painting by Neri di Bicci.*

---

Of the 156 women college presidents in the United States, 105 are nuns.

---

When a new Roman Catholic pope is elected, he is given a ring with a picture of Saint Peter engraved on it. It is called the Fisherman's Ring, and all papal documents must receive its seal. When the pope dies the ring is smashed—no one but the pontiff to whom it was given is allowed to wear it—and a new one is fashioned for his successor. This tradition can be traced back to Saint Peter himself.

---

The first thirty-four popes after Saint Peter were all saints.

## Royalty

Napoleon's coronation balloon.

At the coronation of Napoleon in 1804 a Montgolfier balloon was released over Paris bearing a huge gilded Napoleonic eagle on its gondola. The balloon, unpiloted, drifted for several days until it was caught by a strong wind and blown all the way to Rome. As it passed over the central portion of the city, it narrowly missed a collision with the dome of St. Peter's basilica, then sailed by the tomb of Nero. There the golden eagle came dislodged and crashed down onto the center of the Roman tyrant's sarcophagus. Napoleon, always mindful of omens, promptly discontinued all ballooning in France, and for forty years not a single air balloon was launched in that country.

During the French Revolution grave robbers broke into the tomb of Louis XIV and stole his heart. They sold it to an Englishman, Lord Harcourt, who in turn sold it to another Englishman, the Very Reverend William Buckland, Dean of Westminster. As an experiment, Dean Buckland ate the dried heart for supper one evening and, as far as is known, suffered no ill effects from his peculiar meal.

In the memoirs of Catherine II of Russia, it is recorded that any Russian aristocrat who displeased the queen was forced to squat in the great antechamber of the palace and to remain in that position for several days, mewing like a cat, clucking like a hen, and pecking his food from the floor.

Louis XIV was ruler of France for more than seventy-two years, which made him the longest-reigning European monarch of all time. He came to the throne in 1643 and held it until his death in 1715. Louis's only rival for monarchial longevity in France was his son, Louis XV, who ruled for fifty-nine years.

*Louis XIV,*
*painting by Hyacinthe Rigaud.*

Louis XIV had forty personal wigmakers and almost 1,000 wigs.

When Queen Elizabeth I of England announced her plan to visit the Duke of Bedford, the duke hastily added three new buildings to his castle, installed an artificial lake with three islands at its center, and gathered more than 250 servants who saw to it that every day of the queen's week-long stay was filled with banquets, poetry readings, water festivals, and fireworks.

Ladislaus Cubitas, fourteenth-century king of Poland, was a dwarf.

Ivan the Terrible (1530–1584), czar of Russia and one of the first Russian rulers to open relations with the West, killed his own son in a fit of fury.

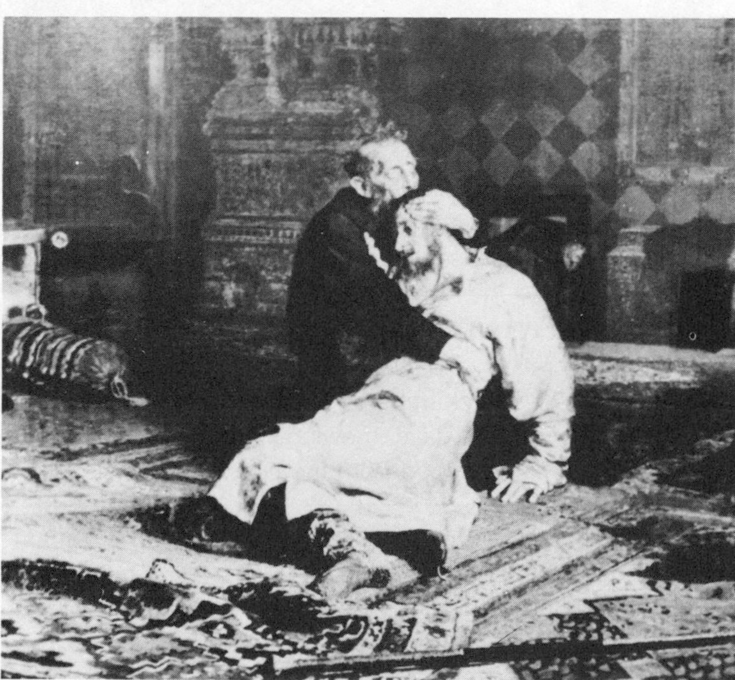

Ivan the Terrible and His Slain Son, *painting by I. Y. Repino.*

The design of the king found on all standard playing-card decks has, with slight alterations, remained the same for three centuries. It is believed to be based on a portrait of the English ruler Charles I (1600–1649). The picture of the queen is of more doubtful origin, but some think it was taken from an early portrait of Queen Elizabeth I.

*King of hearts, from an 18th-century deck of playing cards. Note the name "Charles" at the upper right.*

The Prussian emperor Ferdinand III owned an ivory cane that was encrusted with ninety-three large rubies and had a pair of miniature field glasses tucked inside it.

Charlemagne (742–814), early king of France, was the greatest warrior king of his time, stood 6 feet 4 inches tall, and weighed almost 275 pounds. He had extremely muscular arms and legs, was the finest hunter and rider at his court, and could kill a man with a single blow of his fist. Yet he spoke in a voice so high and squeaky that his contemporaries compared it to the voice of a twelve-year-old.

Anne Boleyn, one of the two unfortunate wives of Henry VIII sent to die in the Tower of London, had six toes on one foot, six fingers on one hand, and three breasts. In medical terminology the condition of having more than two breasts is known as polymazia.

When the Stuart family was restored to the English throne in 1660, one of King Charles II's first acts was to have the body of Oliver Cromwell dug up from its grave and decapitated. Cromwell's head was impaled on a spike and carried through the streets of London, where it was pelted with rocks and garbage.

## The Sea

The salt in sea water comes primarily from the fresh water that flows into the sea. As streams and rivers flow across the land they absorb a great deal of salt from rocks and the earth, and they carry this salt out to sea. There the fresh water evaporates and leaves the salt deposits behind.

---

Tidal waves move faster than any wheeled vehicle on earth. On the open seas they sometimes approach speeds of more than 500 nautical miles per hour.

---

It has been estimated that if all the seas of the earth dried up, they would leave about 4,419,330 cubic miles of rock salt. This would be enough salt to cover the entire United States with a layer 1½ miles deep.

---

According to the U.S. Hydrographic Office, about 2,172 ships have been wrecked at sea in the last hundred years.

*The wreck of the* City of Columbus *in 1884, one of the many shipwrecks of the past century.*

---

The Indian Ocean covers an area of 28,356,300 square miles, extends from Africa to Australia and from Asia to Antarctica, contains 70 million cubic miles of water—and is less than half the size of the Pacific Ocean.

---

During his famous *Ra* voyage across the Atlantic from Africa to Peru, the Scandinavian explorer Thor Heyerdahl reported that he observed oil pollution on forty-three of his fifty-seven days at sea.

---

If the water from all the world's oceans were formed into one sphere, that sphere would be almost one-third as large as the moon.

## Smoking

Women who use oral contraceptives and who smoke a pack of cigarettes a day are twelve times more likely to have a heart attack than women who do neither. Women who smoke two packs a day or more are twenty times more likely to suffer a heart attack than nonsmokers, even if they do not use oral contraceptives.

The Cigarette Dance, *etching by Anders Zorn.*

During World War II, Winston Churchill had a special vault at the Dunhill shop in London, where his cigars were kept. During the blitz a German bomb landed squarely on Dunhill's and blew the building to bits. At two o'clock that morning the manager journeyed to the still-smoking site of the bombing and rummaged through the debris in the cellar until he found what he had come for. ''Sir,'' he reported to the prime minister on the phone shortly afterward, ''your cigars are safe.'' Churchill, who had been puffing cigars regularly since he was twenty years old, reportedly smoked more than 300,000 cigars in his lifetime.

*Winston Churchill with one of his ever-present cigars.*

---

Lord Byron once wrote an ode to a cigar. It was called ''Sublime Tobacco'' and ended with the line ''Give me a cigar.''

---

Smokers suffer 65 percent more colds, 167 percent more nose and throat irritations, and have a 300 percent greater incidence of chronic coughs than nonsmokers.

---

It is possible to go blind from smoking too heavily. A condition known as amblyopia, in which a person's sight grows progressively dimmer, is directly attributable to excessive use of cigarettes. The cure is usually quite simple: stop smoking.

---

In 1640, by order of Pope Urban VIII, Spanish priests were forbidden to smoke cigars.

---

The amount of nicotine the average pack-a-day smoker inhales in a week—400 milligrams—would kill a person instantly if it were taken in all at once.

---

Casanova was the first well-known man ever to smoke a cigarette.

---

If all the packages of cigarettes smoked by Americans each year were laid end to end, they would circle the earth twenty-one times.

---

American Indians made tomahawks that also served as tobacco pipes. The head of such a tomahawk was fashioned into an axe blade on one side and a smoking bowl on the other. The handle was hollow and served as the pipe's stem. During periods of war the tomahawk was used as a weapon; in quiet times it was smoked as a peace pipe. The phrase "burying the hatchet" comes from the Indian custom of burying tomahawks whenever treaties were made.

*A Chippewa tomahawk-pipe.*

---

## Sports

Before 1850, golf balls were made of leather and were stuffed with feathers.

---

In 1866 the world record for the mile run was 4 minutes 12¾ seconds, set by W. G. George in London on August 23. Today that time would be considered a pretty good achievement for a high-school runner.

---

There are bullfights in Detroit. Twelve times a year, at the Cobo Arena, some of the best Spanish and Mexican matadors are featured, as well as several American bullfighters who have been trained in Spain. Bullfights themselves are not illegal in the United States; the matador is simply not allowed to kill the bull. In Detroit, therefore, all fights are ''exhibitions,'' bloodless events that demonstrate the matador's skill, not his ability to make a kill.

---

Lenin Stadium in Moscow has enough seats to accommodate more than 103,000 people.

---

The Stanley Cup, emblematic of ice-hockey supremacy in North America, was donated in 1893 by Canada's then-governor-general, Frederick Arthur, Lord Stanley of Preston. Originally awarded to honor Canada's top amateur team, it eventually became the championship trophy of the professional National Hockey League. Stanley Cup playoffs have been held continuously since 1894, although in the 1918–1919 season the finals were halted by the worldwide influenza epidemic. Oddly, Lord Stanley himself never saw a Stanley Cup game.

---

On June 7, 1950, the Boston Red Sox scored twenty runs against the St. Louis Browns. Next day the Sox beat the Browns by a score of 29 to 4. In two games Boston compiled forty-nine runs.

---

In the 1905 football season, eighteen men were killed in college games in the United States and 159 were permanently injured. At that time, football players wore only light equipment. Punching, linking arms, gouging, and kicking were all part of the action, and the entire team was allowed to line up on the scrimmage line. At least a quarter of all games, reports tell us, ended in mob brawls. In 1905 the Reverend David Buel of Georgetown University reported that one unidentified team had been taught to "strike their opponents in certain delicate parts of the body so as to render them helpless." The large number of deaths and injuries that year prompted President Theodore Roosevelt to establish the National Collegiate Athletic Association, which instituted regulations designed to make college football a less lethal sport.

Out of the Game,
*drawing by W. A. Rogers. Injuries like this were common in pre-1905 college football games.*

---

Sports fans in Brazil sometimes become so impassioned that it was necessary to build a wide moat around the playing field of Rio's 180,000-seat Maracaña Stadium. The moat keeps the crowd from running onto the field, molesting the players, and attacking the referees.

The great Yankee slugger Babe Ruth, who began his career as a pitcher, had a favorite pitching trick that has rarely been duplicated. He was able to throw two baseballs in such a way that the balls remained parallel to each other all the way from his hand to the catcher's glove. Ruth was famous for this stunt and would demonstrate it on request.

Before the Marquis of Queensberry rules for boxing were drawn up in 1867, all prize fights in England and the United States were fought with bare knuckles. Even as late as 1882, the great John L. Sullivan, then boxing champion of the world, rarely fought wearing gloves.

*Championship fight between John Heenan and Tom Sayers, Farmborough, England, April, 1860. Note that both contenders are bare-fisted.*

Have major-league baseball teams ever played a triple-header? Yes, but rarely. Cincinnati played three games at Pittsburgh on the final day of the 1920 season to decide third place in the National League. The first of the three-game series had been rained out, and as there were no make-up dates left, the Reds, leading by two and a half games, seemed to have third locked up. But Pittsburgh protested, and the National League agreed to allow a triple-header to settle the issue on the field. The teams started at noon and completed two full games and six innings of the third before darkness fell. The Reds won two and lost one to clinch third. Perhaps most remarkable was the speed with which the teams played. The twenty-four innings were run off in exactly five hours. Previously, the Pirates had lost a triple-header to Brooklyn in 1890.

---

Since 1967 every senior who has played on the basketball team of De Matha High School, just outside Washington, D.C., has won a college athletic scholarship.

---

In 1910 a football team was penalized 15 yards for an incompleted forward pass.

---

Before 1845, the bases on a baseball field were arranged in a U-shape. Posts or stakes were used instead of bases as we know them, runs were called "aces," and the first team to reach a score of 21 won the game. Even by 1860 baseball was more a social event than a competitive sport. Tea was served during the many "intermissions," and the pitcher threw the ball where the batter asked him to. Bunting was considered a breach of taste.

---

A sport practiced in ancient China consisted of placing two angry male quails in a large glass bowl and watching as the creatures clawed each other to death.

---

In 1822 Timothy Dwight, president of Yale College, forbade all students to play football. Violators were to be reported to the dean and were to be penalized by a fine not to exceed fifty cents.

---

The Pittsburgh Pirates got their name as a result of bad publicity. In 1880 the Pittsburgh team allegedly "pirated" an important player away from Philadelphia and did nothing to smooth over ruffled feelings. Local newspapers angrily called Pittsburgh "a bunch of pirates." The epithet stuck, and eventually became the team's official name.

---

The Aztec and Maya Indians of Mexico and Central America played a complicated kind of ball game not unlike lacrosse. The game, played in a large stadium and witnessed by thousands of spectators, went on for several hours. When the game was finished, the captain of the losing team was slaughtered before the onlookers, his body torn limb from limb, and pieces of his heart passed among the crowd for members of the audience to nibble.

---

In eighteenth- and nineteenth-century Peru, a special type of bullfighting was practiced. The matadors fought the bulls on horseback, and the best fighters were women. The women matadors were known as *capeadoras*. Juanita Brena, a well-known *capeadora* of the nineteenth century, had a distinctive fighting style: she pursued the bull at full tilt riding sidesaddle, a position difficult to maintain even when one is not chasing a bull.

*19th-century mounted matadors.*

---

The practice of identifying baseball players by number was begun by the Yankees in 1929. In 1931 the practice became standard throughout the American League; the National League adopted it in 1933. In 1960 Bill Veeck added players' names to their uniforms.

No high jumper has ever been able to stay off the ground for more than one second.

## Stamps

A stamp worth one penny at the time of its issue in 1856 by the government of British Guiana is worth $100,000 today. It is the rarest stamp in the world—only one of its kind is known to exist.

*The 1856 "one-cent magenta," the world's rarest stamp.*

In 1903 St. Kitts-Nevis issued a stamp showing Christopher Columbus looking over the side of his ship with a telescope. The telescope, however, was not invented until the seventeenth century. In 1958 Germany issued a stamp commemorating the composer Robert Schumann—and behind him they placed sheet music written by Franz Schubert. In 1947 Monaco issued a stamp showing Franklin D. Roosevelt with six fingers on his left hand.

The country of Tonga once issued a stamp shaped like a banana.

From 1950 until 1971, when President Nixon opened relations with Communist China, it was illegal for a collector to purchase or exhibit any stamp printed in China. Such an act was declared by the U.S. Congress to be "trading with the enemy."

Albania once issued a stamp to commemorate the world's greatest smoker. His name was Ahmed Zogu and he reputedly smoked an average of 240 cigarettes—twelve packs—a day.

## Theater

*Peter Pan* was the first English play ever written exclusively for children. Its one notable predecessor, *Bluebell in Fairyland*, was more in the genre of pantomime and operetta than drama.

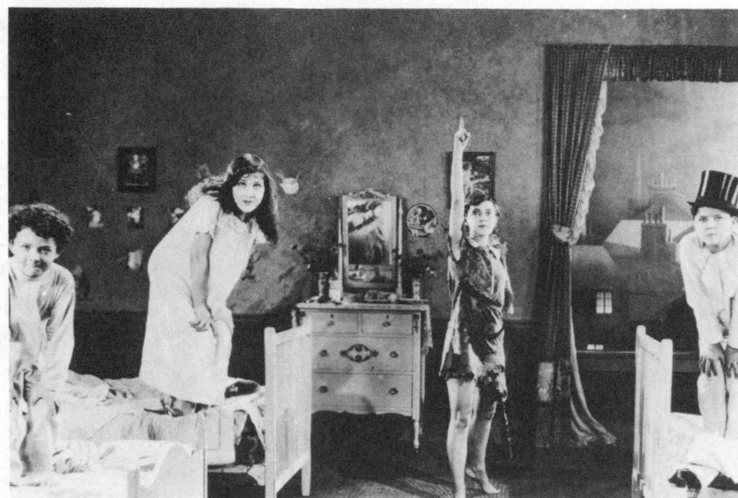

*Scene from a 1925 production of* Peter Pan.

Until the mid-eighteenth century, spectators in English theaters often watched performances while sitting on stage, just a few feet away from the actors. Spectators who did not approve of the production at times tried to bump the performers off the stage. It was not until the great Shakespearean actor David Garrick introduced his theatrical reforms in 1760 that the British audience was entirely relegated to the orchestra and pit.

The play *Chantecler*, written in 1910 by the French playwright Edmond Rostand, features a rooster as the major character.

*Theater poster for* Gentleman Jack, *one of the plays in which ''Gentleman Jim'' Corbett starred.*

The famous boxer James J. Corbett (1866–1933) was also one of the great matinee idols of his time. ''Gentleman'' Jim, after completing an extremely successful career in the ring, made his stage debut in a play called *After Dark* (which is still remembered for introducing the motif of the hero tied to the railroad tracks). His appearance caused a sensation among female theatergoers, and Corbett was soon touring in several other plays in the United States and England. Once, in London, Corbett charged women admission just for the privilege of watching him jump rope and hit a punching bag.

---

Until the twentieth century there was no such thing as a dramatic play in China. All dramas were musicals of a sort—that is, stories were acted out through singing, dancing, and musical accompaniment. Only around 1900 did the Chinese begin producing plays in which dramatic dialogue was the primary means of expression.

*Scene from* The Spectacle of the Sun and Moon, *a 19th-century Chinese drama with musical accompaniment.*

## Transportation and Travel

During their lifetime, more than 50 percent of Americans travel more than a million miles. Most of this distance is logged in automobiles.

---

The first ferryboat in America, which was established in 1630 between Boston and Charleston across the Charles River, charged traders one cent for every 100 pounds of goods transported. Thus the cost of moving a ton of merchandise was the princely sum of twenty cents.

---

In 1976 the total mileage clocked by U.S. passenger cars was more than 1 trillion.

---

One out of every two people in Denmark owns a bicycle. In Northern Ireland there are more bicycles than automobiles.

## The Universe: Stars, Planets, and Space

Our galaxy has approximately 250 billion stars—and it is estimated by astronomers that there are 100 billion other galaxies in the universe.

---

The star Alpha Herculis is twenty-five times larger than the circumference described by the earth's revolution around the sun. This means that twenty-five diameters of our solar orbit would have to be placed end to end to equal the diameter of this star.

---

Astronomers believe that the universe contains one atom for every 88 gallons of space.

---

A pulsar is a small star made up of neutrons so densely packed together that if one the size of a silver dollar landed on earth, it would weigh approximately 100 million tons.

---

In 1910, when it was announced that Halley's Comet would once again pass the earth, hysteria broke out in Europe, based on the belief that the arrival of this comet always heralded catastrophe. The war of 66 A.D. that brought about the fall of Jerusalem, the devastation of Rome by the Huns in 373, the Battle of Hastings in 1066 (it is Halley's Comet that can be seen in the famous Bayeux Tapestry, announcing the death of Harold), and many other tragic events did in fact coincide with the comet's appearance. Whether or not these occurrences actually had anything to do with the comet, anxiety spread throughout Europe as soon as its impending arrival was announced, and thousands of people fled to the mountains for safety. A group of French scientists published a paper claiming that the earth would be poisoned by fumes from the comet's tail. Reports of "comet insanity" and suicide attempts filled the newspapers, and "anticomet pills," guaranteeing protection from the comet's noxious fumes, were bought up eagerly. The comet, however, came and went without much incident—though, it might be noted, World War I began four years later.

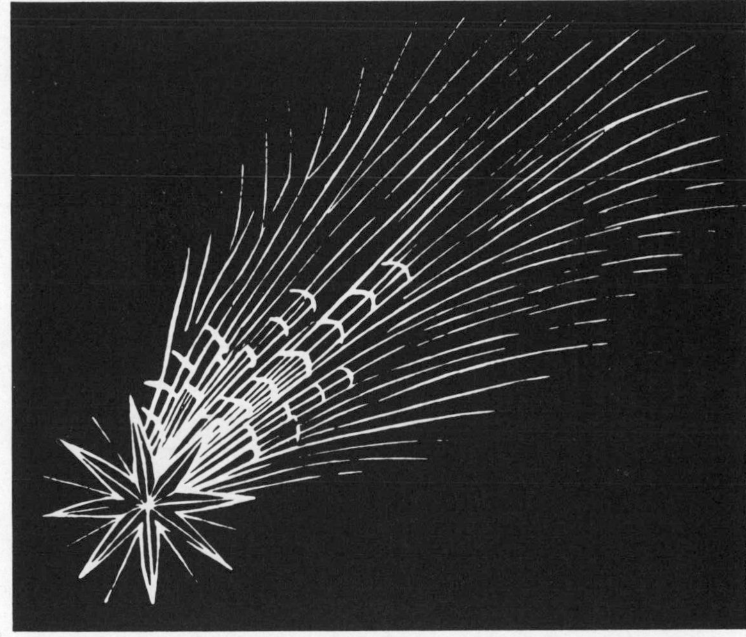

*Representation of Halley's Comet, from the Nuremberg Chronicle.*

---

If the earth were the size of a quarter, the sun would be as large as a 9-foot ball and would be located a football field's distance from the earth. If the entire solar system were the size of a quarter, the sun would be visible only under a microscope, and the nearest star would be 300 feet away. If our whole galaxy were the size of a quarter, our solar system would be less than the size of a molecule. Other galaxies would be from a foot to 1,000 feet away.

---

The sun provides our planet with 126,000,000,000,000 horsepower of energy every day. This means that 54,000 horsepower is delivered to every man, woman, and child on earth in each twenty-four-hour period. This amount of energy equals only about two-billionths of the total energy broadcast into our solar system by the sun each day.

---

A bucket filled with earth would weigh about five times more than the same bucket filled with the substance of the sun. However, the force of gravity is so much greater on the sun that a man weighing 150 pounds on our planet would weigh 2 tons on the sun.

---

Until the mid-sixteenth century, comets were believed to be not astronomical phenomena, but burning vapors that had arisen from distant swamps and were propelled across the sky by fire and light.

---

More than 1 million earths would fit inside the sun.

---

A galaxy of typical size—about 100 billion suns—produces less energy than a single quasar.

---

According to scientists, gold exists on Mars, Mercury, and Venus.

---

A space vehicle must move at a rate of 7 miles per second to escape the earth's gravitational pull. This is equivalent to going from New York to Philadelphia in about twenty seconds.

---

As of 1978 there were approximately 4,500 pieces of equipment revolving around the earth. About 900 of these pieces were satellites; the rest were odd bits of debris.

---

The moon weighs 81 billion tons.

---

A comet's tail always points away from the sun.

*Halley's Comet as depicted in the Bayeux Tapestry.*

Scientists believe that hydrogen comprises approximately 90 to 99 percent of all matter in the universe.

## War and Weapons

During the American Revolution, Congress raised eight companies of soldiers—each numbering 120 men—made up entirely of cripples, invalids, blind men, and men missing arms or legs.

According to *Jane's Fighting Ships,* as of 1978 the Soviet Union had more than twice as many ships in its navy as the United States. This included 35 cruisers (compared with the United States' 27) 220 destroyers (the United States had 129), and 332 submarines (the United States had 120).

In the late fourteenth century, when the fortress of the Knights of St. John in Smyrna was attacked by the legions of the Mongol conqueror Timur, a large reserve fleet of ships arrived to aid the besieged garrison. In response, Timur ordered that the heads of the knights already slain be loaded into a giant catapult and fired at the arriving ships. As soon as the onslaught began, the reserve fleet raised their sails, turned around, and sailed away, leaving the knights to fend for themselves.

---

During World War I, the odds against a French or German soldier being killed were five to one—which meant that one out of every five Frenchmen and Germans who served in that war was killed.

*French infantry soldiers in combat during World War I.*

## Weather

A hailstone weighing more than 1½ pounds once fell on Coffeyville, Kansas. No one was hit.

---

In July, 1861, 366 inches of rain fell in one month on the town of Cherrapunji, India. This is more than 30 feet of water, deeper than many rivers and lakes.

---

A temperature of 134° F was recorded on July 10, 1913, in Death Valley, California. This is only 2.4 degrees cooler than the world's record of 136.4° F, registered in Azizia, Libya, in 1922.

---

In 1966 the mean annual temperature in Plateau Station, Antarctica, was −70° F. If a lightly clothed person were to stand outside in this temperature he or she would freeze to death in approximately 60 seconds.

---

On March 16, 1952, 6 inches of rain fell in one day on the town of Cilaos in the Réunion Islands.

---

According to samplings taken by the National Oceanic Atmospheric Administration, rain water in large areas of the United States has become from a hundred to a thousand times more acidic than it was in the era before fossil fuels. Much of the rain that falls in various parts of the country is almost as acidic as vinegar, reports the survey. The rain in turn affects lakes across the country. In the Adirondack State Park in New York, it is reported that two hundred lakes are now so acidic that they can no longer support fish life. Many scientists believe that the 10 percent decrease in the growth of forests across the northeastern United States is due to the same cause.

*Rain, engraving by Hans Mueller. Rain water in the U.S. is becoming increasingly acidic, threatening fish and plant life.*

---

A serious problem faced by astronomers today is the vast belt of smog encircling the earth and obscuring all telescopic observation. Because of this smog many astronomical observatories are moving to such remote spots as the Andes and the Sahara Desert.

## Weights and Measures

A mile on the ocean and a mile on land are not the same distance. On the ocean, a mile is known as a nautical mile and measures 6,080 feet. A land or statute mile is 5,280 feet.

The weight of a carat (200 milligrams), standard unit of measurement for gemstones, is based on the weight of the carob seed, which was once used as a weighing standard by jewelers in Africa and the Middle East. The word ''carat'' itself is believed to be derived from an Arabic word meaning ''bean'' or ''seed.''

## Wine, Beer, and Spirits

According to the National PTA, 86 to 94 percent of schoolchildren have had some experience with alcoholic beverages by the time they reach high school.

One out of every thirteen adults over twenty years old in the United States is an alcoholic.

Beer was not sold in bottles until 1850. Before then, if a person wished to buy beer, he went to the neighborhood tavern with a bucket or pot made especially for holding beer, had it filled, and brought the brew home.

In the early 1860's, wine almost became extinct in Europe. Sometime around 1860, an insect known as *Phylloxera vitifo-*

*liae* was accidentally brought to Europe from the United States. Closely related to the aphid, it attacked the leaves and roots of the wine-grape vines and soon ravaged the countryside. Within several months it had devastated 2.5 million acres of French grapes, wiped out madeira completely, and reduced the production of wine throughout Europe to a trickle. The destruction was finally checked when a louse-resistant grape stock, which originally came from France, was brought back to Europe from California and the older vine stalks were grafted onto it. To this day, grape stock cultivated before the *Phylloxera* attack in Europe is extremely rare.

---

The martini is the most popular of all alcoholic mixed drinks in the United States, according to the Southern Comfort Corporation. It is followed in popularity by the whiskey sour, the bloody Mary, the Manhattan, the Collins drinks, the screwdriver, the old-fashioned, and the gin and tonic.

*The martini (left) and the old-fashioned, two of America's most popular cocktails.*

---

*Runlet, tierce, puncheon, pipe, gill, tun,* and *firkin* are all terms used by winemakers in the weighing and measuring of wine.

---

A traditional Japanese liquor called *mam* is produced by taking live venomous snakes called *mamushis* (they are related to copperheads), mashing them into a specially prepared fermenting potion, allowing the mixture to age, then collecting the runoff.

---

According to the National Safety Council, coffee is not successful at sobering up a drunk person, and in many cases it may actually *increase* the adverse effects of alcohol.

According to the National Institute of Alcohol Abuse and Alcoholism, liquor may be involved in as many as half the traffic fatalities that occur in the United States.

In 1637, then-Governor Wilhelm Kieft estimated that one-quarter of the shops in Nieuw Amsterdam (soon to become New York) were taverns.

*Huffcup, the mad dog, Father Whoreson, angel's food, dragon's milk, go-by-the-wall, stride well,* and *lift leg* were all common names for beer in Elizabethan England.

Every resident of Nome, Alaska, over fifteen years of age drinks, on the average, 4 gallons of alcoholic beverages a year.

## Miscellaneous

There are more than three hundred clubs in the United States devoted exclusively to model railroading.

*Model railroad cars like this one are a source of interest to thousands of American hobbyists.*

The movie industry's Oscar awards and television's Emmies are no doubt the two best-known media awards in the United States. Here are a few you may know less about:

***Apparel Annie***—A bronze statuette, presented for outstanding promotion in the apparel industry.

***The Barney***—A silver cigarette box engraved with drawings of Barney Google and Snuffy Smith, awarded to the year's best cartoonist.

***The Edgar***—A bust of Edgar Allan Poe, given for the best mystery story of the year.

***The Gertrude***—A silver kangaroo, given by the publishers of Pocket Books to their authors whose books have sold a million or more copies.

***The Winnie***—A bronze female nude, awarded for the year's best fashion design.

---

The National Rifle Association estimates that almost 25 percent of the population of the United States own handguns. It is estimated by the Rifle Association that four handguns are sold over the counter every minute of the day.

*Smith & Wesson revolver, one of the many handguns popular in the U.S.*

---

The chance of two typewriters of the same make typing characters that are identical in terms of alignment and defects is 1 in 3 trillion.

Clocks made before 1687 had only one hand—an hour hand.

*Renaissance clocks, with hour hands only.*

Ivory is used in dental inlays, in the preparation of India ink, in the oil color known as ivory black, and in a food called ivory jelly, which was popular in England in the early twentieth century.

During World War II, the sale of Navajo blankets almost ceased in the United States. The reason for the decline was that the ancient Navajo symbol for the sun, woven into most of the blankets, looked exactly like Hitler's swastika.

Bolivia has had 189 governments since it gained its independence in 1825. This means that Bolivia has had, on the average, more than one government a year for the past 150 years.

All the gold in the world would fit into a single block measuring 18 cubic yards.

In the eighteenth century people bought ink from apothecary shops, where chemists mixed it on the spot and poured it into special bottles. Today these bottles fetch high prices among collectors.

---

One ounce of LSD is enough to make doses for 300,000 people.

---

Pollen never deteriorates. It is one of the few naturally secreted substances that lasts indefinitely.

---

Nobody knows how many people died during the sinking of the *Titanic*. The great ship, which was supposedly sinkproof yet went under in less than three hours, was carrying an unknown number of passengers at the time of its destruction. The British Board of Trade estimated that 1,490 people perished in the disaster. Another British inquiry, however, set the number at 1,503, and an American report listed the number of dead at 1,517. To this day no one knows the exact count.

*The sinking of the* Titanic, *1912.*

---

When discovered in the late 1960s deep in the jungles of Surinam, in northern South America, the Akurio tribe was keeping watch over piles of burning coals. The tribespeople had lost the art of making fire and could maintain it only by continually feeding an already existing flame.

---

At an auction held in March, 1978, at Sotheby's in London, the skull of the famous eighteenth-century Swedish scientist and mystic Emanuel Swedenborg was sold to a Swedish bidder for $3,200. The skull had been stolen scarcely fifty years after Swedenborg's death by a retired sea captain and amateur phrenologist. A century after the theft, the relic showed up in an antique shop in Wales, where it was purchased by Swedenborg's heirs. They kept it until the auction.

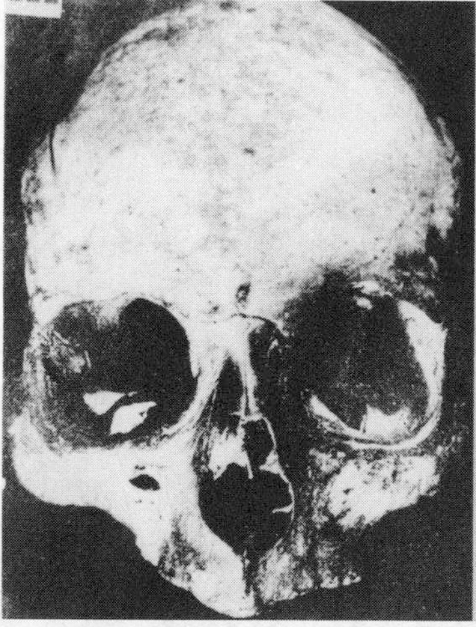

*Emanuel Swendenborg and his valuable skull.*

---

The Emperor Hotel in Tokyo is the world's most erotic hotel. In all rooms there are closed-circuit TV sets that show pornographic movies day and night. Sliding wall panels roll back to reveal mirror-lined walls, and mirrors cover the ceilings, as well. Beds vibrate, revolve, and turn, and waterbeds are available on request. The hallways are scented with exotic perfumes. One room even has a 50-foot waterfall.

---

The motto of the American people, "In God We Trust," was not adopted as the national slogan until 1956.

---

A large number of carpets from Iran are woven with camel's hair.

Approximately 30.8 billion gallons of water are used each day in the United States, or 140 gallons per person. Some 36 percent of this water is used in homes, 36 percent in factories, 14 percent by businesses, and 7 percent for public services like street cleaning and firefighting. The remaining 7 percent is lost through leakages.

*"The Fire," watercolor based on a Currier & Ives lithograph. Firefighters use only a tiny fraction of the U.S. water supply.*

The oldest continuous thoroughfare in the United States is Wilshire Boulevard, a busy street that runs through the heart of downtown Los Angeles. Not only has Wilshire Boulevard been used as a main route for traffic, a pathway for Mexican donkey carts, and a trail for Indians, but this venerable highway was walked upon millions of years ago by prehistoric animals making their way from the mountains to the sea. The La Brea Tar Pits, located on Wilshire Boulevard and today a museum, contain the bones of animals that stopped there for water en route to the ocean, became mired in the tar, and died.

There is an annual spitting-for-distance contest held in Raleigh, Mississippi. Every year, individuals compete to see who can spit the farthest, most accurately, and most compactly. The record to date, held by Don Snyder, is 25 feet 10 inches. Snyder's prize? A gold-plated spittoon.

Japanese jugglers in the nineteenth century performed a feat still discussed among showmen. Displaying several pieces of colored paper, they folded and tore each piece into the shape of a butterfly, then tossed two or three of these cutouts into the air. Using a fan, they then created wind currents to direct the flight of these mock butterflies, causing them to swoop, soar, and circle flowers just as real butterflies do. The act ended with the butterflies alighting on the flowers, fluttering their wings, then flying off the stage in unison. During the entire wondrous exhibition, not a single butterfly was allowed to touch the ground.

No one knows who designed the first American flag. The so-called Stars and Stripes, first displayed on June 14, 1777, is believed by some to have been an early military banner carried into battle during the American Revolution. The notion that it was designed by Betsy Ross has no historical basis.

*The first flag of the American republic.*

# Picture Credits
## Volume One

**Abbreviations**
CP—Culver Pictures
MPG—MPG Picture Collection
NYPL—New York Public Library

7: CP; 8 (top & btm), 9, 10 (top & btm): NYPL; 11: MPG; 12: Museum of Fine Arts, Boston; 13, 14, 15 (top & btm), 16: NYPL; 18 (top): MPG; 18 (btm): Alinari; 19: Museum of Fine Arts, Boston; 22: NYPL; 23 (top): CP; 23 (btm): MPG; 24 (top & btm), 25 (top & ctr): National Library of Medicine, Bethesda, Md.; 25 (btm): NYPL; 26, 28: National Library of Medicine, Bethesda, Md.; 32: Museum of Fine Arts, Boston; 33 (top): The New-York Historical Society; 33 (btm): Alinari; 34: British Museum; 35 (top): CP; 35 (btm): MPG; 36: Museum of Fine Arts, Boston; 39: A.T.&T. Co.; 40: CP; 41: The Metropolitan Museum of Art, N.Y.; 45, 47: NYPL; 48: CP; 50 (top & btm): MPG; 53: Miami Seaquarium; 54; 55 (top & btm): NYPL; 56: **The Oxford Book of Food Plants**, by B. E. Nicholson, Oxford University Press; 57, 58 (top): CP; 58 (btm): Hunt Botanical Library, Pittsburgh, Pa.; 59: The Metropolitan Museum of Art, N.Y.; 60: NYPL; 61: CP; 63 (top): NYPL; 63 (btm): CP; 64: NYPL; 65: National Gallery of Art, Washington, D.C.; 66: CP; 67: The Metropolitan Museum of Art, N.Y.; 69: CP; 72 (top & btm), 73: NYPL; 75, 77: CP; 79: NYPL; 81: Muzeul de Arta, Craiova, Rumania; 83 (top): MPG; 83 (btm): Museum of Fine Arts, Boston; 84: MPG; 86: NYPL; 89 (top & btm): MPG; 90: **Treasure Island**, by Robert Louis Stevenson, Harper & Bros., 1921; 91: MPG; 92: CP; 98: Society of Antiquaries, London; 99: NYPL; 101: **Book of Pirates**, by Howard Pyle, Harper, 1903; 102: CP; 103: NYPL; 104: Library of Congress; 107: CP; 108: Private Collection; 109: NYPL; 110, 111 (top): CP; 111 (ctr): The Metropolitan Museum of Art, N.Y., Crosby Brown Collection; 111 (btm): MPG; 114, 115 (top & btm), 117: NYPL; 118: MPG; 119: NYPL; 120: MPG; 122: Library of Congress; 123: NYPL; 124, 125: MPG; 127, 128: CP; 129: MPG; 132: NYPL; 133 (left): Library of Congress; 133 (rt), 134, 135: MPG; 136: CP; 137: MPG; 138: Library of Congress; 140, 141: MPG; 143: CP; 146: MPG; 147: Library of Congress; 148: The Metropolitan Museum of Art, N.Y.; 149: NYPL; 150: MPG; 152: NYPL; 154: The Metropolitan Museum of Art, N.Y.; 155: Tobacco & Textile Museum, Danville, Va.; 156, 157 (top & btm), 158: NYPL; 159: MPG; 160: NYPL; 161: MPG; 162: National Gallery of Art, Washington, D.C.; 164, 165: MPG; 166: National Portrait Gallery, Smithsonian Institution, Washington, D.C.; 167: NYPL; 168, 169: MPG; 170: CP; 171: Hale Observatories; 173: NYPL; 174: National Aeronautics & Space Administration; 175, 176: NYPL; 177: Insurance Company of North America, Philadelphia, Pa.; 178, 179: MPG; 181: The Library Company of Philadelphia; 182: CP; 184, 185, 186 (top & btm), 187: NYPL; 188: CP; 189: Paul Travis, The Cleveland Museum of Natural History.

# Picture Credits
## Volume Two

MPG - MPG Picture Collection
NYPL - New York Public Library

Page 193: MPG. 194: American Museum of Natural History, New York. 195, 196: NYPL. 197: American Museum of Natural History, New York. 198, 199, 200, 201, 202, 203, 204, 205, 206: NYPL. 207: (top) National Gallery of Art, Washington, DC; (btm) copyright © 1979, Grandma Moses Properties, Inc., New York. 208: (top) Yale University Art Galleries, New Haven, CT; (btm) Ralph Stein Picture Collection. 209: British Tourist Authority. 210: General Motors. 211, 213, 214, 215, 216: NYPL. 217: MPG. 218, 219, 220. National Library of Medicine, Bethesda, MD. 221: American Museum of Natural History, New York. 222: New York *Times*. 223, 224, 225. NYPL. 226: (top) Museum of Fine Arts, Boston; (btm) Sander Davidson, Tulsa, OK. 227: The Arrow Company. 228: The Granger Collection. 230: MPG. 231: NYPL. 232: Bettmann Archives. 233: NYPL. 234, 235, 236. MPG. 237, 238: NYPL. 241: National Archives. 242, 244, 246: NYPL. 247. Historical Pictures Service. 248: MPG. 249: (top) MPG; (btm) Bettmann Archives. 250, 251: NYPL. 252: Bettmann Archives. 253, 254: NYPL. 255. The Granger Collection. 256, 257, 258, 259, 260, 261: NYPL. 262: Cincinnati Art Museum. 263, 264, 265, 267: NYPL. 268: Historical Pictures Service. 269: NYPL. 270: National Library of Medicine, Bethesda, Md. 271, NYPL. 272, *Sports Illustrated*. 274: (top) NYPL, (btm) Bettmann Archives. 275, 276, 277, 278, 279, 280: NYPL. 281. MPG. 282, 285: NYPL. 287: Historical Pictures Service. 289: Museum of the City of New York. 290: MPG. 291, 293, 294: NYPL. 297, 298: Historical Pictures Service. 299, 300: NYPL. 301: MPG. 302: NYPL. 303: MPG. 304 305: NYPL. 307. Metropolitan Museum of Art, New York. 309: Arie de Zanger. 310: MPG. 312: NYPL. 313: Culver Pictures. 314: NYPL. 315: American Museum of Natural History, New York. 316: NYPL. 317: The Granger Collection. 319: Metro-Goldwyn-Mayer. 320: NYPL. 323: Bettmann Archives. 326: NYPL. 327: MPG. 328, 329, 330: NYPL. 332: MPG. 333, 334, 335, 337, 339: NYPL. 340: Library of Congress, Washington DC. 341. MPG. 342: National Library of Medicine, Bethesda, MD. 343, 344, 345. NYPL. 346: Bettmann Archives. 347: NYPL. 348: MPG. 349: Bettmann Archives. 350: MPG. 351: NYPL. 352: Historical Pictures Service. 353: Smithsonian Institution, Washington, DC. 355: MPG. 356: Museum of the City of New York. 358: NYPL. 359: The Granger Collection. 360: (top) Bettmann Archives; (btm) NYPL. 363, 365: Yerkes Observatory, Williams Bay, WI. 366. Historical Pictures Service. 367, 369: NYPL. 370: *Train Collectors Association Quarterly*. 371: NYPL. 372: Historical Pictures Service. 373: The Granger Collection. 374: Wide World. 375: MPG. 376: Historical Pictures Service.